Risky Business

Recent Titles in
Contributions to the Study of Mass Media and Communications

RISKY BUSINESS

COMMUNICATING ISSUES
OF SCIENCE, RISK, AND PUBLIC POLICY

Edited by
Lee Wilkins
and **Philip Patterson**

Foreword by Dorothy Nelkin

Contributions to the Study of
Mass Media and Communications, Number 27

GREENWOOD PRESS
NEW YORK • WESTPORT, CONNECTICUT • LONDON

Library of Congress Cataloging-in-Publication Data

Risky business: communicating issues of science, risk, and public policy / edited by
    Lee Wilkins and Philip Patterson ; foreword by Dorothy Nelkin.
        p.   cm. — (Contributions to the study of mass media and
    communications, ISSN 0732-4456 ; no. 27)
        Includes bibliographical references and index.
        ISBN 0-313-26601-8 (alk. paper)
        1. Mass media and technology. I. Wilkins, Lee. II. Patterson,
    Philip. III. Series.
    P96.T42R57   1991
    302.23–dc20   90-47523

British Library Cataloguing in Publication Data is available.

Library of Congress Catalog Card Number: 90-47523
ISBN: 0-313-26601-8
ISSN: 0732-4456

First published in 1991

Greenwood Press, 88 Post Road West, Westport, CT 06881
An imprint of Greenwood Publishing Group, Inc.

Printed in the United States of America

∞

The paper used in this book complies with the
Permanent Paper Standard issued by the National
Information Standards Organization (Z39.48-1984).

10 9 8 7 6 5 4 3 2 1

Copyright Acknowledgment

The Foreword by Dorothy Nelkin is reprinted with permission from SIPIscope,
published by the Scientists' Institute for Public Information.

To — and for — our families

Contents

Foreword: Why Is Science Writing So Uncritical of Science?

DOROTHY NELKIN

Journalists who write about science and technology are often accused of bias, sensationalism, and antiscience reporting. Indeed, many scientists regard the press, like politics, as a dirty business, threatening the purity of science. Philip Handler, former president of the National Academy of Sciences, wrote that "antiscience attitudes perniciously infiltrate the news media." Industrial scientists, referring to the coverage of toxics, complain that "the media's intent is to show how modern technology is poisoning America," and a media analyst, referring to coverage of antiestablishment views, suggests that "the news media contribute to the corruption of the scientific enterprise."

What images of science and technology are in fact conveyed through the press? As readers scan their magazines and newspapers, what do they find out about scientists? Most readers understand science less through experience than through the filter of language and imagery. Let me suggest some patterns that I see in the language of science writing today.

People read about science in the reporting of very diverse subjects: heart transplants, environmental issues, food additive disputes, the Nobel Prize, scientific discoveries, and scientific fraud. The detailed content of

For more detail and explanation of media coverage of science and Professor Nelkin's criticism of it, see Nelkin, D. (1987). *Selling Science.* New York: W. H. Freeman.

articles ranges broadly, reflecting the diversity of the press and the background of science writers.

There is, however, a remarkable consistency in the imagery. Several metaphorical clusters appear throughout. One is the language of alchemy: miracles, ultimate truths, magic bullets, secret knowledge. Scientists are magicians, miracle workers, wizards.

But increasingly prevalent is an extraordinarily aggressive imagery of warfare, revolution, and frontier. Scientists are pioneers or warriors battling disease, conquering natural forces, competing against the Japanese. The scientists working on the frontier of medical technology or biotechnology are warriors using science as a weapon to fight disease or to win an international or technological struggle. The metaphor of revolution is overused: the computer revolution, the biotechnology revolution, a revolutionary era for U.S. science, a development of revolutionary proportions.

These metaphors add up to an image of science as a solution for intractable dilemmas, a means of certainty in an uncertain world, a source of legitimacy, an institution we can trust. They have been used to mobilize consensus and rebuild comfortable images of progress and national leadership, even at times when these images are challenged.

Of course, one also reads about the perils as well as the promises of science. In the middle of my pile of exuberant heart transplant articles is a cartoon of a doctor observing a patient: "Our hope now is just to get him strong enough to pull his own plug." Journalists today raise some philosophical questions about the difficulty of deciding who will be saved and the value of applying the latest scientific techniques. A Mormon journalist, reporting on the artificial heart, asks, "As the symbol of love, the site of life, the habitat of the soul, can the heart be replaced by a simply mechanical pump?"

But with all the coverage of transplant technology, relatively few reporters follow up on the quality of life of transplant patients, and few touch on the potential ethical consequences of organ scarcity in a market-oriented society. (Is the theme of the film *Coma* so far out?)

THE ULTIMATE PROBLEM SOLVER

Images of science sometimes change, and not always for the better. Take the coverage of psychosurgery: When the technique of lobotomy was developed in the 1950s, scientists regarded it with considerable skepticism, but journalists saw it as a panacea. It was to be a cure for schizophrenia, a relief of pain, a way to release tensions, and a preventative for moral degeneration. By the 1970s, psychosurgery had won greater professional acceptance, but in the press one reads of mutilation, clockwork orange, and emotional vegetables. This reporting reflects changes in social perspectives more than the technique itself.

Science and technology also appear in the press as sources of risk in stories about nuclear power, toxic dumps, and food additives. Reporting the role of science in situations of risk is inherently difficult because of technical uncertainty and scientific disputes. Indeed, the reporting in this area has brought the greatest criticism from scientists.

But what is the image of science in the reporting on risk disputes? A few quotes from the saccharin controversy are suggestive: "The battle royale over the safety of artificial sweeteners is expected to be resolved by scientists next month." "The National Academy of Sciences will definitely resolve the problem once and for all." "Scientists will decide whether saccharin causes cancer." Scientists are the ultimate problem solvers, the experts, the discoverers of truth.

Often reporters covering risk situations express disillusionment. After Three Mile Island a columnist wrote: "They lied. They lied. They lied. They told us it was clean. Did you ever hear such a lie?" But invariably it is not the scientists who lose credibility but the industries, utilities or government agencies. Science is represented as the way out.

The behavior of scientists who engage in controversies or who act as advocates is often reported with cynicism, the "Hertz rent-a-scientist" is described with a tone of concern. So too are incidents of fraud. These incidents are sometimes treated as the pathological behavior of aberrant individuals, sometimes as a reflection of structural problems within science.

However, while consumer fraud is reported as a rip-off, scientific fraud is a scandal, a betrayal, a waste of scientific talent. It tarnishes and taints, besmirches and sullies scientific institutions. Religious metaphors are common: scientists have "succumbed to temptation"; they commit a "scientific sin." This language idealizes science as a pure and awe-inspiring activity, a higher and almost spiritual calling.

Similarly, the fact that scientists may have economic goals is reported with some dismay as a new and distressing problem. Coverage of the increased ties between industry and academic science in high technology fields is extensive, considering how little science policy is usually covered. Pictures of scientists drawing arcane equations on their blackboards have been replaced by photos of them standing in front of corporate growth charts. Researchers are described as "an army that wants their share of the spoils." The dilemma is presented as a polarized choice, profit versus purity, as though the economic influence on science is a new issue. The images again reflect the ideal of a pure science that is the key to progress and the solution to social problems.

SCIENTIFIC SUPERSTARS

This ideal is also revealed in the descriptions of scientists who win the Nobel Prize. Nobel laureates are superstars. They are at the frontier, helping us control the future through science. Articles on the laureates seldom describe their work in detail, except to suggest that it is arcane: "Relatively few persons may fully understand their accomplishments." Rather than the substance of research, the issue most frequently covered is the number of U.S. winners as compared to foreign winners. Indeed, the reports sound strangely similar in style to reports on the Olympics: "Another strong U.S. show." "The winning American style." "We tied a record set in 1972."

Just as their work is arcane, scientists are portrayed as isolated, removed, more than slightly above the rest of us. A striking exception are the few women laureates, who are portrayed in the press as being just like you and me. Marie Mayer is "a brilliant scientist, her children are perfectly darling, and she is so darn pretty that it all seems unfair." In accepting the prize she sees everything "through the starry eyes of a romantic woman." She explains the nucleus of the atom in "a feminine way." (Her metaphor was layers of onions.) The coverage of Rosalyn Yalow was worse, focusing not on her work but on her balancing career and family — and on her clothes. Headline: "She Cooks, She Cleans, She Wins the Nobel Prize." We discover in the first line of a feature on Barbara McClintock that she bakes with walnuts.

The easy recourse to stereotypes perhaps explains the extensive coverage of sociobiology in the press. Here too the language of journalism uncritically reinforces predominant cultural ideas. Genetics is routinely accepted as an explanation of criminal behavior, rape, obesity, and whatever. Why do men cheat on women? "If you get caught fooling around, don't say the devil made you do it. It is your DNA." It explains the importance of a laissez-faire economy, "the invisible hand in the embryo." It explains the difference in math achievement between men and women: "On the towel rack we call our anatomy, nature appears to have hung His and Hers brains."

The comfortable conclusion about sociobiology is that, as one reporter put it, "Science is confirming what poets and parents have long taken for granted." While sociobiology critics are given a voice, they are introduced with adjectives — "radical," or "radically-oriented" — that dismiss their credibility. These critics are described as religious, not scientific, threatening our "freedom to explore nature." There is little critical analysis of the limited evidence supporting the extravagant claims in this field.

The images of science are also affected by what is not covered. Relatively little appears on the methods and social organization of research, or on the choices and priorities involved in major decisions about science and technology. In the effort to personalize science, the scientist becomes a star, distorting the actual structure of research, which is dependent less on stars than on the anonymous work of students, young Ph.D.s, and technicians. In the portrayal of science as a national goal, a source of consensus, there is a sense of inevitability, with little significant social choice.

BEYOND CRITICISM?

What then can we say about the images of science and technology? They are sometimes ambivalent. The tone of optimism about science is often tempered as promises are balanced with perils. The notion of scientists as pure and unsullied professionals is tarnished by their obvious importance in the marketplace, as well as their role in public disputes. And the old Frankenstein image persists, as scientists-as-wizards are often unable to control the consequences of their research: "Modern wizards of science with ultrasophisticated research tools have invented headache remedies, dandelion killers and bug poisons. They have also created a chemical monster — dioxin — an uninvited test-tube guest."

However, the dominant theme in the print media is clear. Scientists are problem solvers, authorities, the ultimate source of truth. They are a resource in "short supply," but necessary for the "brainpower race." The activity called science is portrayed as the key to the future of our high technology, information-based society; it is a factor of production, an explanation of behavior. Yet it is also an arcane activity outside of, indeed, above the sphere of normal human understanding, and therefore beyond serious criticism. While political writers criticize and analyze, science writers elucidate and explain. While newspapers employ critics of art, theater, music, and literature, science is generally spared this critical approach, all of which raises two questions: Why is science writing so uncritical of science? and Why are scientists so critical of the press, so convinced of its antiscience intent?

Acknowledgments

Completing this manuscript, which occurred at times of major changes in both of our lives, would not have been possible without the help of many others.

Foremost among them are two staff members, Pat Hatfield at the University of Colorado–Boulder and Susie Rodman at Oklahoma Christian University, who typed, proofed and checked the book manuscript in a way that was evidence of friendship as well as collegiality. The contributors to this book also have become friends. Their responses to requests for first manuscripts and then editing changes were both timely and gracious. We know that the whole is greater than its parts because of their efforts.

The editors and production staff at Greenwood Publishing Group, beginning with Mary Sive who conceived of this project and continuing through James T. Sabin who saw it to conclusion, also deserve a share of the credit. Their professionalism has been exceptional.

Finally, to all those to whom we owe intellectual debts, and to our families — who cheerfully supported absences and late nights — we cannot thank you enough. This effort would not have been possible without your help.

Introduction

LEE WILKINS AND
PHILIP PATTERSON

In her foreword to this book, Dorothy Nelkin asks two questions: Why is science writing so uncritical of science, and why are scientists so critical of the press? The chapters that follow, in one way or another, address both of these issues.

The book opens with three chapters that critique what has become the new buzzword in science communication: risk. The field of risk communication originally grew out of the notion that people should become informed about hazards such as tornados or earthquakes so they could take individual or collective action to mitigate damages. However, in the early 1980s, when issues of environmental quality began to dominate the agendas of certain federal agencies, the concept of risk communication emerged. Under this new body of scholarship, risk communication was viewed as the one-way transmission of information about various risks in the environment from the expert, scientific community to the lay public. The mass media were seldom viewed as a conduit for such transmission of information, and the public's grasp of risk was generally viewed as inferior to that of the scientific elite.

Robin Gregory, a research associate at Decision Research and former director of the National Science Foundation's division of risk and management science, opens the book with a chapter devoted to risk perception. Gregory, a psychologist, notes that risk perception — or what some scholars in the field have labeled lay rationality — needs to be incorporated in journalistic coverage of risk-related issues. Further, since journalists are much more like lay people than scientific experts when it comes to covering risks, the coverage that they provide may be shaded in unintended ways by their own perceptions of risk. Gregory suggests how journalists should incorporate both expert and lay views of rationality in their coverage of questions of risk.

Sharon Dunwoody and Kurt Neuwirth, both of the University of Wisconsin, take the more general scholarly findings about risk perception and apply them specifically to mediated messages. Dunwoody and Neuwirth argue for a broader definition not only of risk communication but of the role of the audience in seeking and using information about risk. In the process, they provide an important critique on much of the current literature on risk communication as well as a strategy for communicating about risks.

Sharon M. Friedman, head of the journalism program at Lehigh University, completes this trio of chapters and the critique. In an essay drawing heavily from the work of Englishman David Dickson, Friedman explains why both lay and expert rationality are important — if sometimes in conflict — in public consideration of questions of risk. Further, she provides some guidelines for both journalists and policy makers as they make political decisions about risky issues. Friedman's chapter is among the first to blend concepts of both lay and expert rationality without judging one superior to the other. As such, her insights should be particularly important for journalists and policy makers who must often stumble through these conflicting versions of reality in the course of reporting stories or making political decisions about specific risky events.

The next part of the volume is devoted to four essays on media performance. By presenting research on a diversity of topics, from the reporting of medicine and health to technology to natural disasters in both the United States and Japan, the authors analyze media coverage of a variety of scientific issues. The chapters reveal that media coverage of science is shaped by at least two important factors: the influence of individuals who serve as sources and the mandates of professional journalistic norms. These forces provide the media with a world view of science and science-related issues that permeates reporting and editing across specialties and cultures. Taken together with the chapters on risk communication, the authors provide a framework with which to answer Nelkin's first question.

Chapter 4 was written by Robert A. Logan, the director of the Science Journalism Center at the University of Missouri. Logan reviews much of the academic literature on how the media have covered medicine and health during most of the twentieth century. He notes that the original goal of both journalists and health care professionals was the popularization of news of medicine and medical findings. The media have also been used, with somewhat mixed results, to inform the public about issues such as smoking and heart disease. Such popularization has its uses, but, as Logan notes, an uncritical attitude toward medical news promulgates stereotypes and an uncritical acceptance of medical judgments that may have unfortunate effects on the entire health care system. As an alternative, Logan proposes a "secularization" of news of science and medicine, an attitude that would combine critical journalistic coverage with the results of work on public information campaigns. The goal of such secularization, Logan notes, would be to foster a public debate where the understanding and provision of health care is subject to the same analysis accorded many other of society's collective goods.

While secularization may be an alternative to the popularization of medical news, the problem of cultural stereotypes appears to permeate coverage of mental illness. In fact, Russell E. Shain, dean of the College of Communications at Arkansas State University, and Julie Phillips, a science writer in Boulder, Colorado, demonstrate most coverage of mental illness comes in the form of stories about crime rather than the medical problem. As Shain and Phillips note, not only does such coverage perpetuate untrue stereotypes about the mentally ill but it also obscures some of the changes in political society that have made the mentally ill more a part of our everyday lives. The authors suggest how journalists can modify their coverage to include both the individual and the social aspects of the problems they see.

Some understanding of why such events evoke international concern is provided by sociologists Henry Quarantelli of the University of Delaware's Disaster Research Center, and Dennis Wenger, head of Texas A & M's Hazard Reduction and Recovery Center. These distinguished sociologists, in a rare cross-national study, assert that, at least when it comes to disasters, news varies relatively little regardless of culture, country, or media system. These findings are particularly noteworthy because they challenge the current wisdom of much scholarship in mass communication that news production is a culturally dependent commodity. While this chapter certainly cannot settle this important debate, it does provide an alternative framework with which to analyze news and public responses to certain news events. If Quarantelli and Wenger are correct, then it should be possible for journalists in various settings to begin improving their coverage of disastrous events, particularly important in this International Decade of Hazard Reduction.

While Quarantelli and Wenger focus on international comparisons, Everett Rogers and Soon Bum Chang focus on international events as played in the U.S. media. The scholars, both from the Annenberg School for Communications, note that media protrayals of certain kinds of technologically related events and disasters do not always reflect "real life." Their work on AIDS is particularly noteworthy, because it indicates that the agenda setting process is a complex one, particularly for news stories that evolve over time. Finally, Rogers and Chang link media coverage with other activity — for example, governmental funding of certain programs — in an interactive way. This interactive view of the media, science, and public policy characterizes the work in the remainder of the volume as well.

At the end of each of these chapters, the authors suggest how journalists, and sometimes the scientific elite they report on, can alter journalistic behavior. The goal of this part of the book, then, is to note that media coverage of science, broadly construed, follows certain predictable patterns, and that journalists are going to have to critically examine the way they do their jobs before those patterns change.

The next chapters address the assertion that many decisions regarding science, technology, and risk involve conflicting choices. Underlying those choices, whether made by journalists, public policy makers, or the average citizen, are judgments about what and how to publicize and what to keep secret.

Phillip Tompkins, who has studied the organizational communication within the National Aeronautics and Space Administration (NASA) for most of the past 20 years, takes his insights from that organization and applies them to an issue of technology most Americans are deeply concerned about: airline and airport safety. Tompkins's work demonstrates that the values set by people within an organization can influence how that organization handles both potential and real technological accidents. His insights into organization communication are important for both journalists, who must sometimes write about the breakdown of such systems, and policy makers, who must develop or change organizations in ways that will allow them to better cope with technological ambiguity.

While Tompkins's work suggests that privacy is a key component in an organization's attempt to mitigate future hazards, government sometimes confounds privacy with secrecy. David M. Rubin, dean of the S. I. Newhouse School of Journalism and founder of the Center for the Study of War, Peace and the News Media, provides a darker view of this dichotomy. Rubin asserts that, at least when it comes to coverage of science and technology as it is used by the military, the media have been the servants of government in its will to secrecy. Rather than question the underlying assumptions of military policy, journalists, despite fierce attachment to First Amendment rhetoric, appear to have accepted them. The result, Rubin states, is an unwillingness to challenge military policy except when certain other problems, environmental degradation, for example, become overwhelming. Although Rubin makes his argument in a U.S. context, his analysis could be applied to other political systems, particularly if Quarantelli and Wenger's assertions about media coverage of certain types of events are correct.

Sometimes the issue is not what to keep from the public or the media but how to get the most attention. Two chapters examine the ability of the media to increase the salience of a scientific issue.

Deni Elliott, director of the Dartmouth Ethics Center, tackles the problem of media coverage of organ donations and transplants. As her essay indicates, such stories force journalists to re-examine their roles as popularizers of the the latest medical technologies as well as representatives of powerful institutions that may and often do give access to that technology to some individuals while denying it to others. In the midst of these literally life-and-death decisions, Elliott asserts, is also a question of societal good: how can our health care dollars be most effectively spent, even in this age of medical miracles?

The next chapter, by the volume's editors, tackles another political question: when and how certain issues or events "find" a political symbol. Using as a base an analysis of media coverage of the greenhouse effect in 1987 and 1988, the authors show how the media's normal way of doing business, coupled with the vagaries of summer weather, gutted an important political issue of symbolic impact. This chapter, unlike many of the others that precedes it, indicates that the media can dampen as well as amplify political debate on important public policy questions with a scientific base. Such a finding is crucial, particularly if the scientific prediction about the greenhouse century turns out to be more rather than less accurate.

As all the authors in the volume make clear, decisions about science, technology and risk, and media coverage of those questions, are not strictly realms for individual action. They involve what political scientists call the collective good, or the notion that political society can afford some things collectively that individuals within the society cannot. How those choices are made, particularly in the glare of the predictably biased media spotlight, is the focus of the book's penultimate chapter.

Sue O'Brien brings a unique perspective to her analysis of the politics of disaster. During her distinguished career, she has worked as both a print and broadcast journalist, well as a gubernatorial press secretary. In fact, she was Colorado governor Richard Lamm's press secretary for eight years, including the time of the 1982 Denver blizzard. She also covered the Big Thompson flood as a television reporter, and several Denver mayoral campaigns as an editor at the *Denver Post*. O'Brien's contribution is a pragmatic one, for she advises both journalists and politicians how they can and cannot expect to cope with disastrous events.

In the final chapter, the editors return to Nelkin's original questions. They assert that scholarly analysis of media coverage of questions surrounding science and risk indicate not only why journalists are apparently so uncritical of science, but why scientists are apparently equally fearful of the journalistic enterprise.

The reader will note that, throughout this volume, the authors have provided suggestions for how journalists, policy makers, and citizens can work to correct some of the more pervasive problems scholarly analysis of media coverage of science has uncovered. These suggestions are meant to be starting points rather than final goals. Like Sharon Dunwoody, the editors have assumed that the audience for this book is concerned about the issues and willing to begin the critical thinking and action necessary to bring about change. This book was written to encourage such activity. In the coming years, as science, medicine, technology, disaster, and hazards continue to dominate the news and the culture, it will be needed.

Risky Business

1

Risk Perceptions as Substance and Symbol

ROBIN GREGORY

Management of technological risks has been an important topic of theoretical and applied research throughout the 1980s. The widespread public response to accidents such as the Bhopal toxic chemical release or the Exxon Valdez oil spill is indicative of public fears about the effects of technological hazards, as well as public concern for improved risk management. Few today would argue against the view that risk managers need to recognize and effectively address the concerns of the public as well as those of the scientific community.

Until the mid-1970s, however, the management of risk relied largely on calculations of predicted physical harm that reflected the probability and magnitude of an event's consequences to human health. Only recently have researchers begun to analyze the ways in which the public intuitively understands risks and makes judgments concerning the comparative risks of different technologies. One important lesson is that experts and laypersons often disagree about the meaning of risk: the qualities of a hazard can matter as much as the quantity of risk faced by the public. Risk-perception studies (Slovic, 1987a) have been particularly

This author is solely responsible for the views expressed in this chapter. However, the author's thinking about risk perceptions has been greatly influenced by the highly creative and insightful work of his Decision Research colleague Paul Slovic.

influential in making this point, demonstrating that laypersons think of risk as a multidimensional concept that includes psychological responses to such concerns as the voluntariness of exposure, the potential for catastrophe, and the newness of a technology. Studies of risk perception are widely cited by risk managers and play an active role in debates concerning risk policies.

The increased attention given to risk-perception studies in part reflects recent shifts in the decision-making locus of society, with individuals and interest groups today participating in many aspects of public policy development. But it means more: the influence of risk perceptions also derives from a normative position, taken by many risk regulators, that the views of the public should play a large role in defining risk-management priorities. For example, Milton Russell, former assistant administrator for the Environmental Protection Agency (EPA), wrote that "when it comes to protecting health and the environment, it is public, not expert, opinion that counts" (Russell, 1987, p. 20).

But what constitutes a useful description of public risk values? What factors typically affect an individual's attitudes toward risky technologies, products, and activities? To what extent are people's psychological responses predictable or likely to be shaped by the reporting practices of specific local and national news media? Over the past decade, these questions have been debated by researchers and practitioners interested in improving our understanding of the public's perception of risky events. Some answers are now forthcoming, and these will be reviewed and discussed in this chapter. Many other questions, however, remain unanswered and thus serve as reminders of further research needs and limits to the policy effectiveness of our current understanding of risk perceptions.

News media play a special role in developing of the public's perceptions of risk because media serve as a principal link between the technical assessments of experts and the psychological assessments of laypersons. Media also serve a critical role in facilitating two-way communication about risks: from technical experts to the public, and from the public to scientists and government or industry decision makers. This includes communication about the physical effects of a technology, product, or activity, as well as communication about the process by which a risk decision is reached. Considerations such as equity and trust, for example, play important roles in shaping public opinion and can often be influenced by the tone of a reporter's message or by the social, cultural, and historical context within which a risk management discussion is placed. Media also play a role in interpreting scientific findings for the public, providing selective summaries of key information as well as overall assessments of the quality and relevance of a study.

OVERVIEW OF RISK PERCEPTION RESEARCH

The development of a new product or technology will alter the status quo by creating new sources of both benefits and risks. For example, biotechnology offers the promise of significant advances in medical vaccines and therapies but also entails controversial risks. Economists and policy analysts typically assume that decisions are made by balancing the benefits of a proposed project against its costs. Risks to human health and the natural environment represent one important class of potential social costs.

Risk perception research was begun to understand certain puzzling behaviors affecting social responses to natural and technological hazards. The approach assumes that risk is a subjective concept: risk estimates present assumptions and judgments about the past, current, and future state of the world. Risk assessments, therefore, can only reflect the product of cultural practices at one point in time and each individual's unique mental model of risk characteristics, benefits, and costs.

Most current approaches to studying risk perceptions employ psychometric techniques to produce quantitative representations or "cognitive maps" of risk attitudes and perceptions (Slovic, 1987a). In the usual case, people are asked to make judgments about the riskiness of a diverse set of hazards using a numbered (seven- or nine-point) scale. Ratings are typically made regarding the characteristics hypothesized to account for risk perceptions and attitudes, the perceived social benefits, and the number of deaths caused by the hazard. In general, the higher a hazard's score, the higher its perceived risk, the more people want to see its current risks reduced, and the more likely they are to seek strict regulations designed to reduce the risk.

Investigation of these relations through psychophysical scaling and multivariate analysis techniques (e.g., statistical procedures such as factor analysis) has shown that the intercorrelations among a broad domain of risk characteristics can be used to identity two or three underlying, higher order risk perception factors (Slovic, Fischhoff, and Lichtenstein, 1985). Two factors often emerge as the most important. One factor, termed "dread risk," includes such characteristics of a hazard as dread, perceived lack of control, catastrophic potential, fatalities, and the distribution of risks and benefits. Nuclear power generation and waste storage often score highest on the dread factor scale. A second factor, termed "unknown risk," includes such characteristics of a hazard as the extent to which it is observable, known, new, and delayed in its manifestation of harm. Chemical technologies often receive high scores on this factor. The number of people exposed to a risk also may be important, and in some studies this concern has emerged as a third principal factor.

The results of risk perception studies conducted over the past ten years (see Slovic, Fischhoff, and Lichtenstein, 1985; or Kates, Hohenemser, and Kasperson, 1985) indicate that attitudes about technologies clearly involve more than just the expected physical consequences — mortality and morbidity — of a process. They further suggest that people's attitudes about technologies are basically consistent, that perceived characteristics of risks can often be quantified, and that people's expressed opinions are not random or particularly labile. Furthermore, they emphasize that significant differences often exist in how experts and members of the public view the nature of a technological risk and that differences in risk perceptions among experts or different publics (stakeholder groups, for example) may be large. Differences in experts' and laypersons' risk characterizations arise in part because the public's conception of risks often is broader than that of technical experts. Thus, it is not that laypeople ignore quantitative calculations (e.g., those based on the expected value of damages) but that they often place less weight on them as part of an overall risk-evaluation framework.

Several important findings have emerged from psychometric risk studies. First, risk sources often create social and economic impacts that are far greater than would be predicted on the basis of any reasonable estimates of direct harm. These hazards, for example, nuclear power or recombinant DNA research, generally evoke a deeply rooted sense of concern or dread among wide segments of the public and capture the attention of local and national media. As a result, the adverse impacts of these technologies may be amplified over and above any direct effects of facility construction or operation (Kasperson et al., 1988); and occur in advance of, or even in the absence of, any identifiable accidents or events. The first phenomenon is significant because it suggests that events may be important as signals (Slovic, 1987b). The second phenomenon is significant because it suggests that the area around any hazardous activity may become stigmatized (Edelstein, 1988); that is, adverse sociological or economic consequences may accompany even the possibility of hazardous materials production, storage, or use.

Both amplification and stigmatization can lead to psychological, sociological, and economic effects that may not be anticipated in the absence of risk perception studies. Media coverage is often a key contributing factor to the amplification of risks. Events considered by laypersons to be more frequent or more serious than by experts (aircraft collisions, tornadoes), will often receive substantial coverage; others considered more safe (asthma or falls) are less sensational and therefore often remain unreported (Slovic, Fischhoff, and Lichtenstein, 1980). Other considerations also appear to play a role in risk amplification: for example, the appearance of incompetence or callousness on the part of risk managers is likely to foster a split between the perpetrators and victims of an accident (e.g., witness public anger at the delayed response of the Exxon company to the March 1989 Alaska oil spill).

Stigmatization of an area or activity is also likely to be tied to media coverage of a risk exposure. A case in point is provided by recalling the impact on the apple industry following the February 1989 release of a Natural Resources Defense Council (NRDC) report on cancer risks to children from exposure to the growth regulator Alar. NRDC conducted a carefully orchestrated campaign that included targeted releases to specific newspapers and appearances by celebrities on television talk shows. The economic impacts of product stigmatization on the apple industry were severe, with 1990 wholesale apple prices down about one third compared to 1989 and nationwide revenue losses in the apple industry reported to be about $100 million, or roughly 10 percent of 1989 revenues. However, buyers' perceptions also caused the Washington cherry market to shrink, even though the only link to Alar application was one of geography. Similar effects of regional stigmatization were feared by farmers throughout southeastern Washington state during 1986–1987 when a series of newspaper articles focused on DOE's consideration of the area as a site for storing high-level nuclear wastes, leading to fears that local agricultural products would be considered contaminated and no longer could compete on national markets.

Interest in questions of risk amplification and stigmatization has led to the introduction of new analytic methods to the study of risk perceptions. The psychometric studies of perceived risk noted earlier, which used principal components factor analysis, are based on a general class of exploratory multivariate methods for data analysis. A new set of techniques, known as confirmative multivariate methods, is much stronger for testing theories and analyzing the contributions of multiple predictor variables. For example, Bill Burns and Paul Slovic are currently working with Roger Kasperson and his colleagues at Clark University to test empirically a theory of risk amplification based on a data base of 128 hazard event reports selected from the New York *Times* index of newspaper stories from 1977–1987. The use of confirmatory techniques requires the development of an explicit theoretical model linking the characteristics of a risk event, its coverage by the media, and public response. Although this work is still in progress the techniques appear very promising and new risk characteristics already have emerged (e.g., attribution of blame) that help to explain variations in risk levels across items and scenarios.

LIMITS TO USING RISK PERCEPTIONS FOR POLICY PURPOSES

The knowledge that public attitudes about technologies involve more than just the expected mortality caused by a process is clearly relevant to social decision making. The two principal explanatory factors, dread risk and unknown risk, provide important clues about the nature of public concerns. Ratings of dread have been given particular attention because of the frequently observed connection between dreadedness and public opposition to the introduction of a technology or the siting of a facility.

However, the increasing reliance plaed by decision makers on information about the public's perception of risks does not necessarily mean that a risk manager should go along with everything the public says that they want. There are several reasons for caution, some specific to the nature of risk perceptions and others related to general features common to many judgment and decision processes. These reasons serve as a further source of complexity for researchers or reporters desiring to describe public risk perceptions and their implications accurately.

First, risk perceptions generally have been tied to holistic views of technologies, activities, or products (e.g., comparisons between the risks of nuclear power plants, coal-fired plants and hydroelectric dams). Risk managers and reporters typically are concerned about a single risk source: automobiles, cereals, or skiing. Only a few studies of single technologies or products (e.g., work by Kraus and Slovic, 1988 on perceptions of the risks of trains) have been conducted in sufficient depth to provide managers with the type of information needed for many policy choices.

Second, public attitudes concerning risks often will relate to aspects of a technology, activity, or product not directly related to human or environmental health and safety considerations (Gregory, 1989). For example, experimental evidence supports a view that people's attitudes about risk levels may be strongly influenced by their perceived personal benefits from an item, which implies that risk attitudes may provide a net measure (Dyer and Sarin, 1986). This means that information documenting new benefits from a product could reduce its perceived risks without any corresponding reduction in expected health effects. Other cultural considerations — how people feel about the role of government in an industry, such as biotechnology, or the role of the military in developing and using a technology, such as nuclear power — may also affect judgments of perceived riskiness, as could prejudice or misinformation. People's values are legitimate contributors to social policy, but what if those values reflect opinions prohibited by law, such as a distrust of government-sponsored projects because the government hires minorities, or are based on incorrect information, such as a belief that certain physical processes can occur in cases where they cannot? Variations in the source and legitimacy of these different sources of risk attitudes complicate the use of risk information for policy purposes.

Third, desirable criteria for risk management may conflict in ways and for reasons not intuitively obvious. For example, Keeney (1980) has demonstrated that the desire to avoid catastrophes and the desire to achieve a more equitable distribution of risk may not be compatible, because they imply different utility functions: catastrophe avoidance implies risk aversion, whereas equity implies risk proneness. But these are subtle arguments, and concerned laypersons may not appreciate why they are asked to choose between these laudable but inconsistent goals of social policy. In such cases, the decision maker or the risk reporter may be placed in the position of advocating a particular perspective on risk that will be unpopular or, at the extreme, actively opposed by members of the public.[1]

Fourth, reported perceptions of risks are suspect because of the influence of cognitive biases and heuristics, a topic studied in depth by psychologists over the past 15 years (see Kahneman, Slovic, and Tversky, 1982). For example, people tend to simplify because they cannot deal with too many facets of a problem at one time. As a result, probabilities are often quantified in only vague terms, so that low-probability situations may be viewed as impossible; events that are quite different in key respects are viewed as similar because they are easily remembered, as when releases from a chemical plant recall Bhopal; and firmly held opinions are closed to new and perhaps contradictory information, whereas naive views are easily manipulated (Fishhoff, 1985; Slovic, 1986). In addition, the processes by which mental models of risk are formed and the difficulty people have distinguishing between the remotely possible and the probable suggests that one rational response to cognitive quirks, involving use of the media to provide additional information, may not work as intended. To the extent that imaginability serves as a cue to riskiness, merely mentioning some of the possibly adverse consequences of a product or activity may increase its salience and therefore make the product or activity appear more frightening (Morgan et al., 1985).

These reasons argue for caution when applying risk perception results to social policies. However, similar caveats would apply to other inputs to policy: economic measures of value are imperfect, the political process can be biased, and so forth. Risk perception methods were developed to improve our understanding of public concerns about risky technologies, products, and activities. They are multidimensional and frequently messy because that is the way human cognition and judgment operate in the real world of complex problems. They lack the tidiness of a common evaluative basis, in the sense that dollars or utilities are used as bases for measurement, because perceptions are a psychological construct relating to people's attitudes rather than a means for valuation. Risk managers and media reporters of risk events will often be uneasy with this lack of tidiness, the sensitivity of risk perceptions to context, and the multidimensionality of risk concerns. And one appropriate response is certainly to search for underlying factors and models that make order and sense of information about public risk perceptions. However, denying the complexity of risk perceptions by telling too simple a story undermines the credibility of the science, the media, and the storyteller.

RECOMMENDATIONS FOR REPORTING RISK PERCEPTIONS

Risk reporting can be assessed by some of the same criteria used to rate risk management policies: comprehensiveness, objectivity, fairness, and reliability are all important criteria. But each of these terms is, to a large degree, operationally meaningless in the context of describing risk problems and the perceptions held about them. For example, to be comprehensive in covering risk impacts, a reporter must draw from a daunting array of information sources that includes toxicologists, economists, chemists, and psychologists, as well as local and national government officials (see Fischhoff, 1985). To be considered fair a report about risks must first accurately define and then withstand scrutiny from the different participants or stakeholders in a dispute. This constituency will include experts from several disciplines, laypersons from a variety of civic and interest groups, and government regulators. In the usual case, each perspective is likely to present its special view of the world as uniquely persuasive and indispensable.

Coverage of risk problems also must acknowledge and deal with the fundamental role played by uncertainty. Unfortunately, many important risk issues are not well understood by laypersons or experts. For example, at the time of this writing sufficient data exist on the health effects of low-frequency electromagnetic fields (EMF) to indicate probable cause for concern. However, little is known about fundamental dose-response relationships (Is more exposure necessarily worse?) or how to determine critical exposure pathways (Morgan et al., 1987). A policy of simply waiting until more (How much more?) is known is uncomfortable for both regulators and the public. Yet, it is not clear what the story is here and, even in the absence of consensus, media coverage of EMF health risks is likely to stir up additional public worry and concern.

The problem is not a lack of stories. One important story could detail the reasons for disagreement among scientists. Another story could discuss prudent protective actions, a policy of selective avoidance, that would minimally disrupt daily life and reduce the opportunities for exposure. Yet none of these stories is simple or dramatic. There are no clear lines between "good" and "evil" scientists; there is little excitement, and no dramatic benefit, associated with standing farther from one's toaster. Thus it is likely that, for many readers, these stories will lack compelling interest: there is far more subtlety than sensationalism in these topics. Nor is it easy to see how the typical brief story about a complex social issue such as EMF health impacts can score well on criteria such as fairness or comprehensiveness.

This emphasis on uncertainty — of exposure, of effects, of appropriate personal or social responses — underscores the general finding that, in an important sense, risk perceptions do not exist but are made. Defining an acceptable level of risk reflects a constructive decision process undertaken by an individual in the context of his or her family, community, and society. Because risk is associated with nearly all activity, and because there is no single objective criteria of riskiness, there also is no simple method for determining which risks are acceptable and which are not (Fishhoff et al., 1982).

Risks exist in the context of trade-offs in benefits and costs. The different effects associated with the introduction of a risk source are often incommensurate, requiring, for example, that equity of geographic exposure be balanced against monetary cost or the probability of illness to a future generation. Such complex analyses of risk perceptions do not lend themselves to a simple process of gathering and reporting on established facts and values. Instead, facts and values are formed in the context of how the problem is structured, with expert judgments typically taking the lead on facts (e.g., how effective a certain type of scrubber will be in removing pollutant X) and public input typically establishing the relevant domain of values. This means that stories about risks told by the media cannot merely present "the facts" because what is considered important about the problem will change depending on perspective. As a risk story is pieced together, therefore, implicit and explicit decisions are made regarding the appropriate context for risk decision making, and these decisions in turn do much to determine what the story will be.

CONCLUSION

Managing social risks is a problem of great concern to people everywhere. Information about risk perceptions is a basic component of sound risk decision making. For these reasons alone, media reporting of risk perceptions is of great importance.

However, risk perceptions are inherently complex and rarely well behaved. Perceptions of risk are multidimensional, involve unfamiliar trade-offs, and are subject to the same host of cognitive biases as any other facet of human judgment and reasoning. Because perceptions of risk typically relate to concerns of health, safety, and environmental quality, which matter a great deal to people, discussions of risk issues in the media are unlikely to be viewed dispassionately. Risk management involves both a mental and an emotional response. Not only is there substance to every risk story, but there is symbolism and historical context. There are many sides to every risk story, with each side wanting its own perspective to hold a place of prominence. How the story is told will itself shape the definition and magnitude of the problem.

There may be no more challenging topic for responsible reporting than risk perceptions. Coverage by the media will help structure a risk problem and define the key players. Yet the target — defining and analyzing a risk and its social implications — is always moving. Unanimous praise from all sides in a risk dispute is probably impossible. Yet, there may be no better opportunity to interact directly with important social problems and earn a voice in their resolution, if only because how the risk management story is told often determines, to a large extent, the concluding chapters of the tale.

NOTE

1.   In such cases, I would argue in favor of a risk-neutral utility function for lives or for money. This argument is made in Lichtenstein et al. (in press).

2

Coming to Terms with the Impact of Communication on Scientific and Technological Risk Judgments

SHARON DUNWOODY AND
KURT NEUWIRTH

Most discussions of the perception of scientific and technological risk assign communication, whether interpersonal or mediated, a key role in providing individuals with the information needed to make risk judgments. Yet, understanding of how information is selected and used by laypersons to inform risky choices is elusive.

This chapter argues that such an understanding is critical in any risk communication enterprise, but that research to date may have obscured the role information can play for individuals. The chapter explains the confusion precipitated by that research and offers a strategy for examining the influence of information on individual judgments about scientific and technological risk.

Our strategy is grounded in part on concepts derived from existing mass communication literature, a literature that we think has been largely ignored by researchers studying scientific and technological risk perception. But we will also argue that some of the conceptual and operational fuzziness currently plaguing risk communication research handicaps researchers examining the role of communication in other domains; we illustrate this contention by offering some examples of current approaches to mass communication effects that could benefit from increased clarity.

"Risk communication" is a buzz term these days. Thus, its meaning has become diffused and multidimensional. Plough and Krimsky (1987) do a good job of laying out these various dimensions,[1] and a recent report from the National Research Council (1989) takes the extra step of distinguishing between risk messages and risk communication, defining the latter as a process, specifically, "an interactive process of exchange of information and opinion among individuals, groups, and institutions" (p. 2). For purposes of this chapter, risk communication is the relaying of any interpersonal or mediated message that contains information about the existence, nature, severity, or acceptability of a risk. Since risks are ubiquitous, we confine our discussion here to scientific and technological risks and use risk communication to denote scientific and technological risk communication.

PROBLEMS WITH RISK COMMUNICATION STUDIES

Sender-based Bias

Interest in risk communication in the 1980s has paralleled concerns of the scientific community over the adequacy of nonscientists' abilities to make risk judgments. Scientists have long argued that there should be a good fit between estimates of the likelihood of harm in a particular situation and individual judgments about whether or not to abide that situation. That is, they assert that probability of harm and level of worry, with its concomitant behavioral responses, should be positively correlated, and highly so. When a bad fit is uncovered, scientists are likely to blame the receiver. The possibility that differing risk judgments may stem from a difference in underlying values (Douglas and Wildavsky, 1982) is rarely entertained.

Under such circumstances, risk communication becomes synonymous with risk education. Researchers and risk communicators alike assume a knowledge deficit on the part of the receiver and then actively try to reduce that deficit. Among practitioners, such a sender-based assumption results in information campaigns that focus on what nonscientists need to know. Scientists operating within a sender-based perspective (Kahneman and Tversky, 1979; Nisbett et al., 1987) often frame their investigations as expeditions in search of individual limitations. Such work can have value, as potential human limitations often are uncovered. (See Nisbett et al., 1987 for a discussion of human probability reasoning).

But while a sender-based bias places the blame for poor risk judgments squarely in the lap of the receiver, a receiver-based approach focuses instead on how and why individuals make judgments, given the receivers' values. The emphasis becomes understanding ongoing processes rather than trying normatively to change them. In Bradbury's (1989) terms, such a shift means abandoning a conceptual understanding of risk as objective fact in favor of conceptualizing risk as a socially constructed attribute.

Increasing numbers of researchers interested in risk perception are turning from attempts to manipulate receivers to studies that try to understand them. (For a review of this work, see the chapter by Robin Gregory in this book.)

Risk communication research similarly can profit from a receiver-based perspective. Such an approach would call for an examination not just of the effects of communication, but also the processes by which individuals select and use the information available to them. This assumption of an active audience has long been embraced by mass communication researchers within such domains as uses and gratification research. (For a discussion of this area, see McLeod and Becker, 1981).

Risk Perception as a Unidimensional Concept

The assumption that risk is something "out there" to be measured fuels a tendency to view the concept as unidimensional or, at the very least, a messy multidimensional concept that can be captured unidimensionally in the ubiquitous "risk estimate." Such estimates are often defined as "quantitative measures of hazard consequences that can be expressed as conditional probabilities of experiencing harm" (Hohenemser, Kates, and Slovic, 1983, p. 379). If such a measure reasonably captures the likelihood of harm, researchers argue, then reasonable public perceptions of the risk in question should coincide with the estimate. Risk perception, thus, is defined as a measure of the closeness of fit between the risk estimate and individual personal evaluations of the hazards.

Such a definition not only ignores the original multivariate nature of risky situations themselves but also usually renders the concept of risk perception as unidimensional. Even worse, investigators rarely seem to agree on the nature of that single perceptual dimension; some use operationalizations that tap into cognitive dimensions of risk perception (for example, asking individuals to estimate the likelihood that they, personally, might be harmed by a risk), others delve into affective dimensions (asking respondents about their level of worry with respect to a risk), and still others operationalize risk perception as behavioral dimensions (asking respondents about accomplished or intended changes in behavior with respect to a risk). Not surprisingly, most attempts at assessing the congruence between unidimensional risk estimates and unidimensional risk perceptions find little correspondence between the two.

Conceptualizing and operationalizing risk perception as a multidimensional phenomenon seems the far better strategy. Slovic (1987a), for example, defines risk perception as "the judgments people make when they are asked to *characterize* and *evaluate* hazardous activities and technologies" [emphasis added] (p. 280). Slovic, as have others, uses psychophysical scaling and multivariate analysis techniques to produce "cognitive maps of risk attitudes and perceptions" (p. 281). Such maps, argue Slovic and others, illuminate both cognitive and affective dimensions along which individuals locate particular risks.

Another clarification strategy, suggested by Tyler and Cook (1984), calls for separating individuals' perceptions of risk to the community or society at large from their perceptions of their own personal level of risk, distinguishing, in other words, between referential levels. These researchers suggest that different factors will inform these different referential levels. For example, they find that mediated information channels are more likely to be used to inform individual perceptions of societal risk than of personal risk.

We argue here that both the cognitive and affective dimensions and referential level of risk judgment are important distinctions to make when trying to determine the role of information in risky choices, but we find no studies of communication and scientific and technological risk that have employed these more sophisticated conceptualizations of the dependent variable. Studies of the impact of information on risk judgments in other domains have employed one of these clarifying devices but not both (Tyler and Cook, 1984; Sparks and Ogles, 1990).

Focus on Behavioral Change as a Dependent Variable

Within the domain of risky choices, researchers and risk communicators have traditionally focused on behavior as the ultimate dependent variable. Such a goal makes pragmatic sense, particularly when problems are viewed from a sender-based perspective. Information campaigns of all kinds are premised on such goals (see, for example, Rice and Atkin, 1989; Booth, 1988; Salmon, 1989; Shoemaker, 1989).

Certainly, studies have demonstrated relationships, albeit modest, between information use and behavioral change. But such work has also suggested that information may have its greatest impacts on such intermediate variables as knowledge and attitudes, which in turn will influence behavior. If that is the case, then looking for direct, powerful links between information and behavior may actually obscure one's understanding of the specific roles that information can play in risky settings. We argue here that attending to information's impact on such intermediate variables as cognitive and affective responses to risk may offer more insight into the ways in which individuals select and use information than will a focus on behavioral change only.

Doing Communication Research in a Vacuum

Finally, we join other scholars (see, for example, Short, 1984, pp. 720–21) in noting that much of the early risk communication research ignores the wealth of communication studies that could inform the relationship between information and risk judgment. While space does not permit an extensive discussion of the relevant communication literature here, we do note that research across a number of theoretical perspectives tends to find that: individuals are active selectors and processors of information; they use different information channels for different purposes; they attend to information in those channels with varying levels of intensity; they may interpret information available in different channels as differentially applicable to self or society; it makes sense to distinguish between cognition and affect when trying to determine how people think about conundrums in their lives, ranging from selecting a presidential candidate to deciding what to make of radon; and information may influence those cognitive and affective dimensions differentially.

FORGING A CLEARER INFORMATION/RISK JUDGMENT LINK

The problems noted above are not intractable. In this section we propose a strategy for exploring the relationship between information and individual assessments of scientific and technological risks. A recent study we conducted of individual perceptions of the risk presented by the

HIV virus incorporates many of the strategies suggested here. The survey results illustrate some of our points.

The Active Audience

A view of audiences as active information selectors and processors has emerged since mid-century, partly as a by-product of the often unsuccessful search for powerful and systematic media effects. Codified to some extent in the uses and gratifications approach (McLeod and Becker, 1981), which holds that media behavior reflects prior interests and preferences, an active audience view asserts that individuals make decisions to pay attention to and use information available to them across a variety of information channels. Thus, it is the task of the researcher to explore what drives individuals to attend to particular messages.

Dervin (1981) takes the concept another step further, arguing that there are no messages, per se, out there. Instead, individuals construct information from the variety of stimuli around them: "Instead of being seen as having an absolute, accurate, isomorphic relationship with reality, information is seen as being a product, a creation of human observing at specific points in time-space. Information has meaning only in the context of the constraints on the human observing that created it. It is relative to its creator and meaningful only in that context" (p. 75). In the extreme, such a view appears to eschew the possibility of finding any patterns of information use or shared meanings among groups or social aggregates. However, such an approach has merit in that it embraces the idiosyncratic efforts of individuals to extract useful information from their surroundings. For scholars who feel that patterns of information use can indeed be uncovered across individuals, the active audience perspective recommends at least two courses of action:

Looking for Audience Use of a Variety of Channels

Most studies of channel use in developed countries focus on the big four — newspapers, magazines, radio, and television — under the assumption that the mass media account for most of the messages individuals encounter in the course of daily life. Researchers may be right in making such a judgment about sheer volume, but the "bulk" argument ignores the wealth of nonmediated information sources in our environment.

A young man searching for information about AIDS, for example, could certainly encounter relevant stories in the mass media. But think of the additional sources available to him: friends, a physician, someone showing a videotape at a local organizational meeting, a classroom lecture. The social environment of the average individual is information-rich, indeed, and much of that information may be available in nonmediated channels.

As those embroiled in information campaigns have long argued, it is important to look for individuals' penchants for using a variety of chan-nels in order to gain insight into what information is being selected and why.

Why is a tough question to answer, however. Part of the problem is that researchers have often pitted one information channel against another, mediated versus interpersonal, for example, and then pronounced a winner. Such an approach ignores the likelihood that individuals use a variety of information channels simultaneously and for different reasons. Chaffee (1982) argues that one's choice of a particular information channel depends jointly on the accessibility of the channel and one's judgment of the extent to which the information in that channel will be relevant. In other words, individuals may prefer to access a variety of channels, even when gathering information about a single issue. To argue that individuals rely principally on the mass media for information about scientific and technological risks — an assertion often seen in both research and commentary — may oversimplify to the point of uselessness.

Measuring Level of Attention to Messages

The typical media use study operationalizes "use" as exposure over time to a particular medium or, at most, exposure to particular content in a medium. But researchers are increasingly replacing exposure with a more active operationalization: attention.

Attention, they argue, makes better conceptual sense, particularly if one posits an active audience that makes decisions about what available information to attend to and what to ignore. And, indeed, attention seems to work better than simple exposure as a predictor. For example, several researchers have found that attention to media stories dealing with a particular content area had significant effects on knowledge, even after controlling for general exposure to types of media (Chaffee and Choe, 1979; McLeod and McDonald, 1985; Chaffee and Schleuder, 1986). One study that looked at the relationship between media use of and knowledge about science and technology unearthed similar findings: measures of level of attention paid to science and technology stories in the media were more strongly associated with knowledge than were either measures of general exposure to media channels or measures of focused exposure to science and technology stories in those channels (Swindel, Lindstrom, and Sathoff, July 1988).

Risk Judgment as a Multidimensional Concept

One major problem with risk perception as a dependent variable has been that researchers have viewed it as a unidimensional, cognitive concept. According to this view, cognitive information about a risk, that is, a measure of likelihood of harm, is used to reach cognitive, individual decisions about a risky situation (that is, I have a low/high probability of harm from exposure to this risk, and I will act accordingly).

Both research and common sense fail to support such a conceptualization. We argue here for the incorporation of two dimensions in any measurement of risk judgment. We will use the term "risk judgment" instead of "risk perception" because the latter has been used with such abandon that its meaning has been irreparably fuzzed.

Differentiating Affect from Cognition

There exists a lengthy tradition in psychology, as well as in mass communication research, of distinguishing between affective and cognitive variables. We will not get embroiled here in the argument over whether or not these dimensions can be mutually exclusive of one another. Instead, we are drawn to the arguments of Leventhal and Scherer (1987), who assert that while the mechanisms underlying affect and cognition may be partially independent, an individual's affective and cognitive reactions to his or her environment may be intricately interwoven.

Slovic and colleagues have done perhaps the most illuminating work on the multidimensional nature of risk judgment to date (see, for example, Fischhoff, Slovic, and Lichtenstein, 1982; Hohenemser, Kates, and Slovic, 1983; Slovic, 1987a). These researchers have defined a number of dimensions used by nonscientists to make risk judgments, among them the voluntary or involuntary nature of the risk, its catastrophic potential, and the level of risk the hazard poses to future generations. Although many of these dimensions are cognitive in nature, the scientists also posit one dimension, clearly an affective variable, that they label "dread."

But the question of how information may influence these dimensions goes unanswered in many perception studies. We must call on communication research for help.

Researchers in recent years have focused on the mass media's influence on cognition — on what people know. From studies of voting decisions (O'Keefe and Atwood, 1981; Becker and Dunwoody, 1982) to evaluations of health campaigns (Ettema, Brown, and Luepker, 1983; Chaffee, Roser, and Flora, 1989), researchers have found relationships between mediated information and cognition. Often, when scientists have been able to compare the influence of media use on both affect and cognition, they find the biggest impact on the latter (for example, see Sears and Chaffee, 1979).

Information from interpersonal sources is another matter. Relationships with others are loaded with affective attributes, and researchers have long argued that interpersonal influence on affective judgment is far stronger than mass mediated influence. Chaffee (1972) notes that interpersonal channels are more likely to contain "normative" information, while mediated channels are more likely to contain "informational" content.

These findings suggest that differentiating between affective and cognitive dimensions of risk judgment is important to understanding potential media effects. We would expect mass media content to influence primarily the cognitive dimension of risk judgment and information sources with a heavy affective component — interpersonal sources, for example — to be more strongly related to the affective dimension.

Differentiating between Individual- and Societal-level Referents

Risk perception researchers have long lamented the resistance of individuals to regard risks as affecting themselves. Instead, audiences seem to interpret risk statistics as information about others, not about themselves. This tendency to separate personal and general views of the world has been found repeatedly in psychological research (see Tyler and Cook, 1984 for a summary of such research and Weinstein, 1989 for applications to risk perception).

If individuals indeed differentiate between personal and general views of the world, then it seems logical to suggest that they may use information channels differentially to inform those views, and that is what past studies have found. Tyler and Cook (1984) note, "Media impact is found in studies examining judgments at the societal level but not in studies probing judgments at the personal level" (p. 693).

This suggests that the information channels individuals select to inform their personal-level judgments may be different from those preferred for societal-level judgments. Understanding the role of information, then, would require making that referential distinction.

In summary, research is needed premised on an active information-processing audience and, in the search for the roles played by information, that uses a multidimensional model of risk judgment. Figure 2.1 arrays two particularly important sets of dimensions: the cognitive/affective dimension and individual/societal referential dimension.

FIGURE 2.1 — Risk Orientation by Reference Level

REFERENCE LEVEL

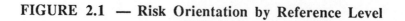

	INDIVIDUAL	SOCIETAL
COGNITIVE	INDIVIDUAL RISK ESTIMATE	SOCIETAL RISK ESTIMATE
AFFECTIVE	INDIVIDUAL AFFECT ESTIMATE	SOCIETAL AFFECT ESTIMATE

RISK ORIENTATION

AN ILLUSTRATION

In fall 1987 we conducted a survey of University of Wisconsin at Madison students' perceptions of Acquired Immune Deficiency Syndrome (AIDS). The design incorporated some of the variables discussed above, and the results illustrate some of our points. Specifically, we were able to look at the impact of exposure and attention to both interpersonal and mediated information channels on cognitive and affective dimensions of risk judgment. Referential levels are not included in this analysis.

The sample consisted of 505 randomly selected undergraduate students. Interviews were conducted by telephone in October 1987 and averaged 27 minutes in duration. Forty percent of the interviews were authenticated through a verification procedure.

Successfully completed interviews totaled 438, a completion rate of 86.7 percent. Only 34 persons (6.7 percent) refused to participate, and another 33 (6.5 percent) were never reached. The sample characteristics matched known population parameters.

Dimensions of Risk Judgment

Respondents were asked parallel questions about the level of risk (cognitive) relative to and their level of worry (affective) about a set of actions and situations (see Table 2.1 for brief descriptions of these variables). Anxiety estimates were measured on a 100-point scale, while the risk estimates spanned 10 orders of magnitude. The latter were transformed into logarithms prior to analysis.

TABLE 2.1
Factor Loadings of Worry and Risk Estimates

	Factors		
Risk and Worry Items	*General Worry*	*Situational Worry*	*Risk Estimation*
(a) Worry about self getting AIDS	.93	−.17	.07
(b) Friends' worry about getting AIDS	.85	−.12	.03
(c) Parents' worry about respondent getting AIDS	.68	−.06	.00
(d) Worry about kissing someone with the AIDS virus	.08	−.91	−.07
(e) Worry about using toilet just after it was used by someone with the AIDS virus	.16	−.63	−.02
(f) Worry about having sex with someone with the AIDS virus but using a condom	.08	−.45	−.02
(g) Estimate of getting AIDS virus by using a toilet just after it was used by someone with the AIDS virus	.08	.12	.78
(h) Estimate of getting AIDS from kissing someone who has the AIDS virus	.16	.31	.65
(i) Estimate of getting AIDS by having sex with someone who has the AIDS virus but using a condom	.07	.16	.46
(j) Estimate that a friend has the AIDS virus	−.20	−.21	.44
(k) Estimate that self will get the AIDS virus	−.35	−.13	.43
Percent Variance	28.4	15.0	10.0

Note: n = 438. Oblique rotation. Factor coefficients are Maximum Likelihood (ML) estimates.

When we factor analyzed the responses, the cognitive and affective dimensions emerged as separate factors. As Table 2.1 shows, affective orientations were grouped into two factors — one general and one focused on specific risky behaviors — while the cognitive risk estimates all loaded onto one factor. These results suggested to us that respondents indeed were distinguishing between cognitive and affective estimations of risk. They also seemed to be differentiating between a more general level of worry about self and anxiety about specific behaviors.

Relationships between Channel Use and Risk Judgment

Table 2.2 offers the results of three regression equations that examine the influence of three blocks of variables — demographics, media exposure, and level of attention to AIDS stories in specific channels — on the cognitive and affective dimensions of risk judgment.

We asked respondents about their use of specific channels of information as well as about their level of attention to AIDS information in those channels.

The most obvious finding of Table 2.2 is that interpersonal channels are the best predictors of both cognitive and affective dimensions of risk judgment. The mass media do not fare well. Exposure to channels and level of attention to AIDS stories in particular channels are equally poorly related to risk judgment; one can find few significant betas.

Yet, those few betas do lend support to our suggestion that the use of mediated channels should be related to the cognitive dimension, not the affective dimension, of risk judgment. Both newspaper exposure and attention to television AIDS stories are negatively related to risk estimate: the more time respondents reported spending with newspapers and the more attention they reported paying to AIDS stories on television, the lower were their estimates of the likelihood of contracting the AIDS virus in general and from specific activities. We cannot say here that media exposure and attention created more or less accurate risk estimates, but simply that mediated channel use was related to lower risk estimates.

We think these data provide preliminary support for the multidimensional nature of risk judgments and for the possibility that individuals may use a variety of information channels to construct meanings that inform their risky choices. Individuals in this study seemed to be using both mass media and interpersonal sources, but while interpersonal sources were used to inform both dimensions of risk

TABLE 2.2
Prediction of Risk Judgments (hierarchical regression)

	Risk Judgments					
	General Worry		Situational Worry		Risk Estimation	
Block	Beta	R^2	Beta	R^2	Beta	R^2
Demographic[a]						
Hispanic	.06		.05		.00	
Gender	.00		−.11*		−.04	
Age	−.01		−.07		.01	
Race	.02	.01	.05	.02	.00	.00
Exposure						
Magazine	−.04		.04		.07	
Television	−.05		.07		.07	
Radio	.08		.08		−.01	
Newspaper	.01		−.01		−.15*	
Interpersonal	.20*	.04*	.09	.02	.22*	.06*
Attention						
Magazine	.08		.00		.01	
Television	−.04		−.04		−.19*	
Radio	.00		.07		.04	
Newspaper	−.02	.00	−.05	.00	.07	.02
Total R^2		.05*		.04		.08*

Note: n = 438. Entries are standardized betas. R^2 is incremental variance for each block.
  [a]Coding: Hispanic (0 = Non-Hispanic); Gender (0 = Male); Race (0 = White).
  *p < .05.

judgment, the mass media were used to inform the cognitive dimension only.

Attention to AIDS information in particular channels did not play a stronger role in influencing risk judgment than did simple channel exposure in this study, but previous studies have provided such strong support for attention as a predictor that we are reluctant to abandon the concept at this time. The lackluster nature of the betas in Table 2.2 could be a function of several things, including the homogeneous nature of the sample. Respondents were university students with similar demographic characteristics and relatively low levels of information use. Given the topic's obvious relevance to these young adults, another possibility is that, under conditions of high salience, the acts of exposure and attention are synonymous. Testing the model on more representative samples of adults and across types of risky situations would be important next steps.

GENERALIZATION

The clarification provided by the multidimensional parsing of risk judgment into cognitive/affective and individual/societal categories shows promise for some other areas of mass communication theory as well. The dependent variables important to a number of communication theories — cultivation analysis, spiral of silence, impersonal impact, agenda-setting — share characteristics either explicitly or implicitly with our risk judgment concept. We offer two examples here to illustrate the point.

Agenda-Setting

The basic agenda-setting hypothesis asserts that the selection and display of issues in the mass media will influence the salience assigned to those issues by audience members and society as a whole. It was first tested empirically by McCombs and Shaw (1972). Publication of the original article was followed relatively quickly by a study confirming the original study's main findings (McLeod, Becker, and Byrnes, 1974). The replication is of particular note not only for its completeness in linking media and audience agendas, but also for distinguishing among three concepts: intrapersonal salience, the respondents' own estimates of the importance of issues at a societal level; community issue salience, usually operationalized as the extent to which respondents discussed particular issues with others; and perceived issue salience, respondents' estimates of the salience levels assigned to issues by members of the society.

Although the first and last concepts are of particular interest here, it is important to note that all three concepts reside at the societal referential level. Agenda-setting does not attend to individual evaluations of the importance of issues to themselves. Instead, it asks individuals to assess the saliencies of society directly (what I think society should do) or perceptually (what I think society thinks we should do). Those categories are both lodged under the societal level in Figure 2.2.

Curiously, the concept of salience or importance upon which the entire agenda-setting enterprise rests has remained largely unexamined. Conventional wisdom holds salience to be cognitive in nature; the one

FIGURE 2.2 — Risk Judgments by Reference Levels: Agenda-setting and Cultivation

THEORY	REFERENCE LEVEL					
	INDIVIDUAL		SOCIETAL		PERCEIVED SOCIETAL	
	RISK JUDGMENT		RISK JUDGMENT		RISK JUDGMENT	
	PROB. ESTIMATE	AFFECT ESTIMATE	PROB. ESTIMATE	AFFECT ESTIMATE	PROB. ESTIMATE	AFFECT ESTIMATE
AGENDA-SETTING						
CURRENT:	NONE	NONE	"INTRAPERSONAL SALIENCE"		"PERCEIVED COMMUNITY SALIENCE"	
PROPOSED:	POSSIBLE	POSSIBLE	PROB. EST. OF OUTCOME FOR EACH ISSUE	AFFECT EST. (NEGATIVE) FOR EACH ISSUE	PROB. EST. OF OUTCOME FOR EACH ISSUE	AFFECT EST. (NEGATIVE) FOR EACH ISSUE
CULTIVATION						
CURRENT:	CHANCE OF VICTIMIZATION	FEAR OF CRIME	"MEAN WORLD"		NONE	NONE
PROPOSED:	PROB. EST. OF CRIME VICTIMIZATION	CRIME AFFECT (WORRY) EST.	SOCIETAL CRIME PROB. ESTIMATE / PROB. OF "POLICE STATE" OUTCOME AS SOLUTION	SOCIETAL CRIME AFFECT ESTIMATE / AFFECT EST. OF "POLICE STATE" OUTCOME AS SOLUTION	POSSIBLE	POSSIBLE

exception to that assumption is in Smith (1987, n.12), who, without elaborating on the meaning of either term, considered salience to fall somewhere between an attitude and a cognition.

A moment's thought reveals the ambiguity inherent in the conventional wisdom, however. An agenda implies a ranking of issues. The ranking consists of cognitive comparisons of value weights assigned to each issue on the agenda. But what is the source of value assigned to each issue? Clearly, some other component is involved.

It is possible that asking respondents to specify, for example, "the most important problem facing the country" generates the following series of decisions: individuals first assess the likelihood of various outcomes, weigh each by some negative value (since we're talking about problems here) associated with the outcome, and then rank the various outcomes to arrive at an answer. For example, an individual may estimate the likelihood of the country being overwhelmed by crime, annihilated by nuclear war, and economically and psychologically damaged by drug use. The person would then assign various levels of negative value to these elements, for example, the individual may fear nuclear war far more than criminal activity. Finally, the individual uses both risk estimates and value weights to rank the options.

Cast in these terms, the dependent variables sound familiar. We are dealing with risk judgment.

Defining salience as a joint function of a risk estimate and an affect estimate implies that previous studies have confounded the two, thus obscuring underlying processes. If we are correct, then such confounding is likely to have underestimated the magnitude and extent of media effects as well. For example, if mass media have their greatest impact on cognitive elements, as is suggested by many researchers, then mixing in the affective can only obscure relationships. If media content does indeed influence both cognitive and affective dimensions, then that can be discovered only by separating them. Media coverage may cause an individual to revise estimates of outcome probabilities, preferences regarding outcomes, or both.

Differentiating between cognitive and affective dimensions of salience is particularly important in instances where information causes both to vary, but in opposite directions. In such situations the net effect of information on salience appears to be zero, while the total effect on both could be quite substantial. Just examining salience would obscure the action.

As Figure 2.2 indicates, the agenda-setting hypothesis could be extended to include individual-level risk judgments. Studies cited previously (e.g., Tyler and Cook, 1984) suggest little possibility of observing mass media effects on these judgments about self, although our AIDS study suggests that one should find an impact of interpersonal communication at the individual level.

The Cultivation Hypothesis

Originally proposed as a macro-level theory linking institutions, television message systems, and mass society (Gerbner, 1973), the cultivation hypothesis has been tested using the individual as the unit of analysis (for a recent review, see Ogles, 1987; for theoretical criticisms, see Newcomb, 1978; for empirical critiques, see Hirsch, 1980, 1981).

In general, researchers have tested only a limited range of possible hypotheses. Despite numerous studies, evidence for cultivation effects is conceded to be meager (Hawkins, Pingree, and Adler, 1987).

Recently, Sparks and Ogles (May 1990) did differentiate between likelihood and fear of victimization at the individual level. They offer support for the argument that mediated information informs estimates of the likelihood of being victimized but not level of worry. Their work should begin to clear up that cognitive/affective confusion, but distinguishing between individual and societal levels of reference may also contribute to conceptual clarity.

The cultivation hypothesis has interesting macro-level implications. Researchers working within the theory have argued, but scarcely tested, that the system of meta messages embedded in television content may affect the course of politics. They argue, for example, that an over-representation of criminal acts and the presentation of police state methods of dealing with crime as normal on television inculcates greater fear of crime and heightens the likelihood that viewers will demand authorities take extreme measures in order to solve the problem.

Notice that at least six variables may be involved in such an argument. Not only would researchers expect television exposure to influence individual- and societal-level risk judgments in both cognitive and affective dimensions, but that a person's societal-level preference for a police state solution would be affected by television exposure as well. This latter concept should have cognitive and affective dimensions, too.

SUMMARY AND IMPLICATIONS

In a recent article in *Science* magazine on national efforts to change behaviors that put individuals at risk for AIDS, reporter William Booth reflected the frustration of many scientists and policy makers at the apparent powerlessness of information. "Most experts agree that knowledge has little, if anything, to do with behavior change," wrote Booth (1988, p. 1238).

Indeed, the experts Booth quoted did feel that information is only weakly related to behavioral change, and they may be right. But information is an important component of dimensions of risk judgment, itself a concept that must ultimately be related to choices individuals make about risky situations.

When individuals have to make risky choices we think they use information intensively to reach decisions. The issue for researchers and policy makers should not be the failure of individuals to use information in risky choice situations, but rather devising more sophisticated ways to discover what channels they use for particular types of information and how they incorporate that information into their decisions.

The strategy proposed here calls for the assumption that individuals are active information seekers and processors. It calls for a willingness to extend the notion of information channels beyond the mass media. And it calls for a more careful conceptualization of the risk judgments into which information is incorporated.

If subsequent empirical work supports the argument that individuals use a variety of channels to inform multiple dimensions of risk judgment, then it will be important for policy makers to take those channels and dimensions into account when designing risk communication efforts. Our work, as does the work of other scholars, suggests that the one-message-fits-all approach is flawed, and that risk managers must understand their communications challenge before tackling it. Here are some examples of questions made relevant by this model:

If risk judgment is a multidimensional phenomenon, then which dimensions do you wish to influence? Depending on the type of channel used, knowledge about a risk may be far easier to influence than level of worry about a risk.

If individuals use various types of information channels to inform their understanding of risky situations, then how do you determine which channels they are likely to use? Such a question may be exceedingly situational, with access to particular channels and individual judgments about the potential relevance of information available in those channels varying across time and space.

For example, if a risky situation has a sudden onset but is rather long lived, one might find individuals relying on mediated messages for both cognitive and affective assistance early in the game but shifting to a reliance on interpersonal channels for affective help later. The argument here is that, while individuals generally may prefer interpersonal channels to mediated ones for informing their risk judgments, few interpersonal channels may be available early in the onset of a risk. Persons may thus be forced to rely on mediated messages for initial risk judgment decisions. As a risky situation matures, one would expect a greater number of interpersonal sources to be available.

One illustration of this particular scenario might be the sudden announcement in a community that an industrial site on the edge of town has just been added to the federal Superfund list. Community members would probably know little about the risk, so information seekers might rely initially on mediated messages to learn about the risk and to make some early decisions about how worried to be. But the passage of time would produce greater and greater reliance on interpersonal sources, both within the community and without. For example, community members might ask representatives of state agencies investigating the site to discuss their findings in town meetings.

If individuals are highly likely to interpret risk information in mediated channels as relevant to society but not to themselves, what can a risk manager do to inform an individual's personal risk judgment? While empirical findings might lead one to conclude that interpersonal communication is the policy maker's best bet, it is important to avoid confusing what is with what might be. Channel accessibility, the likelihood that relevant information will appear on a given channel, and awareness that relevant information is indeed available are all open to intervention and modification. The choice of a channel or mix of channels is one of relative economic efficiency. Thus, we leave open the question of whether or not it is possible to design mediated messages in ways that enhance the likelihood they will be interpreted personally. For example, does personalizing a message — leading a risk story with a brief account of an individual wrestling with the risk — enhance personal interpretation? Do broadcast messages seem more personal than messages conveyed in print?

These questions are a few of many that would confront policy makers and risk managers, should our model hold up under the empirical test. Most of these questions are themselves empirically testable.

This chapter makes a preliminary argument that concepts important to a number of communication theories might, like risk judgment, be a more complex mixture of cognitive and affective attributes than is currently assumed. We have briefly made our case for agenda setting and cultivation theory. Other perspectives that might benefit from such a reconceptualization include spiral of silence, impersonal impact hypothesis, sociotropic voting and symbolic politics, personal optimism/societal pessimism, video malaise, third-person effect, and pluralistic ignorance. Our contention here is not that the primary concepts of interest in these domains are all really risk judgment in disguise, but that many of them may be mixing cognitive and affective dimensions in ways that may submerge their true relationships to information. More careful conceptualization will behoove us all.

NOTES

1. Plough and Krimsky suggest that risk communication has five components: intentionality, content, audience direction, source, and flow. They argue that different definitions of risk communication vary in the "latitude of interpretation" of these elements (p. 6).

3

Risk Management: The Public versus the Technical Experts

Sharon M. Friedman

It is not at all unusual to hear scientists lament, "Why can't the public understand the facts we present and be rational about them?" Often such a question arises because the public becomes very concerned about an environmental risk that a scientist perceives to be minute.

In February 1989, for example, the Natural Resources Defense Council (NRDC) announced children were in danger from eating apples sprayed with Alar. Major school districts in Chicago, New York, and Los Angeles immediately withdrew apples and apple juice from lunch programs.

Was this an irrational act? Was it an isolated case, or do members of the public frequently react irrationally to information dealing with environmental and health risks? Certainly, from the view of many technical experts, they do. But to a number of social science and communication researchers, such actions are not irrational at all. The difference in interpretation is based on a difference in premise.

According to Dorothy Nelkin, risk assessment experts have assumed that evaluating risk is a technical matter that requires better, more accurate scientific information. Once the experts have this information, they

An earlier version of this chapter appeared in *Weaver of Information and Perspectives on Technological Literacy 8* (Spring 1990): 5–7.

believe they simply have to present it to people who should accept the "rational" way to proceed. They assume "that if public fear of risk is defined in terms of inadequate information, then increased technical evidence and better communication of this evidence by knowledgeable experts will allay public concern" (Nelkin, 1988, p. 5). But in their efforts to promote a "rational" view of risk, these experts ignore factors that cannot be quantified. Nelkin points out that

> While some people talk of risk in terms of cost-effective solution, of efficiency; others use the language of "rights," emphasizing moral issues and questions of social responsibility, justice and obligation. Some individuals evaluate risk in statistical terms; others talk of "victims" or "real people." Some define risk as a problem that requires expert solutions; others seek more participatory controls (Nelkin, 1988, pp. 7–8).

Many social scientists believe facts are not the only factors operating in public risk assessment. Values, beliefs and attitudes also play a major role in influencing public actions, and they often override whatever the facts present. For example, a recent poll by the Roper Organization on what the public thinks about environmental risks found that 58 percent considered radiation from nuclear accidents a very serious threat. Yet, only 22 percent considered X-ray radiation a very serious threat, and only 21 percent considered radiation from radon a very serious threat (Russell, 1990).

Because scientific facts do not support these opinions, many technical experts would call them irrational. Not many people live close enough to a nuclear plant to be concerned about potential radiation exposure. The Three Mile Island accident did not appear to harm many people except to subject nearby residents to severe stress. The Chernobyl accident did far more damage, but it still was not as deadly as flooding in Bangladesh or the chemical accident in Bhopal, India.

In contrast, radiation exposure from radon has been called the second largest cause of lung cancer after cigarette smoking by the Surgeon General and the Environmental Protection Agency (EPA). Despite extensive information campaigns to alert and motivate people to test and remediate, the public remains relatively unmoved about radon.

Many technical experts find this behavior irrational. Yet, there are factors lurking below the surface that experts do not take into account.

Slovic, Fischhoff, and Lichtenstein (1982) have found that nuclear power evokes greater feelings of dread among people than do any other activities, except terrorism and warfare. They point out that some of this fear can be attributed to radiation's invisible and irreversible contamination, which can induce cancer and genetic damage, but radiation from radon and X-rays can do that, too.

What radon and X-rays do not bring with them is the fear of catastrophe. Many people believe that a serious accident at a nuclear plant will cause thousands of deaths and severe environmental damage. They also connect, perhaps subliminally, nuclear power to nuclear weapons. Remember, the public first heard about atomic energy relating to a bomb that caused widespread damage and many deaths. And even though people have been told for many years that nuclear plants cannot blow up like nuclear bombs, a 1984 study found that 84 percent of U.S. citizens surveyed thought nuclear plants could explode, although 44 percent thought it was "not very likely" (Inglehard, 1984, p. 1).

So, dread of catastrophe and links to nuclear bombs, factors one would not find in a risk assessment, powerfully influence public attitudes toward nuclear power. And these public attitudes have helped slow down, if not stop, the growth of the nuclear power industry in this country. As public attitudes have impeded this technology, they also can impede others. Scientists fear that when members of the public involve themselves in scientific issues, they will slow down research and affect its applications.

A clear example of this public interference is taking place over fetal tissue research. For a number of years, the United States has banned research using fetal tissue because it comes from aborted fetuses. Caught in the highly emotional abortion issue, this area of scientific research is severely constrained despite the many promises it holds for the public good, such as its use in research for ways to overcome Parkinson's disease.

The clash over public participation in science issues is not new, nor does it only revolve around risk. The turbulent period from the mid-1960s to the early 1970s led to questioning by the public about environmental damage, unregulated technological growth, and the use of weapons developed through technology in the Vietnam War. People began to question whether science's ability to produce new discoveries was outstripping society's ability to control them.

Concern was directed at "the failure of traditional political institutions to prevent the new problems associated with science and technology from emerging and to deal with their results," David Dickson (1984) points out in *The New Politics of Science*. In particular, people argued that these institutions had inserted social values into decision making on scientific and technological issues only when they promoted economic growth or military strength.

To deal with the increasing public demands for change, legislation and new programs encouraged more public participation in decision making. The Federal Advisory Committee Act of 1972 allowed citizens to attend and comment at meetings of federal agency advisory committees. Similar legislation included the National Environmental Protection Act of 1969, the Occupational Safety and Health Act of 1970, the Clean Air Act of 1972, the Water Pollution Control Act of 1972, and the Toxic Substances Control Act of 1976. However, some groups wanted what they considered a more equitable distribution of power, with public access to and control over science and technology (Dickson, 1984, p. 218).

These conflicts point out two different styles of political strategy according to Dickson. The first is a technocratic approach, favored by those who seek a "rational" approach to problems by imposing solutions reached through a con-sensus of experts. The second is a democratic approach, which argues that "the rationality of solutions offered by technical experts is often illusory and that the best protection against this is to have opportunities for wide participation in decision making" (Dickson, 1984, p. 219). This approach calls for participation by federal and state legislative bodies, by the courts, and by public interest groups and labor unions.

The debate over political strategy covered not only technological applications but also the practice of basic research, Dickson relates. Many groups argued that the public has a fundamental right to take part in deciding both where and how research funds should be spent, since taxpayers supported research through tax dollars, shared many of the risks that research created, and benefited from the application of research results.

Such calls for participation posed a fundamental challenge to the agreement reached between the scientific community and the federal government immediately after World War II, Dickson said. Scientists had argued successfully that they could do their best work if the government and the public did not apply political pressures to them or the scientific enterprise. Free from interference, the scientists would, in return, work on research that would eventually benefit society.

Over time, scientists have fiercely defended their freedom to determine their own research directions. During the debates over regulating recombinant DNA research, for example, scientists dramatically compared their plight — their loss of research freedom if regulations were passed — to the persecution of Galileo.

To protect their freedoms, these technical experts have developed defensive techniques to limit programs seeking to redistribute power over science and its social applications. One such strategy has been to control the structure of the decision-making agenda, by deciding, for example, what forms of public participation would be permitted at what stage, and what their final impact would be, Dickson says.

A second defensive technique has been to establish conditions for public participation, such as determining which types of argument will be considered by decision makers, therefore defining what is or is not legitimate. Nowhere can either of these techniques be seen more clearly than in licensing hearings for nuclear power plants held by the Atomic Safety Licensing Board. After many attempts, most citizens and activist groups consider futile efforts to make a serious impact on the outcome of these hearings.

Dickson cites numerous other examples of defensiveness toward demands for greater social accountability on the part of the scientific community, including scientific response to Rachel Carson's *Silent Spring,* boundary setting for the National Science Foundation's (NSF) program in Ethics and Values in Science and Technology, and the development of the Office of Technology Assessment (OTA).

The OTA example is particularly revealing. According to Dickson, a National Academy of Sciences report on OTA and technology assessment warned that "frightened by the untoward side effects of technological change and frustrated by their inability to humanize its direction, 'people with much power and little wisdom will lash out against scientific and technological activity in general, attempting to destroy what they find themselves unable to control.'" While it recommended that public participation be encouraged, the report suggested restricting such participation to "well-defined channels." It also suggested that mechanisms "be provided to filter out for summary treatment truly frivolous or irresponsible claims" (Dickson, 1984, p. 234).

The report makes clear that technology assessment was being proposed as a means of ultimately reinforcing, rather than challenging, the basic patterns of control over science and technology. It was conceived in a political framework that sought to minimize the imposition of publicly determined needs on unwilling private decision makers. Dickson believes that the history of the establishment of OTA and the recombinant DNA debate each reinforced the dominant patterns of control over science and technology by heading off what the scientific establishment considered excessive demands for greater democracy.

For most of the 1980s, particularly in the areas of technology assessment and risk management, technical experts had the upper hand in controlling information and policy. However, toward the end of the decade, as the situation changed in risk management because of an increasing number of conflicts erupting among scientists, the government, and the public, so too did the degree of technocratic control. The rise of the field of risk communication, a subset of risk management, implied that more information, and consequently more power, had to be shared with citizens.

The 1989 report of the National Research Council (NRC) on *Improving Risk Communication* reflected the change in the following way:

> When a decision that may have major political effects by altering the distribution of money, power, and well-being in society is made through procedures that emphasize scientific judgment, scientific disagreements tend to become proxies for political disagreements and political adversaries often express their positions in the language of science (NRC, 1989, p. 67).

People became aware that one could find experts to support just about any position in a technological debate. They also realized that both industry and environmental groups often produced only those scientific arguments that advanced their own goals. The media reported that even the federal government was influenced by various interest groups in its scientific studies. Statements of scientific experts in risk debates became seen by the skeptical members of the public as reflecting political positions rather than unbiased assessments. The effect of the mistrust was to make communication more difficult.

Sheldon Krimsky and Alonzo Plough (1988) say there are two competing models for the interpretation of risk information: one technical for experts and one cultural for the lay public. At the root of this divergence is the distinction between technical and cultural rationality of risk. Quantitative risk analysis, rather than narrowing differences, may actually increase antagonism between the "technosphere" and the "demosphere," as they call them. Casting the issues in a technical language reduces the possibility of a dialogue between the public and the technical elites.

The differing ways of analyzing risk raise a serious question. "Two things deserving respect, namely scientific rationality and democracy (the rights of local communities to express their will on issues of health and safety), are in conflict. How does one proceed?" ask Krimsky and Plough.

Scientists suggest educating the public into thinking about the problem the way they do, and accepting notions of expert rationality. This tactic is "directed specifically at reducing the opposition between the demosphere and the technosphere from the expert's perspective." Within this context, "risk communication is the responsibility of elites and falls into the general rubric of 'public understanding of science'" (Krimsky and Plough, 1988, p. 303).

However, some segments of the public reject such approaches and demand a greater say on risk issues. Once again, legislation helps to provide greater public input. Superfund and other right-to-know legislation requires dissemination of information that citizens can use to heighten their political involvement.

Even the NRC — a prestigious scientific organization — suggests that the public must be involved more. In the introduction to its 1989 report on risk communication it says:

> Only a few experts possess the best knowledge available to estimate accurately the extent of the possible harm or the likelihood of its occurrence. But while great weight needs to be given to the specialized knowledge of these experts, democratic principles require that the decisions be controlled by officials, generally nonspecialists, who are answerable to the public (NRC, 1989, p. 14).

The NRC report goes on to warn that "to remain democratic, a society must find ways to put specialized knowledge into the service of public choice and keep it from becoming the basis of power for an elite" (p. 15).

Risk communication has arisen in the past five years as a field that attempts to do just that — share information about risk-laden issues with the public. The new concern with informing the public has several motivating sources, not entirely consistent with each other, including:

1. a requirement for or desire by government to inform;
2. a desire by government or industry officials to overcome opposition to decisions;
3. a desire to share power between government and public groups;
4. a desire to develop effective alternatives to direct regulatory control (NRC, 1989, p. 16).

To many people, risk communication initially meant a one-way message developed by technical experts about a risk likely to persuade an uninformed and passive public. However, risk communicators and technical experts quickly found that efforts that included extensive cost-benefit arguments or that told people which option was the best for them had little effect. This happened for several reasons, according to the NRC report.

"First, costs and benefits are not equally distributed across a society," the report stated (p. 22). For any particular option, the people who will experience the highest cost will try to convince others that the option is not good and that another should be selected. So, in risk issues, the interests of different groups collide, and this collision cannot be resolved by simply informing people about the likely effects of each option.

"Second, people do not agree about which harms are most worth avoiding or which benefits are most worth seeking," the report continues (p. 20). Conflicts about technological issues pit opposing values against each other. The NRC believes these conflicting values must be debated and weighed in a political process.

"Third, citizens of a democracy expect to participate in debate about controversial political issues and about institutional mechanisms to which they sometimes delegate decision-making power" (p. 20). The report explains, "A problem formulation that appears to substitute technical analysis for political debate, or to disenfranchise people who lack technical training, or to treat technical analysis as more important to decision making than the clash of values and interests is bound to elicit resentment from people" (NRC, 1989, p. 20). The NRC strongly emphasizes that technological choices are value laden.

What many risk communication researchers are finding out is that communication of risk in an environmental controversy takes many forms. As Krimsky and Plough's case studies suggest, multiple generators of risk information — including nonofficial sources — play a key role in the overall risk communication scenario. Risk communications resemble tangled webs rather than parallel series of sender-receiver interactions.

They chose the tangled web metaphor because of several factors that evolved from their case studies. First, they found that there are many potentially influential voices in risk controversy, and it is often not possible to anticipate which will dominate. Second, because of constant interplay, risk communication messages become tangled and may result in unpredictable social outcomes. Third, risk messages come in many forms and reflect diverse modes of communication (Krimsky and Plough, 1988, p. 298).

All of this means that under particular circumstances it is difficult for any single communicator, even a government agency, to establish the boundaries of risk communication for an issue. In their case studies, Krimsky and Plough found that technical information often does not play a dominant role in a risk communication controversy. Local values and safety and economic concerns often predominate, and, as much as experts would like technical information to be the driving force behind a risk decision, this is unlikely when there is uncertainty about the data and where there are important social and economic questions involved.

To move away from the model of a one-way technocratic message, the NRC report redefines risk communication as "an interactive process of exchange of information and opinion among individuals, groups and institutions. It involves multiple messages about the nature of risk and other messages, not strictly about risk, that express concerns, opinions, or reactions to risk messages or to legal and institutional arrangements for risk management" (NRC, 1989, p. 21).

But expressing or even believing that risk communication is a larger and more complex situation will not ensure a more democratic approach to risk management. Even if technical information does not play a dominant role in a risk communication controversy, it plays such a role in a risk management decisions.

Technical experts still dominate the risk management scene. Because of their influence, it is questionable whether risk management can ever truly become a democratic process. Because technical experts interpret the data, they can define and set limits on the topics to be evaluated. Unless backed by very strong public and media support, topics that citizens seek to add to a particular risk debate do not seem to carry as much weight with decision makers.

In their roles as advisers to local, state, and federal government agencies, these same technical experts often provide strong views that promote their own opinions and scientific beliefs. Rarely do they speak to what they see as the "irrational" side of the debate. Government scientists and administrators, although professing concern about public attitudes and actions, depend on technical interpretations, such as the one-in-a-million safety limit that the EPA uses regarding carcinogenic risks from chemicals. If environmental groups want to make changes, they must accept the challenge of the technical data and argue their validity.

Because risk management is so dominated by technical experts, some groups, including Congress, the mass media, and citizen action organizations work to safeguard democratic input into risk decision making. Sometimes congressional representatives try to provide such safeguards with the laws they devise. Such laws as the National Environmental Protection Act, which set up the process of requiring environmental impact statements (EIS), provide an opportunity for citizen participation. However, one wonders how many citizens or groups over the years won out over technical experts in pursuit of change through the EIS process. Congress is also heavily influenced by vested interests that do not reflect citizens' viewpoints, and this can weaken protection of democratic participation. Congress's 1990 revision of the Clean Air Act was heavily influenced by such interests.

Even specific right-to-know laws, such as Title III of the Superfund Amendment and Reauthorization Act, do not always ensure democratic access. As Title III's first deadline approached for providing emission data to the mass media and citizens, industries trained their executives to explain this information in the best possible light for them. And while a limited number of reporters have used this information to alert their communities to hazardous emissions, others have said they cannot interpret what the data mean unless they go to industrial spokespersons or scientific experts, who put their own "spin" on the information.

While not reporting everything that they perhaps should, the mass media do provide some guarantee of democratic input by calling attention to citizen concerns. Unfortunately, this attention is often superficial and fleeting. Although some publications and broadcast stations have helped lead campaigns for change through editorials and investigative reports on environmental issues, the majority have not (Friedman and Friedman, 1988; Friedman, Gorney, and Egolf, 1987; Walters, Wilkins, and Walters, 1989).

It only has been because of the strong public environmental concerns voiced in the late 1980s that many newspapers have re-established an environmental beat for reporters. Most individuals who hold this beat are not trained in science and cannot question the data used by the technical experts, so, while they can and do pit expert against expert, they can only call attention to risk issues and, if they are skillful and responsible, educate a few readers or viewers about the situation. But, unless a groundswell of public concern and perhaps outrage occurs, public access to decision making about risk is not generally achieved by this route.

The most dedicated group pursuing input into risk management is composed of those who help stir up the public concern and outrage: the environmental and citizen activists. They seek entry into risk decision making. However, an organization usually must have national stature, such as the Environmental Defense Fund or the National Wildlife Federation, to have standing in the debate. Local citizens and environmental groups have to not only demonstrate that they represent a significant number of people in the community, but they must also show that they can understand and interpret the technical data. Otherwise, they will be dismissed and labeled as "kooks and nuts," as were antinuclear power forces at TMI in Harrisburg, Pennsylvania.

Efforts by these three and other segments of society to achieve democratic access to risk management have only been mildly effective in selected situations. For widespread democratic access to occur, citizens will have to be accepted by decision makers as experts in their own right.

This means decision makers will have to take what Krimsky and Plough call the cultural approach to risk issues.

The cultural approach requires that two forms of rationality be applied to risk: technical and experiential. Both make contributions to the problem of constructing and analyzing a risk event, but neither is sufficient. The model says that both expert and citizen approaches to a risk event can be logical and coherent on their own terms. Cultural reason does not deny the role of technical reason, but simply extends it. Cultural rationality does not separate the context from the content of risk analysis; rather, it seeks technical knowledge but incorporates it within a broader decision framework.

If decision makers were to take such an approach, it is possible that risk management would become more democratic. How efficient this process would be, or how expensive, remains to be seen. It would probably be considered fairer by individuals and activist groups because it would give them a greater voice. It would be considered less fair by corporations and government agencies because their influence would be diminished.

Would it really work? Yes, according to Krimsky and Plough, if technical experts and government officials began to appreciate and respect the logic of the local culture toward risk events, and if citizens tried to understand the scientific aspects of the risk situation. There would then be a chance that an agreement on management of risk issues would be reached. Until such a change in the process occurs, the seesaw of information and power will continue between the technocratic and democratic power structures.

4

Popularization versus Secularization: Media Coverage of Health

ROBERT A. LOGAN

INTRODUCTION

For more than 200 years, the improvement of public health has been a benchmark to assess social progress in the United States (Starr, 1982; World Health Organization [WHO], 1958). Public diffusion of medical information and health tips always has been a fundamental U.S. governmental and social priority. In the nineteenth century, the practice and acceptance of folk medicine was blamed for undermining public understanding of health, acceptance of the growing science of biomedicine, and the institutionalization of health care delivery. Poor public health knowledge and epidemics of diphtheria, syphilis, and typhoid fever convinced urban United States public health officials at the end of the nineteenth century to use the news media to counter public misinformation and encourage more therapeutic health care practices (Ziphorn, 1988). The rapid institutionalization of medicine paralleled new interest in the mass media's portrayal of health from 1930–65 (Krieghbaum, 1967).

Recent opinion surveys reveal that the news media are now the public's most important source of health information and an important information source for physicians (Simpkins and Brenner, 1984; O'Keefe, 1970). Public interest in reading about health has increased steadily during the past decade (Bogart, 1981; Gollin and Salisburg,

1986; Stone, 1987). As mass communications evolved as a scholarly discipline and the news media became a vital source of health information, the news media's portrayal of health became a significant scholarly issue to researchers as well as an important social issue to physicians (Bogart, 1981; "Newspaper Science," 1986; "Who's Writing," 1988; Pettegrew and Logan, 1987).

This chapter explores how the news media cover health issues and mass media campaigns to improve public health behaviors. Health is operationally defined by the WHO as "a state of complete physical, mental, and social well being and not merely the absence of disease or infirmity" (WHO, 1958). The chapter sections explore the theoretical framework that underpins the news media's role in conveying health news and information; research about the news media's performance; the effectiveness of mass media contributions to public health campaigns; and a critique of recent work with some theoretical alternatives.

POPULARIZATION OF HEALTH AND MEDICINE

The role of the press has been consistently perceived by journalists and physicians as literally popularizing, or translating, biomedical developments and providing health tips to lay audiences to improve public health (Tobey, 1971; Burnham, 1987; Stephenson, 1973). Transmitting medical news is viewed as a one-way information flow beginning with refereed medical journals, expert physicians, and public health officials. These experts provide medical information to journalists, who then popularize specialized biomedical knowledge for lay readers and viewers (Stephenson, 1973; Tobey, 1971). Increases in public knowledge about medicine are designed to engender these socially desirable effects: decreases in public superstition about health care, more public acceptance for organized medicine's preferred approaches to biomedical treatment, changes in actual public health care behaviors (in the therapeutic direction set by health care officials), resulting improvements in national health care statistics, and increased public support for medical research and health facilities via tax monies and private contributions (Burnham, 1987; Laetsch, 1987; Haff, 1976). The press's role as the lay source of health information results in a parallel media responsibility for both the quality of the nation's health and medical information environment and the state of public health (Burnham, 1987).

The popularization model for news coverage of organized medicine historically represents a theory of information diffusion as well as public persuasion (Stephenson, 1973; Haff, 1976). From its beginnings a century ago, the news media's coverage of medicine implied support for the scientific and political agenda of the nation's health care delivery system, a stance that has contrasted with media coverage of government and big business (Tobey, 1971; Logan, 1985; Greenberg, 1974; Warner, 1989).

The results of popularization have been mixed. News reporting has been linked to functional increases in the public's biomedical literacy (Stephenson, 1973; Tobey, 1971; Laetsch, 1987; Haff, 1976; Turow, 1989). However, other studies have found current low levels of public health literacy in the United States and widespread belief in superstitions about health (Burnham, 1987; Laetsch, 1987; American Association for the Advancement of Science, 1989a, 1989b; Miller, 1989, 1986, 1983).

To some critics, the inability of the press to engender improvement in biomedical and scientific literacy demonstrates the dubious efficacy of using the news media to inform persons about health and science. Physicians and scientists are encouraged to curtail their reliance on the news media. Critics suggest using alternative strategies to improve public knowledge about health care and medicine (Trachtman, 1981). Biomedical journalism should be written for well-educated "attentive publics," rather than lay audiences (Prewitt, 1982, 1983).

Despite evidence of poor biomedical literacy, many scholars maintain that the news media are not exclusively responsible for the quality of the nation's public biomedical knowledge and health environment. The press, the health care delivery system, educators, and citizens are perceived to share responsibility for what Americans know about biomedicine and therapeutic health-seeking behavioral patterns. Cooperation between the health care delivery system and the news media remains a viable strategy to inform the lay public about medicine, health, and science. Improved public knowledge about health and enhanced public credibility of journalism, biomedicine, and science are maintained as realistic and important future goals (Nelkin, 1984, 1987; Perlman, 1974; Cohn, 1963, 1989a; O'Leary, 1986; Kotulak, 1989).

Although the influence of journalism on biomedical literacy is currently an issue, popularization's defenders and critics agree on three points: the press is perceived as a liaison to translate biomedical research and events into lay language, the press is partly responsible for the levels of public health knowledge in the United States, and improvement in the press's performance indicates how seriously the news media accept their role in improving the quality of the life in the United States (Logan, 1985).

The willingness of journalists earlier in this century to tie their efforts to improvements in biomedical literacy set a framework to assess future mass communications problems. Popularization posits that accurate, impartial, and comprehensive biomedical news will lead to a better informed public, while inaccurate, partial, and one-sided health information contributes to biomedical illiteracy. If the premise is theoretically sound, then the proposals that journalists should write mostly for elite audiences or bolster press-physician relations to improve the accuracy and comprehensiveness of news reporting may be logical remedies. But, research shows that popularization suffers from several fundamental weaknesses that undermine its value as a theory of mass communication. There is surprising evidence that the accuracy, impartiality, and comprehensiveness of news is not directly tied to what one knows about medicine, or a person's health care behavior.

Two recurring themes of this chapter are: whether popularization's narrow parameters need to be reassessed to improve public understanding of medicine and if an ongoing problem with assessing press performance has been the traditional consensus about the news media's role in translating health and medical information.

PRESS PERFORMANCE

The evaluation of the press's performance in medical and health reporting is an important research issue. Kotulak (1989) provides a journalist's perspective about what medical and health news is and how the range of biomedical stories has changed.

Health and biomedical journalists report primarily about well-known diseases, the safety of medical procedures, and the frontiers of medical research. Journalistic attention to a disease varies according to the significance of its perceived threat to public health. Acquired Immune Deficiency Syndrome (AIDS), cancer, heart disease, and stroke dominate today's coverage in comparison with smallpox, rabies, botulism, typhus, and other diseases that dominated medical news attention earlier in this century (Ziphorn, 1988; Russell, 1986).

The safety of surgical techniques, rating the cost and quality of medical care, new research about specific diseases, and biological causes of illness and substance abuse (alcohol, drugs, and tobacco) are of perennial interest to medical writers and readers.

In the 1970s and 1980s, former subdivisions between medical and environmental writing blurred because of new understandings of public health risks caused by industrial and natural environmental hazards. Contemporary medical and health reporting now partially encompasses environmental health threats to animals and humans. Other biomedically related, important, and newsworthy topics include abortion research and safety, global warming, and recombinant DNA. The spectrum of medical news and the resulting pressures on medical writers to improve news selection, reporting, writing are increasing (Russell, 1986).

NEWS REPORTING

The evaluation of medical news reporting usually begins with assessments of reportorial accuracy. Scientists have found a low number of errors in science and biomedical news stories. But, the definition of accuracy to scientists and physicians may be broader than factual errors (Dunwoody, 1982; Dunwoody and Ryan, 1985; Tichenor et al., 1970). Although factual errors are rare, physicians dislike distortions in health and medical news, which are defined as press reports that are oversimplified and sensationalized (Winsten, 1985; Hart, 1984).

In stories where medical news is oversimplified and sensationalized, journalists tend to overemphasize the uniqueness of the information they present, exaggerate both original findings and assertions, and undervalue the subtle qualifications that biomedical researchers make in explaining their findings (Fahnestock, 1986). However, distortions, oversimplifications, and mistakes are often the result of attempts to gather news under deadline pressures and rarely reflect premeditated journalistic inattention to detail (Nelkin, 1987; Perlman, 1974).

But professional norms are not the only source of distortion. Medical journalists write about too many staged events that are often managed by public relations offices within hospitals, clinics, journals, or physician interest groups (Freimuth, et al., 1984a, 1984b; Wilkins, 1987; Nelkin, 1987). The overemphasis on a packaged preparation of medical news reinforces journalistic dependence on established, well-organized sources for news within federal, state, and local governments, large public health facilities, well-established medical journals, and large research universities. (Shepard, 1979, 1981). For example, in reporting on recombinant DNA research, journalists covered breaking events and relied on well-established, prepackaged sources. The resulting stories tended to be disjointed. Too little attention was paid to physicians and researchers who challenged conventional research or wisdom (Pfund and Hofstadter, 1981) .

The emphasis on staged events coupled with a reliance on well-known experts results in an underemphasis on the sociological, cultural, ethical, historical, and educational contexts underlying medical news (Wilkins and Patterson, 1987; Altimore, 1982). An analysis of news reporting about the toxic chemical spill on public health in Bhopal, India, showed significant attention to statements in press conferences officiated by government, industry, or well-known scientists, with parallel inattention to the sociological, cultural, ethical, historical, educational, scientific, or biomedical contexts under which the chemical spill's medical risks could be assessed by the public (Wilkins, 1987, 1989).

Other scholars assert these aggregate journalistic errors cause unnecessary alarm about the energy and chemical industries. Such news coverage creates unmerited public distrust of the stewardship of U.S. federal agencies, such as the Environmental Protection Agency (EPA) and the Food and Drug Administration (FDA), as well as major energy, chemical, and food processing corporations (Efron, 1985; Whelan, 1985).

Efron and Whelan's finding that news reporting is unfavorable to government, industry, and mainstream scientific opinion seems to contradict other analyses. (It is important to note that Whelan's research is often supported by industry, and she was funded in 1989 by Uniroyal, the makers of the chemical Alar, to combat negative publicity of the chemical industry.) Medical journalists are occasionally unskeptical of information provided by government, industry, universities, and public interest groups. Almost all medical journalists agree that reporters should be equally skeptical of all sources of information. However, as Cohn (1989b) notes, some medical journalists lack the skills to critically evaluate scientific research.

The pitfalls of not challenging scientific data are explained by Warner (1989), who finds that the news media rarely counter the tobacco industry's assertions about the impact of smoking on health. The press covers tobacco and other scientific controversies by enabling official sources either to speak unchallenged or let spokespersons for opposing groups criticize each other's work. As the recent manipulation of the press regarding the safety of Alar and its unquestioned coverage of the medical value of Retin A demonstrate, an independent evaluation by the press of the comparative merits of scientific arguments and evidence is often missing.

NEWS WRITING

Research about biomedical news writing has discussed the overuse of human drama, the dearth of coping information, how the form of news can dictate content, and the use of metaphor to shape public opinion. Although Blakeslee (1986) defends judicious reporting about the human angle of biomedical and scientific research, she adds that medical journalists should also describe biomedical procedures and provide a context to help readers understand how and why changes in health care practices occur. Journalists should be more responsive to public fears and instruct readers how to constructively cope with biomedical risks (Wilkins and Patterson, 1987).

The wire service inverted pyramid style and feature approaches to news writing can dictate news content (Nelkin, 1987; Altheide, 1985). Critics of news writing and reporting often fail to understand that a degree of superficiality and partiality in news stories is an inevitable by-product of forcing journalists to convey complex ideas within conventional news frameworks.

Words, and not just their form, are also problematic. Franklin (1986) suggests that reporters judiciously use literary devices to explain the challenges and science of medicine. Metaphors and analogies should illuminate and elucidate difficult concepts to help readers understand how biomedical procedures work. Written images describing the heart as a pump, for example, help readers understand its function, if not its form. But metaphors and written images can frame a reader's impression of events and eventually help shape public opinion about biomedicine and science. Metaphors and images "help to create the judgmental biases that underlie public policy" (Nelkin, 1987, p. 80).

Besides shading opinion with word choice or literary description, the language of news can reinforce stereotypes about disease and accompanying social prejudices. Despite the fact that the aggregate of new stories about AIDS follow wire service guidelines of accuracy, impartiality, and dispassion, AIDS reporting adds a subtext: "The unsafe behavior that produces AIDS is judged to be more than a weakness. It is indulgence, delinquency — addictions to chemicals that are illegal and to sex are regarded as deviant" (Sontag, 1989, p. 25).

Sontag's objections to AIDS coverage reflect a long-standing sociological critique of journalism. Medical journalists can set an agenda of how health issues are publicly perceived by raising them in the first place — which provides social legitimacy — and by the aggregate of news approaches, news selection, as well as the selective use of words and phrases. All these journalistic decisions can inadvertently reflect prevailing viewpoints about health, disease, the role of patients and providers, and prejudices about the distribution of health care services among socioeconomic groups.

In the news coverage of AIDS, for example, its subtext occasionally reinforces prevailing social norms about fear of death and disease, gays, drug addicts, and sexually active persons with multiple partners, and affects the distribution of medical resources to these groups. AIDS coverage also reveals how important the language of news is to those who perceive themselves as socially deviant. Persons with AIDS may find themselves more victimized by news coverage and society than by the disease itself (Shilts, 1987; Kinsella, 1989).

While reinforcement of social norms and prejudices is an inadvertent and unintentioned by-product of biomedical news coverage, its consistent recurrence raises serious ethical issues for medical journalists and the future of medical journalism training. Understanding how language shapes opinion and how language and news approaches reinforce stereotypes should be treated far more seriously than it is in journalism schools or within the news media professions. The recent progress that has been made in helping journalists understand the national importance and implied biases in news selection (see the next section) should be extended to journalistic sensitivity to semantics.

GATEKEEPING

In addition to news reporting and writing techniques, significant journalistic bias is introduced when medical journalists decide what stories to cover. "Whether we like it or not, we journalists have become gatekeepers. In some measure our choices of what will be reported, and how the data will be reported, set the national agenda vis-à-vis health risks. In a sense, we [journalists] have become part of the regulatory machinery" (Cohn, 1989a, p. 42).

Biomedical news selection is constricted within several levels of decision making by journalists and health care professionals. Biomedical gatekeeping begins with the influence of a few professional journals — especially, the *Journal of the American Medical Association* and the *New England Journal of Medicine* — that confer legitimacy to medical issues and status on published researchers (Winsten, 1985). The same major medical journals, especially the *New England Journal of Medicine,* partially control journalistic access to information (and apply a secondary level of gatekeeping) by not permitting researchers to release findings until research is published within the journal (Perlman, 1974; Cohn, 1963; Russell, 1986).

The gatekeeping process continues with the press's overuse of physicians and experts who publish in major journals, or have an unusual ability to communicate with reporters and the public (Goodell, 1977). Journalists tend to interview medical celebrities for news stories, to the exclusion of less-known medical experts (Shepard, 1979, 1981). Journalists also confer status on a small number of peers who have an unusual influence on what other biomedical and science reporters choose to cover (Dunwoody, 1980; Danielian and Resse, 1989; Resse and Danielian, 1989).

The influence of the New York *Times* to establish drug abuse as a journalistic priority in 1986 provides an example (Danielian and Resse, 1989; Resse and Danielian, 1989). Once the *Times* increased the frequency of reporting about drug abuse and moved drug abuse stories to the front page, most of the nation's other newspapers and television networks devoted more prime news time or space to cover drug abuse (Shoemaker, Wanta, and Leggett, 1989).

The result of gatekeeping by publication in a few journals, withholding access by some journal editors, consistent use of medical celebrities as news sources, and the influential news selection patterns of distinguished journalists is often criticized as producing a lack of pluralism in medical news (Nelkin, 1984; Haff, 1976; Wilkins, 1987; Winsten, 1985). The way in which gatekeeping within the health care delivery system and newsrooms influences the nation's health agenda demonstrates a growing journalistic understanding of the impact of news coverage on public affairs. Exploring how gatekeeping contributes to public well-being broadens the understanding of the potentially adverse impact of routine practices in journalism and the health care delivery system. Journalists need better access to medical news and should widen their routines in deciding what stories to cover.

OTHER INSIGHTS

Some research about mass communication takes an even broader view of media performance. Reviewing news media coverage in the early 1980s of health risks from AIDS, nuclear power, and toxic spills, Nelkin concludes most major U.S. newspapers, television networks, and wire services displayed a "reasonable degree of accuracy, comprehensiveness and impartiality" (1984, p. 72). A less optimistic appraisal of 12 years of news reporting about smoking is reported by Whelan et al. (1981), who find few news articles that could be classified as antismoking. Similarly, Freimuth et al. (1984a, 1984b) find news reporting about cancer gives the impression that "everything causes cancer," and journalists made little effort to dispel public misconceptions about the incidence and prevalence of cancer.

The portrayal of health in commercial television programs and commercials provides persistent public misconceptions about obesity, alcohol abuse, the need for medical treatment and incidence of illness among health care professionals (Gerbner et al., 1981). Twenty-five years of television medical dramas either directly supported the public policy agendas of major medical organizations, such as the American Medical Association, or provided false impressions about the equitable availability of health care delivery in the United States (Turow, 1989).

One recent trend in press criticism is its break from accepting popularization as the underlying rationale for why the news media should cover medicine. While the impact of accuracy and impartiality of health reporting on public education remains the foundation of media criticism, medical news is now seen as having a more holistic role than increasing how much the public knows about medicine or supporting the agenda of the health care delivery system. Indeed, medical news criticism seems to be broadening to consider the role of the news media and a revised view of medical journalism's ethics and public responsibilities. Some of these changes parallel scholarship about the use of mass media to influence public health, as explained below.

MASS MEDIA AND PUBLIC HEALTH CAMPAIGNS

Although evidence critical of journalistic and media performance in the United States is mixed, it has become public policy in the United States and most Western nations to attempt to "reverse adverse effects of the mass media's portrayal of health care by barring some forms of advertising or by (public information) campaigns set along more therapeutic lines" (Pettegrew and Logan, 1987, p. 690). Television commercials for smoking and many alcoholic beverages are banned in the United States, and restrictions have been placed on advertising food products for children.

Mass communication researchers have contributed to applied public health campaigns in three areas: prevention of smoking, prevention of drug and alcohol abuse, and reduction of cardiovascular disease.

Cardiovascular media campaigns are more successful than smoking or substance abuse campaigns in shifting public opinion, attitudes, and actual behavior in intended directions (Simpkins and Brenner, 1984). Most campaigns about smoking or drug and alcohol abuse report only significant linkages between mass media exposure and increases in public awareness (Pettegrew and Logan, 1987). But in the Stanford Heart Disease Prevention Program from 1972–75, mass media campaigns heightened public awareness and increased public knowledge about the importance of preventing heart disease. The campaigns also resulted in weight reduction, reduced cigarette smoking, and improved cholesterol and blood pressure levels (Farquhar et al., 1983).

Subsequent studies at Stanford (Farquhar, Maccoby, and Solomon, 1984; Chaffee and Roser, 1986) and the Minnesota Heart Health Project (Pavlik et al., 1985; Finnegan and Loken, 1985) reconfirm linkages between mass media campaigns and changes in audience awareness, and heart disease knowledge and improvements in therapeutic health-seeking behaviors. In contrast with smoking and substance abuse campaign research, the approaches at Stanford and Minnesota coordinated mass media information with interpersonal instruction in community clinics, schools, and physicians' offices to inform the public about therapeutic health behaviors. The combination of mass media plus interpersonal influences may explain the relative success of the Stanford and Minnesota programs. In addition, multifactor cardiovascular risk reduction occurred in a city where mass media information without supplemental personal instruction was available (Farquhar 1983). Maccoby and Alexander add that "if mass media alone . . . can lead to results in behavioral change, then there is far more hope for health campaigns than was previously suspected" (1980, p. 369) .

The acknowledged uncertainty about the influences of mass media on public information, attitudes, and behavioral changes in the early 1980s led to an emphasis in the research to distinguish the impact of mass media use from interpersonal instruction, peer groups, and other social influences (Chaffee and Roser, 1986).

While there is considerable evidence that mass media campaigns can influence public awareness about substance abuse and prevention of smoking and heart disease, the reasons for shifts in public attitudes and actual behavioral changes have been difficult to distinguish empirically. The role of the mass media in comparison with social changes, peer groups, and interpersonal instruction is under active investigation (Pettegrew and Logan, 1987).

CAMPAIGNS AND NEWS MEDIA PERFORMANCE

A review of campaign research in the 1970s finds that most efforts are one-dimensionally centered on the use of newspapers, radio, and television to create persuasive messages (Atkin, 1981). Most campaign research reflects a linear model of social learning theory (Simpkins and Brenner, 1984). The model begins with mass media content and traces the transfer of media messages on public awareness, information gain (how much someone remembers), long-range increases in medical knowledge, opinion shifts, efforts to seek peer reinforcement, perceived self-enhancement gained by improving health, and changes in one's health or health habits. However useful as a research framework, the model omits public expectations of the news media, health advertising, physicians, health care, the quality of news and programming, and how people define good health. Most media campaign research overlooks much of the context of how a person converges on both mass media and health.

A second significant omission in mass media research is the examination of the broader impact of the mass media's role as a social institution in presenting health information to the public. The role of the mass media in conjunction with health care providers is assumed to be socially therapeutic. But medical sociologists maintain that the mass media glamorize the health care delivery system and sanction a social dependence on physicians as the sole providers of health (Callahan, 1989; Payer, 1988).

However, an over-reliance on medical providers and medical technology is unwise public policy, because Americans may not be prepared for limits to equitable health care delivery in the future. The institutionalization of health care is both socially deleterious and pernicious (Illich, 1976). Although the influence of the health care delivery system as a social institution is well reflected in medical sociology, the mass media's role in maintaining institutional privileges is not encompassed in social learning theory and is often missing from current scholarship about popularization.

The developing emphasis on how people converge on health and the critique of the news media's role in institutionalizing health care exposes the theoretical limitations of popularization. Popularization has been more than a description of the media's roles and responsibilities; its goals were operationalized as the anticipated result of mass media campaigns. In seminal campaign research, the goals of mass media use were social learning and changes in attitude and behavior. To influence social learning to maximally use mass media, researchers began by measuring differences in the credibility of sources, message strategies, and comparative media channels (radio, television, and newspapers versus interpersonal sources).

Although it was found there are differences in source credibility and types of message appeals, and that supplementing mass media with interpersonal influences improved a campaign's impact, the efficacy of media campaigns remained mixed. Some early oversights included missing the relative influence of community, family, religion, cultural norms, personal opinions, values, and beliefs on how a person attends to health and the relative influence of these same factors on how a person attends to media messages about health.

These oversights not only revealed popularization's limitations, recent changes in research strategies to incorporate how persons converge on health and media reflect an evolution of a new theory of science communication, which I call secularization.

Secularization emphasizes the public communication of science and a dialogue among the public, the media, and the health care delivery system, in contrast with the one-way flow from providers to the press to the public once considered axiomatic. Recent research has yielded more insight about the effects of media campaigns, probably because the interaction between mass media and human beings is better conceived.

Media campaign scholarship also parallels some developments in journalism criticism and is conceptually ahead in one area. A recent challenge to journalism criticism in media campaign research is to reconceive the role of the press and other mass media with more public participation, or convergence on medical issues, in mind. The rejection of popularization as a basis to analyze the news media's *raison d'être* is consistent with both journalism criticism and media campaign research.

In addition, as research strategies become more sophisticated, another area to explore is the context of advertising, shopping, and health compared with other media experiences. Researchers still ignore that the success of advertising commercial health-related products might be related to the context of shopping in a store, rather than the credibility of the source, the persuasiveness of an advertisement, the appropriateness of the channel, or individual attitudes about health in conjunction with the influence of peer groups and community norms and practices.

The normal barriers between health awareness and one's attitude and behavioral change, for example, are remarkably removed when a person learns about commercial health-related products in an advertisement and then shops in a store. For most Americans, shopping is the primary form of recreation and an example of what Stephenson (1967) termed "play."

The beguiling incentive to try new toothpastes, vitamin supplements, or dermatological creams in a store, coupled with an awareness of commercial health products created by the mass media, create a maximally nonthreatening atmosphere for behavioral change. This atmosphere is missing in almost every other type of health communication environment where health options are dictated by medical "experts." Some campaigns to encourage Americans to improve their health practices might be more successful, in other words, if the advertising-shopping linkage could be mimicked. Certainly, the context surrounding how persons converge on commercial advertising and shop needs to be better understood to explain why ads that encourage alcohol, smoking, and legal drug consumption are often more successful than similarly well-produced commercials that encourage the reverse.

SECULARIZATION AS AN ALTERNATIVE TO POPULARIZATION

Popularization is underpined by social learning theory. Its mechanistic concepts of information transfer reflect beliefs deeply held by physicians and scientists. Both biomedicine's self-righting process and its intellectual advancement are seen as hinged on a freedom from social values, which are unprofessional sources of "noise" or represent interprofessional communication errors (Graham, 1981). The scientific belief in the therapeutic by-product of value free information explains why popularization is conceived as the transfer of data provided to journalists by scientists, who are the optimal sources to prevent entropy in the diffusion of public information (Stephenson, 1973). Similarly, deficiencies or improvements in the public's health knowledge, declining public support for biomedicine, and stalled progress in improving national health care indicators are seen linked to the messages journalists convey.

But a mechanistic theory of social learning reflects a false conception of how communication really proceeds in both biomedicine and society. The interaction of social values and scientific decision making occurs at every level of biomedical inquiry. The communication of biomedicine is infused with values that underlie theoretical concepts and research approaches, stirs up the passions that lead to biomedical interest, and reinforces professional commitment and learning (Graham, 1981).

The public communication of biomedicine, in turn, should be grounded via a similar dialogue that places an emphasis on the values health care providers and the public bring to medical issues. (Stephenson, 1973; Yankelovich, 1982; Logan, 1985; Wilkins, 1987).

Such an emphasis might solve several underlying problems in the public communication of medicine discussed by Yankelovich (1982). First, providers and journalists have misunderstood that participation and dialogue are a prerequisite for social learning and interest, not vice versa. Popularization results in a public perception that providers should dominate what becomes news. Citizens, therefore, have little to say about the development of science and biomedicine in American life. The press is similarly held in poor regard because journalists are perceived as part of a system that supports the status quo. As a result, public distrust and poor understanding of health remains despite an abundance of biomedical information (Logan, 1989).

To enhance the public's understanding of medicine, Yankelovich (1982) proposes to supplement reports of biomedical research findings with discussions of public and professional values about biomedical issues. Although better journalistic understanding of statistics, aggressive reporting, and less reliance on public relations are seen as desirable, many scholars agree that initiating a public dialogue about medicine may be a higher social priority. At the same time, Yankelovich criticizes as counterproductive proposals to curtail lay access to health news (Prewitt, 1982; Trachtman, 1981; and Burnham, 1987).

A social dialogue about the values underlying the science and delivery of biomedicine represents the evolution of popularization into secularization. A secularization perspective is highly consistent with Dewey's view of the press's social ethics. To Dewey (1927, 1916), an active rather than a passive audience creates a democratic, open society and engenders the formation of social consensus. Nurturing a public to be actively interested in health and biomedicine is certainly as desirable as increasing public knowledge about health, and might eventually lead to better health behaviors.

Dialogues about a number of public health issues are currently needed in the United States. Some issues the news media might cover include equitable medical care, medical insurance, infant mortality rates, malpractice insurance, provider-patient relations, the high cost of organ transplantation, AIDS treatment, emergency medicine, intensive care, conception and contraception technology, the wisdom of the cost of mapping the human genome, and patient privacy.

Providers and the public disagree about all of these issues and current disagreements are often based more on values than scientific evidence. An interest group's values can influence legislative opinion and public policy, sometimes without an accessible public debate regarding the wisdom of spending public monies to support parochial biomedical causes. It is precisely this type of exclusion and limitation from public participation that makes citizens cynical about the social ethics within the health care delivery system and news media.

To discuss public health issues via a secularization approach, the press should cover how interest groups perceive issues and provide an overview that clarifies the merits of differing arguments. This would allow persons to participate in public policy and redress the longstanding oversight that health and health policy first depends on communication among providers and patients, not dictation by experts or the best organized interest group, about what health care or health policy should be.

A dialogue that welcomes opinions about biomedical issues and seeks to provide access for all points of view greatly improves the climate that encourages people to become more biomedically literate. Better informed patients and providers might help reverse declining public support and respect for the health care delivery system. But if the press and providers continue to ignore how society converges on health issues, the credibility of both the health care delivery system and the news media will continue to decline.

A commitment to secularization does not supersede a continuing obligation to report about biomedical science. The science of medicine still needs to be thoroughly covered with consideration of the hidden biases in language use and news selection, as well as increased attention to the merits of conflicting scientific evidence. Although there is little evidence that the diffusion of accurate medical news singularly improves biomedical literacy or support for the health care delivery system, this finding does not provide an excuse for health and medical sections to emphasize pseudoscience, legitimize medical superstitions, or discuss aspects of medical research that are not scientifically grounded.

Finally, it is time to bring the insights from campaign research and media criticism to implement new strategies to improve public understanding of health and medicine. It seems both ethical and logical to initiate a new dialogue about public health in the news media with a renewed commitment to assessing the scientific merits of biomedical research and ideas. Since the public is keenly concerned about medical care and health issues, a new type of journalism that tries to engage providers and the public and provides the best available biomedical evidence should be well received. A revised approach to medical news coverage also may engender more appreciation for health care providers and the journalists who write about medicine.

5

The Stigma of Mental Illness: Labeling and Stereotyping in the News

RUSSELL E. SHAIN AND
JULIE PHILLIPS

INTRODUCTION

Medical treatment of mentally ill persons has made significant progress since seventeenth-century England, where the public paid to watch the antics of the possessed and the crazy. Whether media treatment has made similar progress is questionable. For example, Portland, Oregon, residents opened their newspapers June 26, 1985, to a shocking front page color photograph. A Portland man, who had been seeing one of the city's more prominent psychiatrists, walked into his doctor's office and emptied a shotgun into the doctor's chest. The photograph showed the accused assailant being taken from the scene with blood splatters clearly visible on his face.

This newspaper scene reinforces a stereotype that the mentally ill are violent and dangerous. Buried deep within the story is the fact that the alleged murderer had shown few signs of mental illness other than seeing a psychiatrist or walking down the street talking to himself. A sidebar inside the paper quoted local psychiatrists saying they do not fear their patients. Despite such disclaimers, the stereotype is frequently reinforced. Headlines blare the violent connection: "Sniper had tried therapy," or "Schizophrenic captor wanted to die." Other stories tie mental illness to violence with little or no justification.

For example, a United Press International (UPI) story began, "A young mother with a history of mental illness stabbed her two young children to death with a bayonet Sunday, [and] then tried to kill herself by swallowing cleaning agents, investigators said." The only suggestion of mental illness in the rest of the story was a statement by her husband. Whether her mental illness was related to the murder was unknown, but the implication was clear.

The association with violence is only part of a cultural stigma that tends to be attached to the mentally ill. In a landmark study during the 1950s, Jim Nunnally at the University of Illinois concluded,

> One of the most important findings is that there is a "negative halo" associated with mentally ill; they are regarded as all things bad. . . . Presentations of mental health problems in the mass media have been stylized to fit the requirements of fiction and drama. The symptoms of mental illness are exaggerated, the causes and treatments are greatly oversimplified and often erroneous, and mental illness usually appears in a context of "horror," sin, and violence (Nunnally, 1961, p. 233).

Signorielli concluded that television's "dramatic needs result in overemphasizing the native and stigmatized images of the mentally ill, such as violence, bizarre behavior and failure" (1989, p. 329). These dangerous and helpless images contribute to a cultural view of a group that is already stigmatized and often shunned: "Television portrayals do little to convince the public that people can recover from mental illness and become productive members of society" (Signorielli, 1989, p. 330).

Gerbner noted that the media's depiction of mental illness makes "it easier to behave toward the subjects of the depictions in abnormal and irrational ways." He added that the mentally ill are a "lightening rod for pent-up insecurities" and demonstrate "the moral and physical price to be paid for deviance" (1961, p. 22).

Stigmatized, the mentally ill find themselves confronted not only by medical problems but also by the expectations of society. Foucault (1965) has called the mentally ill the lepers of the modern Western world. They are labeled, at worst, as violent and dangerous, and at best as weird curiosities. They know it and society knows it, and if they forget, the media remind everyone.

Nunnally suggested that the media could assist in reducing stigma by better informing the public better about mental disorders, making them more understandable. A multitude of informational campaigns in the ensuing 25 years changed little. Research scientist Joseph Cocozza (Cocozza, Melnick, and Steadman, 1978) argued the campaigns were misdirected: "Most attempts appear to be aimed at ignorance rather than fear. Yet it is the fear and the mistrust of the mentally ill which are most salient to the public and appear to lead to their rejection of the mentally ill" (Cocozza, Melnick, and Steadman, 1978, p. 22).

One difficulty with campaigns providing information about the "true" nature of mental illness is that they are addressing deeply imbedded stigmatizing social myths. Stigma itself "is a social construct — a reflection of culture itself. . . . People qualify as stigmatized only within the context of a particular culture, historic events, or economic, political, or social situation" (Ainby, Becker, and Coleman, 1986, p. 4). In cultural terms, the 30 years of information campaigns are relatively short term, particularly when, as Gerbner demonstrated, other parts of media culture are reinforcing rather than dispelling the stigma.

Gerbner examined one aspect of media culture: televised fiction. But it was just one aspect of media culture. News accounts compose another large segment of the culture, a segment largely unexamined since Nunnally's study until 1984. Tankard and Adelson (1982) analyzed advice columns in 1979 but paid no attention to news accounts. The research reported in this article attempted to add another element of understanding to the culture and symbols that stigmatize mental illness. The effort is incomplete, of course, until it also examines nonmedia culture in an effort, as James W. Carey phrased it, "to build up models of reality . . . of differing types of symbols — verbal, written, mathematical, gestural, kinesthetics — and by differing symbolic forms — art, science, journalism, ideology, speech, religion, mythology" (Carey, 1979, p. 323).

This chapter, thus, reports on news portrayals of mental illness in 1983 and 1988. It attempts to establish a general image of the mentally ill in contemporary news accounts and compares contemporary portrayals to the results of Nunnally's study. To the extent that media content reflects social conditions, contemporary content of the media should reflect the many changes that have occurred in the lives of the mentally ill during the past 30 years. When Nunnally's study was conducted, 77 percent of the mentally ill were confined in institutions. By 1979, 72 percent were outpatients. In 1955 the mentally ill were out of sight, out of mind. Today the mentally ill are very much in sight and in mind.

RESEARCH PROCEDURES

Two content analyses were conducted. The first was performed on 210 UPI stories appearing between April 6 and September 13, 1983. Articles were retrieved from the DIALOG Information Service database. Five primary descriptors were used to retrieve the stories: mental illness, schizoph-, psychotic, psychiatric hospital, and mental patient. A total of 236 stories were retrieved, 210 of which were analyzed. The remaining 26 items were discarded because they were national or international briefs or news summaries rather than complete stories.

The second analysis used a constructed 1988 month of stories from the NEXIS database of newspapers. A total of 43 stories were selected from the *Los Angeles Times,* New York *Times, Newsday,* and *Boston Globe.* Based on the previous experience and advice of psychiatric professionals, 20 primary descriptors were used to retrieve the stories: anorexia, dementia, insane, insanity, major depression, manic depression, mental depression, mental hospital, mental illness, mentally ill, mental patient, paranoi-, phobia, psychiatric hospital, psychiatric treatment, psychopath, psychotic, and schizophreni-. Stories that included these descriptors were discarded if they were not relevant to the image of the mentally ill.

The stories were analyzed in two steps. After the coding form was developed, four persons pretested it and made some recommendations for change. Two coders then analyzed every UPI story, reconciling any differences before coding was finalized. One coder analyzed the newspaper stories. The coding unit for most items was the story as a whole. Some items used words or sentences as the unit of analysis.

Nunnally's study used a sample of daily newspapers and other media. The UPI database was used instead of newspapers because of the ease of accessibility in 1984 and in anticipation of doing a news selection analysis for a sample of newspapers at a later date.

1983: A TRAIL OF VIOLENCE

The 1983 UPI stories included strong associations between mental illness and violent crime. A total of 147 persons were identified in the stories as mentally ill, mental patients, or former mental patients. Of these, 118 were implicated in violent crimes — usually murder or mass murder. Former mental patients, more than any other category, were identified with committing violent crimes. A total of 86 percent of former mental patients, 79 percent of the mentally ill, and 65 percent of those labeled in news accounts as mental patients were linked with violent crimes. By contrast, only 14 percent of the non–mentally ill characters in these stories were tied to violent crimes. Only five of the 147 were described as making a positive contribution to society.

A total of 210 UPI stories were analyzed. Five were subsequently discarded because they used schizophrenic in a nonmedical sense, such as schizophrenic economic indicators. The remaining stories included as many as 23 references to mental illness and as few as one.

Two-thirds of the stories mentioned mental illness in the first quarter of the text. Mental illness was the primary focus of 27 stories, the secondary focus of 63, and incidental to the focus of 115.

A total of 126 stories were classified as crime and vice in accordance with the American Newspaper Publishers Association (ANPA) story definitions. Other frequent story categories were government with 25, science 19, and foreign affairs 11.

In 147 stories, someone was specifically identified as mentally ill, a mental patient, or a former mental patient.

The percentage of former mental patients in these stories who committed violent crimes appears to be at odds with reality. Cocozza, Melick, and Steadman (1978) found that 1.7 percent of former mental patients in New York were arrested for committing a violent crime, compared to the 86 percent in UPI stories.

One reason that the mentally ill involved in violent crime appeared disproportionately often in UPI stories is that violent crimes, more than nonviolent events, become continuing stories. Almost 60 percent of the UPI stories were follow-ups. They often portrayed a continuing series of frequently violent events; 71 percent of the stories analyzed tended to focus on crime and vice more than did initial stories (46 percent). Thus, stories that linked mental illness and crime ran more often and reinforced the stereotypical association between mental illness and violence.

Despite their relative longevity, stories of violent crime provided little information about mental illness and, in fact, usually contained few references to mental illness. A total of 75 percent of the stories that contained fewer than three references to mental illness were crime and vice stories. The references usually appeared in the first sentence of the story and served as labels much like age, address, and occupation.

People labeled generically as mentally ill, mental patients, former mental patients, and psychotic were almost all implicated in violent crime. Those whose mental illness was specified were less likely to be linked to violent crimes.

Such stories were much less likely to addresses the causes, treatments, or consequences of mental illness. Only 14 percent of violent crime stories mention causes of mental illness, compared to 37 percent of nonviolent stories. About half of the violent stories and two-thirds of the nonviolent mentioned treatment, although description of treatment in violent stories was often restricted to mentioning that a violent former mental patient had previously been committed to a mental hospital. These references associated hospitalization with the tendency to be violent rather than inform or clarify the treatment of mental illness. Stories that specified mental illnesses tended to have more information than did those that used the general labels.

Nunnally (1961) found that media portrayals of the mentally ill reinforced a number of myths and misconceptions. Twenty-five years later the results of the UPI analysis confirmed this situation (Table 5.1). The stories overwhelmingly (75 percent) portrayed the mentally ill as looking and acting different. About 45 percent indicated that the mentally ill are somehow different in appearance and behavior than "normal" people. The same percentage supported the misconception that most people who receive treatment for a mental illness are not very worthwhile.

However, some positive changes occurred. In 1961, Nunnally wrote that news accounts often portrayed people receiving treatment for mental illness as not really needing it. In 1983, more than half the stories presented the opposite view: people who receive treatment need it. In fact, no one was portrayed as receiving unneeded treatment.

Another positive result was that 10 percent or less of the stories supported the last four of Nunnally's "misconceptions": Mental disorder is brought on by organic factors like poor diet; Mental disorder is brought on by organic factors like nervous system diseases; Mental disorder is associated with physical symptoms like brain damage; and Mental disorders can be cured by "physical means." These misconceptions were regarded as such at the time of Nunnally's study. Scientific discoveries since then have shown that, indeed, physical causes like drug and alcohol abuse, heredity, and abnormalities of brain chemistry can lead to and compound mental illness.

FIVE YEARS LATER: VIOLENCE AND HELPLESSNESS

Helplessness joined dangerousness as the dominant symbols of mental illness in the newspaper stories of 1988.

TABLE 5.1
Common Misconceptions in UPI Stories (in percent)

Misconception	Support	Refute	Irrelevant
Mentally ill look, act differently	75	1	24
Mentally ill are recognizably different from "normal" people	45	24	31
People who remain mentally ill do not try to get better	18	4	78
Most people who receive treatment do not need it	—	52	48
Most people who receive treatment for mental illness are not very worthwhile	45	7	48
Mental health can be maintained by strong people in the environment	9	1	90
Little can be done to cure mental disorder	6	13	81
An individual's state of mental health depends on pressures in the environment	16	1	83
Mental problems are caused by physical exhaustion or financial or social problems	12	1	87
An individual's well being depends on personal history, particularly childhood	12	2	86
Emotional difficulties are relatively unimportant problems that cause little damage to people who experience them	1	38	62
Mental disorder is brought on by organic factors like poor diet	6	1	94
Mental disorder is brought on by organic factors like nervous system diseases	7	—	93
Mental disorder is associated with physical symptoms like brain damage	7	—	93
Mental disorders can be cured by "physical" means	10	—	90

A total of 43 stories were selected in 1988 from the NEXIS database, most from either the *Los Angeles Times* (17) or the New York *Times* (16). *Newsday* contributed eight stories and the *Boston Globe* (4). Most were in either the general (15) or the metro (12) sections of the newspapers. Four of the stories were national and three each were regional, sports, and opinion, or what was called "view." Twenty-three stories were hard news and 14 were features. Six were analyses. In contrast, the UPI stories of 1983 were overwhelmingly hard news.

The stories had as many as 17 references to mental illness and as few as one. Slightly less than two-thirds of the stories (65 percent) mentioned mental illness in the first quarter of the text. More than a third (37 percent) mentioned it in the lead. A total of 20 of the 43 stories had mental illness as the primary focus, and 23 had it as the secondary focus.

One major difference between the 1983 and 1988 results showed up in the distribution of stories among American Newspaper Publishers Association content categories. A total of 62 percent of the UPI stories on mental illness fell into the crime and vice category. Only 16 percent of the newspaper stories in 1988 featured crime and vice. The 1988 stories were much more evenly divided among the categories: 19 percent human interest, 19 percent legal, 14 percent science, 14 percent government, and 18 percent among several other categories. The more uniform distribution of stories among categories could reflect changes in society and the way the mentally ill are regarded. It also could be a function of differences in the ways in which wire services and newspapers approach news. Wire services tend to convey breaking news to their members in a timely fashion. Newspapers have deadlines that allow more time to study an issue and explore its complex meanings.

Despite the decline in crime stories, the dangerousness of the mentally ill remained a central focus for the largest plurality (37 percent) of the stories. In fact, 44 percent of the mentally ill in the stories committed violent crimes. Perhaps more importantly, though, particularly in contrast with 1983's results, 56 percent did not commit a violent crime.

This shift reflected the emergence of two new themes in 1988: helplessness (found in 21 percent of the stories) and homelessness (12 percent). Other frequent themes were institutionalization (9 percent), social costs (7 percent), and funding (7 percent). The attention to helplessness and homelessness may have reflected a new sensitivity of journalists to the circumstances of mental illness. It could also reflect pack journalism. Homelessness stories have become particular favorites throughout the country during holidays and freezing temperatures.

Whatever the reason, newspaper stories tended to include more soft news and analyses than did UPI stories. Hard news was more likely to focus on dangerousness and soft news or other issues. Two-thirds of hard news stories in 1988 had dangerousness as the primary issue. Seventy-one percent of the feature stories focused on issues other than dangerousness.

Newspaper stories in 1988 tended to pay more attention to causes and treatments than did the 1983 stories. Thirty percent of the stories suggested a cause and 72 percent a treatment, compared to 23 percent and 55 percent in 1983. Crisis and distress (38 percent), childhood experiences (31 percent), and trauma (19 percent) were the most frequently mentioned causes. Hospitalization (48 percent) was the most frequent treatment, a sharp contrast to reality in this age of deinstitutionalization. Counseling (24 percent) and medication (17 percent) also were frequent ways of treating mental illness.

Attention to causes and treatments increased in 1988 in both violent and nonviolent stories. Twice as many 1988 violent stories included suggestions of causes (26 percent compared to 14 percent in 1983), and one-third more included mention of treatments (63 percent compared to 48 percent). Nonviolent stories also paid more attention to causes and treatments, but the increases were not as great (43 percent versus 37 percent for causes, and 78 percent versus 66 percent for treatments).

TWO SIDES OF A STIGMA

Both sets of stories clearly associated the mentally ill, mental patients, and former mental patients with violent crime, reaffirming a cultural stigma of dangerousness and unpredictability. These results are similar to what Nunnally (1961) found in the 1950s and Gerbner (1968) in the 1970s. The emergence of helplessness in 1988 as another frequent characterization provided another, if equally sigmatizing, view of mental illness.

In contrast to Nunnally's finding of a paucity of accurate information about mental illness in the media, the UPI stories contained a bit more and somewhat better information. The 1988 newspaper stories increased their informational content even more. However, informative stories often did not identify some individuals as mentally ill. They did not personalize mental illness for readers. When readers are given little opportunity to understand the daily lives and experiences of the vast majority of the nonviolent mentally ill, mental illness becomes an impersonal condition that happens to someone outside the psychological proximity of the reader. Most news stories personalized mental illness only in connection with violent crime.

Reporting by stereotype or label with little regard for the precise meaning or implication of the label resembles the reporting of other minority groups, particularly ethnic minorities. Ethnic minorities have organized to try to change media coverage. However, the mentally ill would be at a disadvantage if they attempted to repeat this process. Mental illness often means that people have difficulty organizing their own lives much less other people. In addition, identifying oneself as a former mental patient by itself can bring discrimination and stigma.

Perhaps the greatest danger in news accounts is when the overall effect is not to inform but to alarm. That is what occurs when news portrays the mentally ill as violent, dangerous, and unpredictable. Stories should have at least some measure of justification before tying mental illness to violence.

Consider, for example, a front page story from the *Boston Globe* on November 20, 1988 ("Quality of Care Questioned," p. 1). In what could be interpreted as an appropriate attempt to improve treatment for the mentally ill, the story spotlights a staffing shortage at New Hampshire Hospital. The shortage, however, focuses on danger, leaving the impression that the lives of staff are in jeopardy. "A critical staff shortage at New Hampshire Hospital has jeopardized safety and the quality of care at the institution, according to health workers who say the problem threatens to undo a decade of progress at the state psychiatric hospital," said the story. The article continued by giving example after example of violence: patients punching workers and stabbing them with pencils, for example.

Only at the end of the article does the writer reveal that New Hampshire Hospital is "home to the state's most seriously ill psychiatric patients." All psychiatric patients are tainted by the early paragraphs of the article, which leave an impression that they are dangerous to anyone around them. Letting the reader know early in the story that this institution houses the "most seriously ill" would have softened the impression of a link between mental illness and dangerousness.

Long Island *Newsday* portrayed such a link without generalizing it to include all the mentally ill by delaying the mention of the illness and focusing on actions without attributing motivation ("Ex-Student," March 4, 1988, p. 9). The lead said, "A former New York City Technical College student was convicted yesterday of killing one person and critically wounding four others in a 29-minute shooting rampage at the school's downtown Brooklyn campus." Not until the fourth paragraph from the end is the accused's mental illness introduced. The delay in linking mental illness with the murders lessened the possibility that the readers would generalize this particular schizophrenic's problems to include all schizophrenics.

Delaying the mental illness link, however, does not necessarily lessen the association with danger. Consider, for example, a New York *Times* story ("Murder for Thrill Described at a Trial," March 4, 1988, p. 19) with a lead focusing on action rather than linking mental illness and danger: "A 15-year-old defendant on trial here for murder is said to have killed a classmate for a thrill, then showed the corpse to friends who stayed mum about the killing for weeks."

The *Times* delayed the mental illness link until the fifth paragraph, but that paragraph left a misleading impression about the mentally ill as a group: "The defense attorney, John Philip White, painted another picture, describing the youth as a mentally ill child from a troubled home whose use of the stimulant Ritalin contributed to his murderous actions. 'In this case is the insidious element of mental illness with the overlying thread of Ritalin,' Mr. White told the jury."

The association of mental illness with dangerousness, without explanation or justification, confirms a social stigma that the mentally ill are to be feared and avoided. Earlier civilizations felt that physical deformities implied moral failings. Frequent association of mental illness with violence in contemporary culture attributes similar moral failings to today's mental ill: "From reading the media, one would infer a much stronger relationship between mental illness and violent behavior than actually exists. . . . Taken together the research in this field shows no relationship between mental disorder in general and violent behavior in general," noted law professor John Monahan (Monahan, 1984).

Psychiatrist Linda Teplin pointed out, "The real problem is that any history a person has of a mental disorder is always mentioned prominently in news coverage" (Teplin, 1984). Her research (Teplin, 1985) shows that mentally ill persons are no more likely to be violent and dangerous than other people. "Because mental disorder is linked with crime [in news stories], it implies a causal relationship. . . . Our data do not support that. It makes as much sense to always give a person's eye color as it does their mental status" (Teplin, 1984).

This deeply held but erroneous belief that the mentally ill are more dangerous than other people is reinforced each time a reporter or editor uses mental illness as a label to identify and, by implication, explain the actions of someone accused of committing a violent crime. "This assumption that any history of mental disorder per se is relevant to a news story should not be automatic. Reporters need to take the time to find out whether a person's mental disorder plausibly had something to do with their crime, or not use it. It's no more reasonable to associate mental illness with crime in general than it would be to blame tuberculosis" (Monahan, 1984).

The coverage of Henry Lee Lucas in 1983 illustrates the point. A digest item in the *Denver Post* lured readers with this teaser: "A formal mental patient convicted of murdering his mother and charged with two Texas slayings gave authorities more details to back up his claims that he killed 100 women in at least 16 states." The story appeared under a headline which read: "Ex-Mental Patient Tells Police He's Killed 100

Women." Only at the end of the story is it disclosed that Lucas's mental hospitalization occurred 23 years before the murders.

To assume a connection between Lucas's hospitalization and the alleged murders is to assume that all mental illness is lifelong and incurable. The Lucas story made only two references to his mental history. The first was in the lead and was exploited sensationally and stereotypically. The other came in the last paragraph. Such a use of the mental illness tag labels and stigmatizes.

Lucas, called a former mental patient, murderer, and necrophiliac, appeared in news accounts dozens of times, each time reinforcing the supposed association between mental illness and violence. Later stories cast doubts about Lucas's claims of mass murder. Yet, the link between violence and mental illness had been established and repeatedly reinforced.

The link, of course, is sometimes relevant and newsworthy. After the 1983 murders of three members of a Chino, California, family and its young houseguest, public safety required journalists to report that suspect Kevin Cooper was a mental hospital escapee wanted in Pennsylvania for rape and other crimes: "It would have been preposterous to imagine reporting the [John] Hinckley case without the issue of mental disorder arising," observed Monahan, who testified for the prosecution in that case. "But one example doesn't justify that someone's psychiatric history causes crime" (Monahan, 1984).

Nor does the fact that Hinckley was found not guilty by reason of insanity mean that droves of criminals avoid punishment with such a plea. In a study of public perception, Monahan explained:

> State legislators estimated that 40 percent of all defendants used the insanity defense to escape conviction. The truth is the insanity defense succeeds in less than one percent of the cases. . . . You have to ask. Where do people get this crazy idea? From reading the newspaper. Insanity cases always make the front page; run-of-the-mill liquor store robberies don't (Monahan, 1984).

By prominently reporting trials involving the insanity defense or crimes in which the suspect has a history of mental disorder, journalists feed society's phobia of the mentally ill. However, such stereotyping is not monolithic. News does include thoughtful articles about mental illness. During the last five years mental health organizations and professionals have conducted a campaign to improve treatment of the mentally ill by the news media. The 1988 study of newspapers suggests the campaign might have had some impact. Newspapers covered a wider variety of the problems of the mentally ill, such as homelessness and discrimination, and printed informative features on the biochemistry of mental illness.

The news media should pay careful attention to the implications of labeling even if they are not forced to do so by the mentally ill or others. An editor of the *Dayton Daily News* took an important step in this direction when he instructed his staff to refrain from including references to a person's mental hospitalization history in headlines "unless we are certain of the absolute relevance to the crime" ("Name? Age? Address? Race?" 1965).

This advice should be heeded at other papers. In addition, reporters should follow these strategies:

Omit references to a person's mental status or history unless it is directly relevant to a story. A crime suspect's mental disorder is not newsworthy in and of itself. To report the disorder is to imply a connection between mental illness and violence that is both unfair and untrue.

If a criminal suspect is at large and considered dangerous, mental status may be relevant.

If mental status or mental illness is relevant to the story, explain how and why. Three or fewer references to mental status, according to the UPI study, is often indicative of labeling. So, as a rule of thumb, if there are three or fewer references to mental illness in a story, reporters and editors should eliminate the references or explain them.

Be precise when using such terms as psycho, schizophrenic, mentally ill, mental patient, former mental patient, mentally deranged. These terms, used without explanation or definition, are merely labels.

Be aware that event-oriented news can reinforce public misperception of the mentally ill. The insanity defense and violent crime are newsworthy and frequently covered but, in the total picture, relatively rare. Discrimination against the mentally ill is widespread but seldom covered.

Reporters should write stories about the personal experiences of the mentally ill and their families. Stories might include problems in the daily lives of the mentally ill, discrimination and prejudice, homelessness, and positive contributions to society by former mental patients.

Journalists are a product of their own culture. They need to understand this reality. It may be that they can seldom escape their own cultures, but increasing awareness and sensitivity would alleviate stigmatizing predispositions. Twenty-five years ago in language that is now obviously dated, *Columbia Journalism Review* addressed stereotyping of a different nature: "When is a man's race a legitimate part of his identification in the news? Is description of a person as a 'Negro' — particularly in a crime story — discriminatory? Or is it a detail like age, occupation, or address?" The publication's answer then was: "Identify a person by race only if his race is pertinent to the story" ("Name? Age? Address? Race?" 1965, p. 40). Journalists would do well to heed this advice today; identify a person by mental health only when mental health is pertinent to the story.

6

Media Coverage of Technology Issues: Ethiopian Drought of 1984, AIDS, Challenger, and Chernobyl

EVERETT M. ROGERS AND SOON BUM CHANG

This chapter explores how four technology-related news issues gained a place on the U.S. media agenda during the 1980s and how these stories were played. Our main variable of interest in these analyses is the amount of mass media coverage given to a news issue over time. We measure media coverage as the number of news stories in three national newspapers — the New York *Times,* the *Los Angeles Times,* and the Washington *Post* — and in the evening news programs of the three U.S. television networks — NBC, ABC, and CBS.

The four news issues of study are:

The *1984 Ethiopian drought,* a slow-onset disaster that received heavy media coverage in the United States after October 23, 1984, when the first news film about the Ethiopian famine was broadcast by NBC. At that time, the drought had already been underway for about five years, killing several million head of livestock and an estimated 1 million people. The Associated Press (AP) annual survey of newspaper editors rated the Ethiopian drought as the sixth most important news event of 1984. The drought was a complicated technology failure, resulting from desertification caused by the destruction of trees used for cooking and heating fuel by a rapidly increasing population, which was in turn a result of yet other causes.

AIDS (Acquired Immune Deficiency Syndrome) was first diagnosed in the United States in May 1981. The epidemic began to receive considerable media coverage in mid-1985, and then stayed relatively high on the U.S. media agenda for the next four or five years. The AP annual survey of newspaper editors ranked the Rock Hudson AIDS story as the fifth most important news event of 1985, and in 1987 ranked the spread of the AIDS virus as the eighth most important news story.

The *Challenger explosion* on January 28, 1986 was a technology failure resulting in a quick-onset disaster. It was ranked in the AP survey of newspaper editors as the top news story of 1986. The Challenger disaster had major impacts on the National Aeronautics and Space Administration (NASA), the private companies involved, such as Morton Thiokol, and on the U.S. public's attitudes toward the space program (Miller, 1987).

The *Chernobyl explosion,* another technology failure, occurred on April 26, 1986, when the nuclear reactor at the Chernobyl power plant in the Soviet Union's Ukraine exploded. The quick-onset Chernobyl disaster received a considerable amount of coverage from the U.S. mass media, but then rapidly dropped off the media agenda. The AP survey of newspaper editors ranked the Chernobyl explosion as the third most important news story of 1986.

Our theoretical perspective is the agenda-setting process (McCombs and Shaw, 1972; Rogers and Dearing, 1988), and is operationalized in the following research questions: How important is a "real life indicator," like the number of deaths, the role of the New York *Times* and the White House, and spatial distance from a technological event (e.g., Kiev and Ethiopia) in explaining the amount of U.S. media coverage given to an issue? What are the effects of media coverage on public opinion (as indexed by national polls), regarding policy responses, such as federal funding for AIDS, and other indicators, such as the stock market price of Morton Thiokol after the Challenger explosion?

THE AGENDA-SETTING PROCESS

An agenda is a set of events and issues given at a point in time, a hierarchy of importance (Rogers and Dearing, 1988, p. 556). Events are discrete happenings limited by space and time, while issues are defined as involving cumulative news coverage of a series of related events that fit together in a broad category. For instance, the drug-related deaths of basketball star Len Bias and professional football player Don Rogers in mid-1986 were news events that helped put the issue of drug abuse higher on the national agenda (Danielian and Reese, 1989; Merriam, 1989). Agenda setting has been studied regarding such news issues as the Vietnam War, Watergate, a federal auto safety law, abortion, drug abuse, and the Sahel drought and other natural disasters (Rogers and Dearing, 1988).

Scholarly research on agenda setting stems directly from Bernard Cohen (1963, p. 3), who observed that the press

> May not be successful much of the time in telling people *what to think,* but it is stunningly successful in telling its readers *what to think about.* . . . The world will look different to different people, depending . . . on the map that is drawn for them by writers, editors, and publishers of the papers they read [emphasis added].

Cohen's metaphor alerted media scholars to the agenda-setting process, but empirical support did not begin until McCombs and Shaw's (1972) study of how the mass media set the agenda during the 1968 presidential campaign in Chapel Hill, North Carolina. Since 1972, more than 200 scholarly publications about agenda setting have appeared. This past research linked three main components of the agenda-setting process: the media agenda, measured by the amount of news coverage given to an issue of study; the public agenda, indexed by public responses to sample surveys about the issue; and the policy agenda, indicated by the decisions of policy elites about the issue.

The relationship between media agenda and public agenda has been well established. Much less scholarly attention has been devoted to how the media agenda is set (Chang, 1989). It is conventionally believed that the U.S. media's agenda-setting process is influenced by the amount of news coverage given to a news issue by influential newspapers such as the New York *Times,* by media gatekeepers such as editors and news managers, and by certain spectacular news events like, for example, the 1989 oil spill by the Exxon Valdez in Alaska, which influenced the larger environment issue in the United States.

Agenda-setting studies often include in their analysis a "real world indicator" of the importance of an issue. In the present study, for example, we use the number of diagnosed AIDS cases in the United States by the Centers for Disease Control (CDC) as a month by month real world indicator. Past research shows that the real world indicator of the seriousness of an issue is often not highly related to the amount of mass media coverage given to the issue. Other factors evidently intervene. For example, the number of drug related deaths in the United States changed only slightly during the 1980s, while media attention given to the drug issue increased tremendously, evidently as a result of the championing of the drug problem by the White House and the first lady (Danielian and Reese, 1989).

THE 1984 ETHIOPIAN DROUGHT

A drought is one type of slow-onset issue in which the agenda-setting function of the mass media can be observed rather clearly, as shown by research on media coverage of the Sahel drought of the 1970s (Morentz, 1979; Rogers and Kincaid, 1981, pp. 57–60). The first news article about the Sahel drought appeared in late 1972, after the drought had been underway for five years. When *Le Monde,* the influential French newspaper, and the New York *Times* began to provide extensive news coverage of the Sahel drought, food relief was sent from the United States and Europe.

The Ethiopian drought of 1984 followed a similar pattern of delayed news coverage. Human overpopulation led to the denuding of trees and shrubs for firewood. The environmental balance of the region was changed, decreasing transpiration of moisture into the air, leading to decreasing rainfall. Drought and famine resulted. The drought and famine was most severe in the two break-away provinces of Ethiopia — Eritrea and Tigre — which received little food aid from the national government of Ethiopia because of political conflict. During the early 1980s, people and livestock continued to die from the Ethiopian drought, but without attracting media attention.

Mohammed Amin, an East African news photographer stationed in Nairobi, Kenya, obtained a visa and permission to visit relief camps in Ethiopia in 1984. The BBC's Michael Buerk accompanied Amin and narrated his footage. The video news essay captured the human pathos of the Ethiopian drought at the relief camp of Korem.

First broadcast by the BBC in England, the story immediately had a strong public impact. The NBC bureau in London transmitted the BBC story by satellite to NBC headquarters in New York. Tom Brokaw, an NBC anchor, insisted that the three-and-a-half minute news film be broadcast on the NBC evening news on October 23, 1984. The impact in America was strong. Donations poured in to Save the Children, a relief agency mentioned by Brokaw at the end of the report. Within a week,

ABC and CBS broadcast news stories on the Ethiopian disaster (Boyer, 1985b; Boot, 1985). The U.S. government reversed its previous policy and sent massive food aid to Ethiopia. Rock musicians in England and then in the United States organized relief activities, such as the July 13, 1985, Live Aid concert, which raised more than $60 million for food relief in Ethiopia.

AIDS

The epidemic began in the United States in mid-1981, when AIDS was diagnosed among gay men living in New York, San Francisco, and Los Angeles. For the next four years, until mid-1985, the media gave relatively little attention to AIDS. Then two events put AIDS on the media agenda: the illness and death of movie actor Rock Hudson, and public protests that kept a young Indiana boy with AIDS, Ryan White, from attending public school. These two news events, as we show later in this chapter, changed the meaning of AIDS for news people and the U.S. public. The issue of AIDS remained high on the U.S. media agenda from 1985 to 1990. Such persistency of media coverage is unusual. One reason for such consistency is that various AIDS subissues rose and fell on the agenda, keeping the overall issue a high priority.

The first AIDS cases in 1981 represented a scientific puzzle, but, after several years of biomedical research, the AIDS virus was identified, means of transmission were determined, and a test for the presence of the virus was devised. Despite massive federal investment in AIDS research, a cure for the disease had still not been found by mid-1990, when 132,510 AIDS cases were reported in the United States by the CDC. The epidemic represents a special type of technological issue, in that scientists are unable to find a cure, and that they respond through public information campaigns, for example, urging people to practice "safe sex."

CHALLENGER EXPLOSION

On January 28, 1986, millions watched as the spaceship Challenger exploded a few minutes after take-off. Hours prior to the tragedy, project engineers at Morton Thiokol, a Utah company that constructed part of the Challenger, pleaded with NASA authorities to delay the launch. They feared that the cold temperature would cause the booster rocket's O rings to malfunction. The engineers were overruled by Thiokol management. The President's Commission (1986, p. 82), investigating the causes of the incident concluded, "the Thiokol management reversed its position and recommended the launch of 51-L, at the urging of Marshall [an intermediary vendor] and contrary to the views of its engineers in order to accommodate a major customer."

Explosion of the space shuttle killed all seven crew members, including Christy McAuliffe, a schoolteacher. The disaster was the first in-flight catastrophic accident of the U.S. space program. The event sent shock waves through NASA, the White House, Congress, and the U.S. public (Miller, 1987, p. 1; Riffe and Stovall, 1989).

For most Americans, the NASA space program and the shuttle represented the major achievement of American science and technology in the previous decade (Miller, 1987, p. 50). The Challenger disaster rendered that achievement problematic. The President's Commission on the Challenger, commonly called the Rogers Commission (after its chairperson, William Rogers), made its report public in mid-1986, resulting in another peak in media attention.

CHERNOBYL DISASTER

At 1:23 A.M. on Saturday, April 26, 1986, an explosion occurred at the Chernobyl nuclear power plant near Kiev in the Ukraine. Flames from a fire in the core shot half a mile into the sky. The next day, 49,000 people were evacuated from within a 30-kilometer radius of the plant. Two days later, radiation was detected on the clothing of employees reporting for work at a Swedish nuclear plant, and the source was traced to Chernobyl. Soviet television that evening, April 28, briefly noted that a nuclear accident had occurred. The Soviets announced there were two fatalities, but United Press International (UPI) reported that 2,000 people were dead. On April 30, the *New York Post* claimed that 15,000 dead had been buried in a nuclear disposal site.

Later the reactor was entombed in an above-ground jacket of concrete, and the area under the reactor foundation was removed. Secretary Mikhail Gorbachov gave a television address about the Chernobyl disaster on May 16, 1984, 16 days after the accident. Within three months 23 people had died from the disaster, most from radiation exposure, and 250 died over the next three years. On May 30, 1986, 34 days after the accident, UPI retracted its claim of 2,000 dead. Our content analysis shows that the U.S. media generally treated the Chernobyl disaster in the context of the cold war conflict between the two nations, charging or implying that the Soviets were covering up the true death toll.

The considerable U.S. media coverage of the Chernobyl disaster was in part due to prior experience with the 1979 nuclear accident at Three Mile Island, near Harrisburg, Pennsylvania (Dorman and Hirsch, 1986). CBS Evening News, for example, gave the Chernobyl disaster 129 minutes of air time in the 31 days after it was discovered, with the disaster completely dominating the news program for the first six days.

MEDIA COVERAGE

The media agenda for each of the four issues of study is measured by the number of news stories about the issue published or broadcast in six major U.S. mass media: the New York *Times,* the *Los Angeles Times,* the Washington *Post,* ABC, NBC, and CBS. We identified news stories about the four issues in the indexes for each of the six media, the *New York Times Index,* for example, and the Vanderbilt Television News Archive index for the three television networks.

Figure 6.1 shows the distribution over time of the number of news stories in the New York *Times* about the four issues of study. News coverage by the other five media shows a similar cyclical rise and fall pattern over time. This oscillating pattern of media coverage occurs because television time and newspaper space are limited resources, while potential new issues are continuously seeking to replace previously important issues (Downs, 1972). However, an old news issue can remain on the media agenda through the continuous addition of new information, which recasts the issue in new ways, as occurred for the issue of AIDS.

CONSISTENCY OF NEWS COVERAGE

When one medium carried a relatively large number of news stories about an issue, so did the other five media of study, as Figures 6.2 and 6.3 show for the Ethiopian famine. A similar degree of convergence in coverage also occurred for the other three issues. Correlations averaged about 80 (64 percent of common variance) between the number of news stories about an issue in any two of the six media outlets on a month by month basis. T he media outlets studied generally agreed on the amount of coverage they give to our issues of study.

FIGURE 6.1 — The New York *Times* News Coverage of the Four Technology-Related Issues

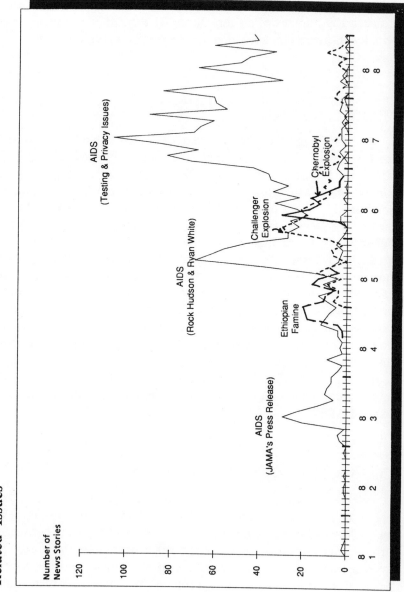

FIGURE 6.2 — Three U.S. Newspapers Covered the Ethiopian Drought with a High Degree of Consistency Over Time

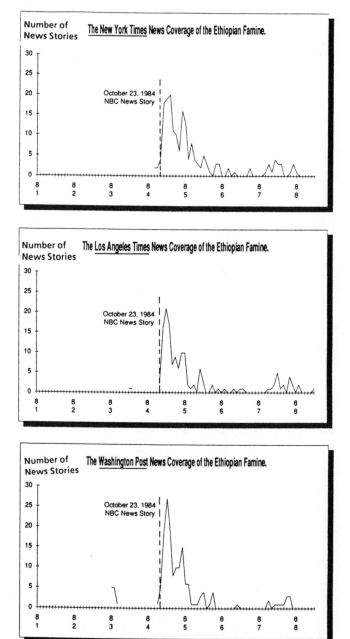

FIGURE 6.3 — Three U.S. Television Networks Covered the Ethiopian Drought with a High Degree of Consistency Over Time

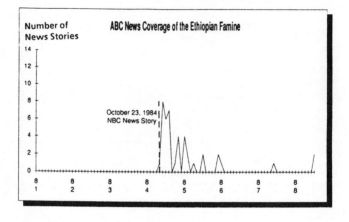

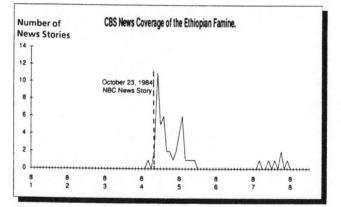

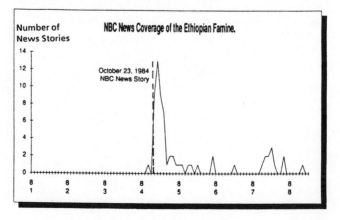

HOW THE MEDIA AGENDA WAS
SET FOR THE ISSUE OF AIDS

AIDS was placed on the U.S. media agenda as a result of the two news events in mid-1985 (Figure 6.4) concerning Rock Hudson and Ryan White. As a result, AIDS was perceived in a more humane and personalized way. Earlier news stories had focused on CDC statistics about the increasing number of AIDS cases.

The number of news stories about AIDS in the six media studied increased tremendously from an average of 14 per month before the Rock Hudson and Ryan White stories, to 143 per month after July 1985 (Figure 6.4). This tenfold increase did not happen because there were 129 more news stories each month about Hudson and White, but because a variety of aspects of the AIDS issue had now become newsworthy: "In interview after interview . . . , journalists and public health authorities alike agreed that it was Hudson who finally — belatedly, tragically — propelled AIDS into the public consciousness and onto the front page" (Shaw, 1987b).

Each of the two news events set off an AIDS subissue: public figures with AIDS in the case of Rock Hudson, and children with AIDS in the case of Ryan White. Each subissue represented a genre of AIDS reporting that then continued. Thus, the general issue of AIDS was kept in the public eye.

We identified 13 AIDS subissues over the 91 months of our time series. As one AIDS subissue declined in the amount of media coverage that it received, another one of the 13 AIDS subissues rose in the degree of media attention that it was given, so that the general issue of AIDS remained high on the U.S. media agenda for several years. Through new emphases and information, such as that created by biomedical research findings, an issue, once on the media agenda, can rise, fall, and then rise again, as new subissues gain and then lose media coverage.

We can better understand the impact of the Hudson and White news events in setting the U.S. media agenda for AIDS by considering several other news events that occurred prior to mid-1985, but which did not set the media agenda:

December 1982: The AIDS virus is found in the U.S. blood supply.
January 1983: CDC announces that heterosexual contact is a means of AIDS virus transmission.
March 1984: Identification of the AIDS virus is announced.
January 1985: Announcement of a blood test for AIDS virus antibodies.

FIGURE 6.4 — The Impact of the Rock Hudson and Ryan White News Events on the Number of News Stories about the Issue of AIDS, June, 1981 through December, 1988 (91 months)

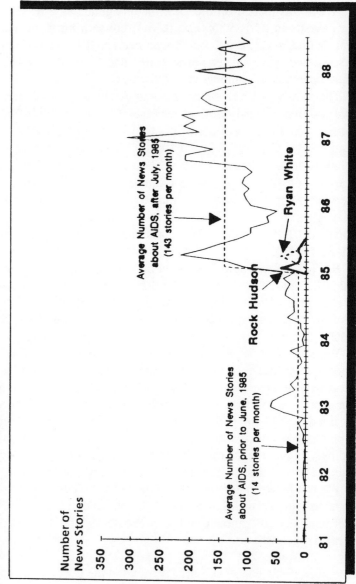

None of these important scientific findings led to major news coverage of AIDS. Science did not set the media agenda for the issue of AIDS (Check, 1987). Instead, the media "found" the AIDS story in two very human and emotional events.

SLOW ONSET OF THE MEDIA AGENDA: THE WHITE HOUSE AND AIDS

After the first four years of the AIDS epidemic, a point at which 9,944 people had AIDS, according to CDC statistics, the issue of AIDS was still not on the media agenda. The six media outlets each averaged only 2.3 news stories per month about AIDS prior to July 1985 (see Figure 6.4), and seldom did these news stories appear on the front page or at the top of an evening television newscast. For example, the New York *Times* did not publish a front page story about AIDS until May 25, 1983 — 23 months into the epidemic.

A four-year time lag in the media reporting of a rapidly spreading epidemic seems almost incredible in hindsight. Why were the national mass media so slow to respond? One reason lies with two potentially powerful organizations that often play a key role in setting the national agenda for various issues in the United States: the New York *Times* and the White House. Neither the New York *Times* nor the president played their usual agenda-setting role for the issue of AIDS.

A U.S. president can create media interest in any particular issue simply by giving a speech about it. President Ronald Reagan chose not to do so until May 1987, 72 months into the AIDS epidemic, a point at which 35,121 AIDS cases had been reported by the CDC. During the early years of the epidemic, the Reagan administration generally ignored the issue of AIDS. The White House was then eager to cut the domestic budget to help offset major increases for military defense. AIDS represented a serious federal budget threat to the White House, and so it was ignored (Shilts, 1987).

The conventional public health strategy is to throw every available resource at an epidemic as quickly as possible. The White House response to AIDS contrasts with the response to Legionnaire's Disease in the 1970s, perhaps due to who contracted each disease. If AIDS had been an epidemic among wealthy, white, older males, the federal response to AIDS might have been different.

Legionnaire's Disease killed 29 individuals in 1976. It received more media coverage in a few weeks than AIDS did from 1981 through mid-1984. The New York *Times* published 62 news stories on Legionnaire's

Disease in August and September 1976; 11 stories were on page one. The New York *Times* published only 7 stories about AIDS in the first 19 months of the AIDS epidemic. AIDS made the front page of the *Times* for the eleventh time when the epidemic was more than four years old, when there were 12,000 AIDS cases and 6,000 dead (Shaw, 1987a).

ROLE OF THE NEW YORK *TIMES*

Like the president, the editor of a prestigious newspaper such as the New York *Times* can influence the national media agenda by simply publishing front page stories about it. Our discussions as well as Shaw's (1987a) with the editorial staff at the New York *Times* indicate that the newspaper's management did not view AIDS as newsworthy in the early years of the epidemic, from 1981 through mid-1985. The *Times*'s top decision makers continued an editorial policy of avoiding the word gay as a synonym for homosexual until mid-1987 (Shaw, 1987a).

When the New York *Times* did carry news stories about AIDS, they generally were not prominently placed. The New York *Times* published its first page one story about AIDS 12 months later than the *Los Angeles Times,* 10 months later than the Washington *Post,* 11 months later than the Philadelphia *Inquirer,* and 11 months later than the San Francisco *Chronicle* (Shaw, 1987a). The *Chronicle* led other big city newspapers in its coverage of the AIDS story, with much of the credit for the *Chronicle*'s early coverage of AIDS going to one reporter, Randy Shilts (Kinsella, 1988, 1990).

The U.S. media rarely published or broadcast news stories about AIDS during the pre-1985 period, and then only because certain individual news persons became personally concerned about AIDS, often through knowing someone with AIDS. These journalistic heroes persisted in reporting the AIDS story prior to 1985, despite the threat posed to their journalistic careers (Kinsella, 1988, 1990).

TIME-SERIES ANALYSIS OF AIDS
MEDIA AGENDA SETTING

In addition to the role of the White House and the New York *Times,* several other factors help explain how the issue of AIDS climbed the U.S. media agenda. First is the science agenda, which we measured by analyzing the content of four medical and science journals: *Science, New England Journal of Medicine, Journal of the American Medical*

Association, and *Mortality and Morbidity Weekly Report* (the official journal of the CDC). These four journals published 1,314 articles about AIDS during the 91 months of our study — June 1981 through December 1988. We expected the science agenda to be related positively to the media agenda for AIDS.

Second is the polling agenda, as measured by the number of poll questions regarding AIDS asked in national surveys. Presumably, media organizations expect to get a return on their considerable investment in polls through higher television ratings and increased newspaper circulation resulting from reporting their AIDS poll results. Here is a unique situation in which the media actively create news by sponsoring polls (Dearing, 1989). From the Roper Center for Public Opinion Research, we obtained 1,084 poll questions asked in 110 different surveys. The first poll questions about AIDS were asked in national polls for the 22 months from August 21, 1983, to June 30, 1985. This same period was characterized by relatively low media coverage of AIDS, as noted previously. About two-thirds of the AIDS polls were sponsored by mass media organizations.

Third is the number of AIDS cases reported to the CDC, the real world indicator for AIDS.

Fourth is the policy agenda, measured here as the amount of federal funds for AIDS research, education, and testing. Although through funding allocations within the CDC some federal funds were spent for AIDS research as early as fiscal year 1981, Congress first officially allocated federal funds for AIDS in 1983. As shown in Figure 6.5, Congress has approximately doubled AIDS funding each year since.

Each of these four independent variables is related to our dependent variable — the number of news stories about AIDS per month. While the four independent variables are each positively related to AIDS media coverage, they are also intercorrelated with each other. These intercorrelations, however, may be spurious due to serial correlation among the observations of each variable over time. The past observations of a variable may influence the present observation of that variable. In order to determine the unique contribution of each of the four independent variables in explaining the dependent variable, we must first identify the influence of the past history of the dependent variable on itself. We used the Box and Jenkins (1976) procedure to determine the degree to which our variable of study was related to itself in a previous month. We found an R^2 for the media agenda of 9.6 percent, indicating the amount of variance in the dependent variable explained by itself with a four-month lag.

FIGURE 6.5 — Federal Funds for AIDS Research, Education, and Testing per Year and the Number of News Stories about AIDS (Six Mass Media Combined, June 1981 through December 1988)

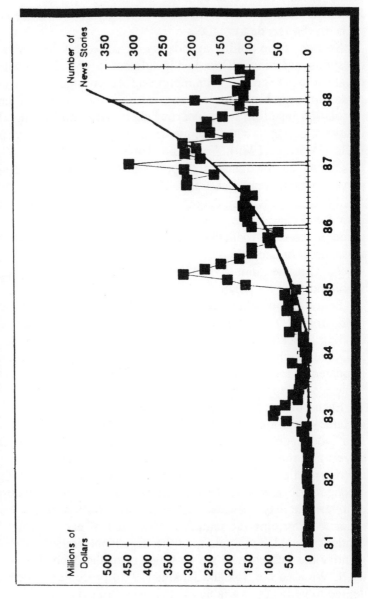

The second step consisted of investigating causal relationships over time among the four independent time-series and the dependent time-series, with various months of time lag of the four independent variable time-series in explaining the dependent time-series (Cassidy, 1981).

Figure 6.6 shows that three independent time-series, the science agenda, the polling agenda, and the number of AIDS cases, jointly set the media agenda, each with different time lags. The policy agenda is dropped in our multivariate analysis because it does not make a contribution in explaining the media agenda over time. About 47 percent of the variance in the media agenda was explained by the three independent time-series, while the influence of the media agenda on itself was about 10 percent of the variance explained.

One of the important conclusions of our time-series analysis is that the number of AIDS cases had an overall negative influence upon the media agenda. The number of news stories lagged behind the growing number of AIDS cases during the 1980s.

We did not have detailed, data of a comparable nature acquired over a period of time for the other three issues of study: the Ethiopian drought, the Challenger explosion, and the Chernobyl disaster. We know that the Challenger and Chernobyl issues were quick-onset in nature; they immediately jumped high on the U.S. media agenda. Several years were required before the Ethiopian drought got on the media agenda, but it climbed to the top very quickly once NBC broadcast the three-and-a-half minutes of video news about the famine on October 23, 1984.

IMPACT ON PUBLIC AND POLICY AGENDAS

Here we return to our second research question: What is the impact of media coverage of an issue?

First consider the issue of AIDS. The mass media positively influenced the polling agenda over time, and the way in which the AIDS issue was portrayed in the mass media influenced the way in which survey questions addressed the issue of AIDS (Dearing, 1989). Unfortunately for scholarly purposes, the U.S. public was not polled about AIDS at regular intervals during the 91 months of our study. Despite the periods when no poll questions were asked, certain trends in the public agenda for AIDS over time can be observed.

Despite the lack of media attention, the adult population of the United States became aware of AIDS relatively early and soon learned how AIDS could, and could not, be transmitted. By April, 1983, 77 percent of a national sample reported that they had heard or read about a disease

FIGURE 6.6 — Multivariate Analysis of the Media Agenda Time-Series (N = 71 months)

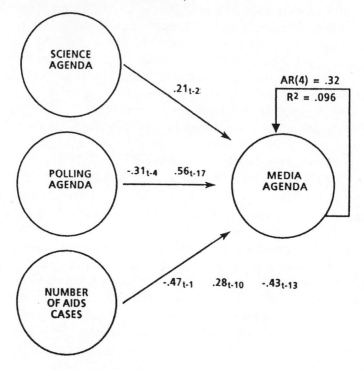

Total variance explained = R^2 = .566
Incremental variance explained = R^2 = .47
The model predicting the media agenda over time is:

$$MA = .12 + .21SA_{t-2} - .31PA_{t-4} + .56PA_{5-17} - .47NOA_{5-1} + .28NOA_{t-10} - .43NOA_{t-13}$$

where MA is the media agenda, SA is the science agenda, PA is the polling agenda, and NOA is the number of AIDS cases.

called AIDS; this figure increased to 91 percent by mid-1983 and then increased slowly to 98 percent by early 1986.

Only 3 percent of the respondents in an April 1987 poll ranked AIDS as the most important problem facing the United States. But when respondents were asked the most important health problem facing the United States, AIDS rose to top importance, over cancer and heart disease, by late 1986, when 33 percent ranked AIDS as the greatest health problem facing the nation, a figure that increased to 70 percent in April 1987.

National survey respondents also reported major life style changes as a result of the AIDS epidemic: from September 1985 to March 1987, condom use to prevent AIDS increased from 2 percent to 11 percent, monogamous sexual relationships were reported as increasing from 10 percent to 19 percent, and reported sexual abstinence increased from 2 percent to 8 percent.

Our analysis of national poll results shows that public awareness of AIDS increased relatively rapidly and early, especially during the first two years of the epidemic when media coverage of AIDS was still quite low; early public confusion existed about the means of transmission of the AIDS virus, which later decreased; relative to other health problems in the United States, AIDS, since mid-1986, has been considered by far the most important; and certain life style changes have occurred as a result of AIDS.

The mass media influence on the public agenda is suggested by the fact that alternative means of communication about AIDS could hardly have operated so rapidly in reaching so many individuals. For instance, in 1987 only 10 percent of the U.S. public said in a national poll that they knew someone with AIDS, so interpersonal communication about AIDS seems to have been limited.

The mass media also positively influenced the policy agenda about AIDS. Congress has approximately doubled administration requests for AIDS funding each year during a period of federal budget-cutting (see Figure 6.5).

The October 23, 1984, BBC broadcast of Mohammed Amin's film of the Korem refugee camp was viewed by Bob Geldof, an Irish rock musician, who set in motion a huge fund-raising activity by U.S. and British rock musicians. The food aid campaign for Ethiopia culminated in the July 1985 Live Aid Concert. More importantly, U.S. media coverage of the Ethiopian drought immediately changed the U.S. government's policy toward Ethiopia, so that $1 billion worth of food aid was shipped in 1984–85.

The January 1986 Challenger explosion led to a higher degree of public support for NASA's space program and for the shuttle program in particular (Miller, 1987, p. i). By evening of the day following the mid-morning explosion, 18 hours after the accident, 95 percent of American adults said they had seen television news pictures of the exploding shuttle (Miller, 1987, p. 10). The accident was highly visual, a perfect television event. It had a strong emotional impact: 6 percent of American adults said they attended a local memorial service for the deceased crew members; 78 percent said they watched all or part of the memorial service in Houston on television; 54 percent reported that they cried or felt like crying (Miller, 1987, p. 16).

The impact on Morton Thiokol, the Utah-based contractor that built the defective O-rings, was immediate and devastating. The selling price of Morton Thiokol's stock on the New York Exchange dropped by 20 percent within an hour of the Challenger explosion, while trading volume escalated. A month or two after the explosion, Morton Thiokol's stock had returned to its predisaster level. But for Morton Thiokol, Martin-Marietta, and other NASA contractors, the Challenger disaster represented plant closings, layoffs, and severe financial setbacks.

The Chernobyl nuclear accident also had a variety of consequences. The May 1986 disaster sparked discussion among policy makers in several nations about the need to improve methods for disseminating international warnings and other information about a national disaster. Almost no new nuclear power plants have been built anywhere in the United States since the disaster, or since the 1979 Three Mile Island accident.

CONCLUSIONS

This chapter began with two research questions, which we now answer. First, how important is a real world indicator, like the number of deaths, the role of the New York *Times* and the White House, and the spatial distance from a technological event (e.g., Kiev and Ethiopia) in explaining the amount of media coverage given to an issue?

Our analysis shows that a real world indicator, such as the number of AIDS cases, is negatively related to the amount of media coverage given to the issue, but with a lag factor of up to about a year in this relationship. Our results support the findings of past studies that show real world indicators are not highly related to media coverage of an issue.

The New York *Times* can put a technology-related issue on the U.S. media agenda, as it did, for example, in the case of Love Canal (Ploughman, 1984) and radon (Mazur, 1987). In the case of AIDS, the New York *Times* and the inactive role of the White House seem to have retarded placing the epidemic on the national media agenda. By not playing their usual agenda-setting roles, these two powerful institutions may have slowed the AIDS issue from getting on the media agenda until mid-1985, when Rock Hudson and Ryan White personalized and humanized AIDS.

Spatial factors were important in keeping the Ethiopian drought off the U.S. media agenda for several years, as editors and other media gatekeepers generally reacted toward the story as "just more starving Africans." Then, one short video news clip broadcast by NBC on October 23, 1984, put the drought on the national agenda.

Second, what are the effects of media coverage on public opinion, as indexed by national polls, on policy responses (e.g., federal funding) and other indicators (e.g., the stock market price of Morton Thiokol after the Challenger explosion)?

Media agenda setting of the four issues of study had an important impact on government funding for AIDS research, education, and testing; for federal government food aid to Ethiopia; and for NASA appropriations. The agenda-setting process of the mass media can be one important cause of social change.

POLICY IMPLICATIONS

Our findings suggest the following implications:

The four-year delay before the issue of AIDS got on the U.S. media agenda suggests that the U.S. mass media may need an improved early warning surveillance system for certain slow-onset issues.

The cases of AIDS and the Ethiopian drought suggest that individual newspeople can, when personally committed to a particular issue, champion the issue in their mass medium.

The degree of scientific attention given to publishing research results about the AIDS epidemic was only modestly related to the amount of mass media attention given to the AIDS issue (see Figure 6.6), and four important scientific findings, such as identifying the AIDS virus and the announcement of a blood test for virus antibodies, did not put the issue of AIDS on the media agenda. Instead, two human interest news events in mid-1985 involving Rock Hudson and Ryan White put the epidemic on the U.S. media agenda by humanizing and personalizing the issue of AIDS.

A technology-related issue such as the 1986 Chernobyl disaster was interpreted by the U.S. media in the context of U.S./Soviet international relationships as was the 1979 nuclear accident at Three Mile Island. Similarly, the 1989 San Francisco earthquake was given meaning by the media in comparing it to the 1906 San Francisco earthquake, the 1985 Mexico City earthquake, and the 1988

Armenian earthquake. Such comparisons help the media give meaning to an issue for the audience.

While the six national media studied here are consistent in the amount of news coverage they gave to four technology-related issues, they may differ in what they report about an issue. Thus, one can understand how the media can tell their audience what to think about (the agenda-setting function) without telling them what to think (Cohen, 1963).

7

A Cross-Societal Comparison of Disaster News: Reporting in Japan and the United States

E. L. QUARANTELLI AND
DENNIS WENGER

During 1984–85, sociologists from the Disaster Research Center (DRC) at the University of Delaware and social scientists associated with the Institute of Mass Communication and Journalism at the University of Tokyo undertook a joint research project on mass media reporting of news about disasters in both countries. Using a common, although not identical, research design, the Americans studied local community-level reporting of a major hurricane — Hurricane Alicia in the Houston, Texas, area in 1983 — and a major sudden flood around Tulsa, Oklahoma, in 1984. The Japanese concurrently researched the reporting of two similar disasters: floods around Nagasaki in 1982 and an earthquake in the Tohoku district in 1983. After the field data had been mostly analyzed, the researchers from both societies held a meeting in the United States to compare their findings.

The conclusions drawn at that meeting, as well as other, later interview comparisons and content analyses, are summarized in this chapter. We additionally point out the new questions generated by our findings. Despite the considerable sociocultural contrasts between the two societies, far more similarities than differences were found in mass media reporting of disaster news, and this is explained in the last part of the chapter along with some policy implications.

The research within the United States focused upon organizational and content analysis of mostly local but, to some extent, also national media operations. Researchers obtained a general profile of the total community mass media involvement in the disaster. This necessitated obtaining surveylike data from a universe of 35 radio stations, seven television stations, and three daily newspapers in the Houston-Galveston area, and from ten radio stations, six television stations, and two daily newspapers in the Tulsa area. We also developed a detailed case study of the major television, radio, and newspaper outlets in both Houston and Tulsa.

Through 49 in-depth interviews in Houston and 22 similar interviews in Tulsa, data were gathered allowing a comparison of normal time operations and organizational structure during the emergencies.

Available content — television and radio programs and one of the newspapers — from these major outlets was also systematically analyzed. (For example, all issues of the Houston newspaper were examined from three days before the hurricane to two weeks afterwards; a total of 160 hurricane-related stories were found). In addition, a limited content analysis was also done on some of the national television, radio, and newspaper coverage of the disasters, and we had access to two audience surveys in Houston.

The Japanese researchers also had a three-fold focus. They examined the news gathering and processing activities of the various mass media that operated in the disasters they studied. They also gave special attention to the role and effectiveness of the mass communication system in providing disaster warnings. Finally, the ability of the system to fulfill audience needs for specific types of information during the disasters was studied through two random samples of 1,000 local residents in the affected areas.

While the data analyses were not identical, the examination of the survey data, the organizational analysis undertaken, and the content analyses done in Japan roughly paralleled what DRC did in the United States. (For more details on the data gathering and analyses undertaken by the Japanese researchers, see Hiroi, Mikami, and Miyata, 1985.)

There are some limitations to the study. Our basic focus was on local news reporting at the emergency time period of the disasters. It dealt with only two natural disasters in both countries. Furthermore, while the disasters were major in that they disrupted the routine functioning of the local communities they affected, none approached the status of catastrophe. Also, while we undertook some content analyses of the national radio and television network outlets, we did not directly study the intraorganizational behavior of the networks involved. Moreover, there was no examination of the activities or contents of the wire services, or the views of the mass media held by the emergency organizations involved. (For topics that might be studied, see Quarantelli, 1980, 1989.)

Nonetheless, our cross-societal comparative research is the first systematic one of its kind ever undertaken. Also, our in-depth and concurrent examination of radio, television, and newspaper organizations in reporting disaster news is the first with such a focus. (For some later work, see Wenger and Quarantelli, 1989.) Given this, it would appear significant that we found far more similarities than differences in the local Japanese and American mass media organizational responses to disasters.

THE SIMILARITIES

We first discuss ten outstanding similarities in our comparative data analysis. The following statements are not advanced in any particular order of importance because our data do not allow such a hierarchical differentiation. However, although they are stated in flat form, we do consider the propositions as tentative hypotheses that can eventually be brought to a more systematic test, not only in Japan and the United States, but also in other societies with different social, political, and economic structures and mass communication systems.

Disasters as Major News Stories

In both countries, disasters were treated as the most important news stories in the communities at the time they occurred. During the emergency time period at some of the local media outlets, practically nothing was reported that was not disaster related. For several days, almost all other aspects of community life were given secondary attention by the local mass communication systems. National and international news was scanty and usually only locally disseminated through extracommunity sources, like regular on-the-hour national network news reports.

This may appear to be stating the obvious, but it is not necessarily a generalization that holds across all social systems. For example, until recently in the Soviet Union — and even now in some African countries — it is known that manifestly major domestic disasters were not even mentioned in either local or national mass media news stories (Sanders,

1986; Shabad, 1986). The existence of a disaster does not automatically mean that it will be treated as news. Leaving aside societal, political, and ideological differences surrounding definitions of news, our generalization raises a question of what mass communication systems will treat as disasters. Is the AIDS epidemic handled as a disaster story anywhere? What accounts for the known differentiation between reporting local, domestic, and foreign disasters? (See Gans, 1980, for such differences in American national media news stories.)

Similar Cross-media Differences in Use and Exposure at Times of Disasters

In both Japan and the United States, the differences in use of and exposure to various media were quite similar. For example, in both countries the electronic media were relied upon most heavily by the public during the immediate postimpact emergency period. The increasing communication output from the electronic media was matched by increasing exposure on the part of the audience. In disasters where electric power was disrupted, radio stations played the key role, in part because victims can use battery-powered radios. However, where power was not disrupted, television appeared to be the primary medium for distributing information during the phases of relief and restoration.

While these may be unexceptional observations, our findings raise the question of why television was the preferred medium. Japanese audiences are accustomed to listening during normal times to regular on-the-hour and half-hour radio broadcasts of news stories.

Intramedia Style Differences in Reporting Disasters

In both Japan and the United States, differences in the nature of the content was observed across organizations within the same medium. For example, television networks in the United States covered disasters with different story lines or themes. For ABC the story was one of danger, threat, and the helplessness of ordinary people to control the ravages of nature. CBS, on the other hand, painted a picture of calm, technological enlightenment. In Japan, the NHK radio broadcasts reported damage and destruction, while the commercial network, ABC, tried to respond to citizens' requests for contact with their families. Although supported by the work of Nimmo (1984; see also Nimmo and Combs, 1985), who reported similar differences of American network television coverage of the Three Mile Island nuclear plant accident, these observations are not inherently obvious.

It might be asked how conscious mass media organizations are of their styles, and whether there are cross-societal similarities. Equally as important, in what way, if any, do intramedia style differences affect audience exposure to and use of mass media content? Another worthwhile question is, Are there also style differences among the print media? Anecdotal and impressionistic observations would seem to support the idea, but systematic empirical documentation is not currently available.

Initial Lack of Accurate Information about Impact

In both countries, local media personnel faced the problem of a lack of information about the magnitude and scope of disaster impacts. In Japan, the broadcasting media personnel faced delays of two hours or more in obtaining details about the events. Similarly, reporters in the United States complained about the difficulty of getting early and detailed information from community officials.

To a considerable extent in both countries, local mass media systems had limited, selective, incomplete, and, in some cases, incorrect information in the immediate aftermath of disaster (also reported for Canadian mass media by Scanlon and Alldred, 1982). This is not surprising given that a similar lack of information prevails among emergency organizations and community officials (Quarantelli, 1985). Nevertheless, the observations imply a number of additional research questions.

What difference does the lack of information make in what the media report? Does the lack of information contribute to media-perpetuated myths about disaster behavior? How are emergency organization officials and private citizens affected by the kind of information available? Is the emphasis on accuracy misplaced, given that relevance of information might be a more meaningful criteria in the emergency time period of disasters? (See Scanlon, Luukko, and Morton, 1978; also for some Japanese work see Hiroi, Mikami, and Miyata, 1985.)

The Command Post View of Disaster

Mass media field representatives within the United States tend to rely upon official sources for their information in constructing stories about both disasters and civil disturbances (Quarantelli, 1981; this is also confirmed for natural disasters by Sood, Stockdale, and Rogers, 1987). Journalists usually ignore nontraditional sources. As a result, what is usually reported is a "command post" view of the disaster. This is one possible perspective, but it is only one of many different orientations possible regarding a disaster. For example, other possible perspectives would include on-the-line operational personnel, such as police and fire officers, disaster victims, relief workers from outside the community, foreign researchers, distant relatives and friends of victims, and community residents who were not affected. Therefore, news coverage is somewhat limited and reflects a more formal, top-down, governmental and social control perspective than any other possible view.

Our data from Houston and Tulsa reconfirmed this general observation. Moreover, there was also a similar reliance on top official sources in Japan. National and prefectural officials were the primary sources for many stories and were generally the first persons to whom field reporters turned. There was almost no use of nontraditional sources.

To describe the command post perspective is one thing; to explain it is another. Moreover, what are the consequences of the command post perspective? For instance, does it contribute to disaster mythologies, such as looting and antisocial behavior, that are the understandable interests of social control agencies like the police?

Diminution of the Gatekeeping Process

The normal gatekeeping process of radio stations is altered during the emergency time period of disasters in the United States (Waxman, 1973). Various steps in the process are eliminated, and a condition of "open gates" becomes operative. Information is gathered by the station, either through its own initiative or calls from the public, and disseminated through the media without undergoing the normal editing or gatekeeping process (see also Sood, 1982).

Again, we observed this pattern in both Japan and the United States. Radio stations aired information immediately; normal validity checks were ignored in both societies. But the pattern was more noticeable at radio stations. The gatekeeping process was less altered in television reporting and remained almost untouched in newspaper organizations.

Why is the decrease in the gatekeeping process more likely to occur in radio rather than other media? While there are several plausible explanations, none have been systematically studied. (We have more recently examined some possibilities; see Wenger and Quarantelli, 1989). There is also a question of why gatekeeping, which works well for the mass communication system during normal times, is apparently less functional during emergencies.

Personalized Media Use in Disasters

In both societies, the electronic media, particularly radio, was often significantly altered in one important aspect: it often became a very elaborate mechanism for interpersonal and not just mass communication. In Japan, thousands of personal messages about safety, location, or concern were broadcast. These were directed to specific relatives and friends of the victims. People would call radio stations with messages that were frequently aired verbatim. A similar pattern was observed in the United States, although to a lesser degree.

But it is not clear what leads broadcasters to engage in a practice that is rather deviant in normal times; in fact, personal messages by the electronic media on an everyday basis are prohibited by law in the United States. Of research interest, too, would be a content analysis of such messages and a study of how audiences use them.

Weak Planning for Disasters by Mass Media

In both Japan and the United States, planning on the part of mass communication outlets for disaster operations was relatively weak. It was not totally absent; a few media groups, especially certain larger organizations, gave some systematic thought to the coverage of major stories on disasters. But, on the whole, the local organizational response pattern in the emergency time period of disasters either followed established routines or were emergent and ad hoc in nature.

Why do mass media systems generally not undertake planning for disaster coverage? (For a comparison with the planning for civil disturbances, see Kueneman and Wright, 1976.) Even in those rare cases where there is systematic planning, it is almost always focused only on one kind of disaster agent, like hurricanes in some southern communities or earthquakes in certain California cities. We would hypothesize that it is because most mass media organizations see themselves primarily as observers and reporters — their everyday view — of disasters rather than as possible victims or part of the responding community actors in the emergency. This seems a reasonable supposition, but the supporting empirical data for the idea does not currently exist.

Socio-organizational and Technical Problems

Since systematic disaster planning by mass media groups in both societies is limited, it was not surprising to find that the problems they encountered in covering stories were dramatically similar. Mobilizing media personnel and resources in both Japan and the United States was problematic. There were, for example, difficulties in both settings in finding higher level management personnel when the emergency developed. Disruption of telephone service generated similar kinds of technical problems for media operations. Communication difficulties arose in both societies due to the convergence of calls and requests for information from citizens. Altered and ad hoc decision making in media organizations occurred in both Japan and the United States, sometimes as a result of the absence of personnel or equipment.

It is difficult to see any common or differentiating dimensions in the difficulties observed. However, we would think further research could establish which problems would be likely to occur earlier than others, and which are more difficult to solve or handle. In addition, all the observed problems seemed to be related both to the degree of, or lack of, mass media preparedness planning and the constraints created by the physical impact of the disaster agent. (Some of these issues have been addressed in our more recent research; see Wenger and Quarantelli, 1989.)

Alterations in Mass Media Organizations during Disasters

In both Japan and the United States there were alterations in news gathering activities, news processing, and the decision-making structures of the local mass media organizations. The everyday or usual pattern of assignment of reporters in the field, the allocation of resources, and relationships between editors and staff personnel were altered. Also, a team approach to news gathering emerged very strongly in both societies.

Many new research questions are generated by these findings. Why is there a curvilinear relationship between size of the mass media outlet and changes in operations (see Friedman, 1987)? How are the alterations affected both by the media technology used and work time schedules of news organizations? In addition, it is not clear what the implications are from observations of the more centralized activities at control points such as the newsroom and the more decentralized decision making undertaken by reporters in the field. This dialectic in decision making at different levels of an organization is not peculiar to the mass media area (see

Quarantelli, 1985), but the consequences for what is done and produced by way of news stories have not been traced.

While the above are the major similarities we observed, there were also others that, for various reasons, we could not document as well. For example, it seemed that in both societies the local mass media outlets were important in providing critical information wanted by the general public. However, the Japanese, who more systematically studied this matter, found that not all citizens wanted what was provided. Also, although the mass media systems appeared to provide the bulk of the warnings people received of the impending disasters, in both societies some persons were never reached despite the massive dissemination of warning messages by the local mass communications system (see Ledingham and Masel-Walters, 1984).

THE DIFFERENCES

Let us now turn to a discussion of the far fewer differences we noted in the mass media disaster operations in the two societies. There were some differences in how local and extracommunity mass media groups, even within the same larger social organization, related to one another in the two societies. For example, in the tsunami disaster in Nagasaki, extensive assistance was given to the local NHK television station by other NHK stations from different parts of Japan. As many as 95 staff members arrived from NHK headquarters in Tokyo, and several neighboring stations assisted the local station in its local coverage. These mass media personnel brought with them ten ENG cameras, four editing units, two ENG cars, three helicopters, and a facsimile machine that became a part of the resource base of the local station. Although network personnel often converge upon disaster areas in the United States and sometime use the facilities of local stations (well dramatized in the recent mass media coverage of the earthquake in San Francisco), they are present to generate stories for their network programs, not to help the local station in its coverage. This altruism on the part of the other units within the network is not found in the United States and is not likely to develop given the competitive work norms that exist in American society.

Also, the content of the disaster coverage disseminated by the national networks in the two countries differed somewhat. There are four time zones within the continental United States; all of Japan is within one time zone. One consequence at the national network level is that in the United States, except for some breaking stories, there is an effort to avoid current time references in a news story. (To say that a hurricane will reach land at 10:00 A.M. is not too meaningful in the state of Florida, which cuts across two time zones.) Japanese journalists, in contrast to their American counterparts, do not need to update news stories that will be telecast three hours later on the west coast after their initial reporting on the east coast.

Finally, there are some legal differences that influence the operations of the mass communication systems. For example, NHK in Japan, in addition to its normal news-gathering function, has the legal responsibility of being a part of the emergency response system. The Meteorological Service Law, for instance, mandates that if the Japan Meteorological Agency issues a warning of weather conditions or of a tsunami, NHK must broadcast it promptly and exactly as the message was issued. Also, according to the Disaster Countermeasures Basic Law, NHK is identified as one of the public corporations for disaster mitigation; it is legally bound to gather and broadcast relevant information to the public at times of disaster. The commercial broadcasting companies and newspapers are not bound by these same laws. However, they voluntarily subscribe to them and attempt to play an important role in the emergency response.

Within the United States, however, there are no legal requirements that mass media outlets must participate in an emergency warning response, although obviously the majority do so. There certainly is no obligation to pass on warning messages exactly as they are issued by the U.S. National Weather Service; in fact, many radio and television stations use private weather services or even their own forecasters. Furthermore, within the United States many mass media representatives do not view themselves as being a part of the community emergency response effort; they see themselves as being somehow outside the social system, observing, chronicling, and evaluating its performance. In fact, disaster researchers have consistently observed that representatives of the local mass media are among the most difficult of all organizational personnel to convince and to get to participate directly in overall community disaster planning (Wenger and Quarantelli, 1989).

ACCOUNTING FOR THE OBSERVATIONS

Why are there far more similarities than differences? Can our findings be extrapolated elsewhere? Clearly, our answers are tentative.

Our general approach is that the similarities found have to do with the evolution of social institutions. Generally speaking, all the major social institutional systems fall into one of two categories. On the one hand, there are traditional institutions organized around such activities as family life, economic exchanges, religious worship, political power, and so forth. These social institutions have existed for a long time in human history. On the other hand, there are a set of social institutions that have only relatively recently evolved, such as those organized around activities like science, medicine, sports, and so forth. The mass media system is one of these newer institutions, having evolved as a distinctly identifiable entity only this century (see McQuail, 1984; Wright, 1986; DeFleur and Ball-Rokeach, 1989).

Apart from the time of their origins, the traditional and newer social institutions differ in how much they are specifically culturally bound. The older or traditional institutions tend to reflect the specific sociocultural settings in which they are embedded. But the newer or more recently evolved ones are less culturally bound. A heart transplant operation, chemical experiment, or soccer match will generally be undertaken in the same way, irrespective of whether it takes place in China, Chile, Iran, Libya, Romania, South Africa, or any other society in the world. On the other hand, the political institutions may be superficially similar but fundamentally different, depending on the country involved. (Almost all nations everywhere have a representative form of governmental legislative structure, but few would argue that all are real democracies.)

Our basic thesis is that the mass communication system is one of the less culturally bound of all social institutions. We are not alone in this view. The point is well made by Jacobson and Deutschmann (1962), who wrote:

> Journalism has idiosyncratic tendencies in various countries, but these are more than outweighed by the common usages of the profession. . . . And when a public event of world-wide importance occurs, such as the projecting of a human being in a space vehicle into orbit around the world, or the detonation of a nuclear device, there are few places where the news does not penetrate quickly.

The authors note that the similarity of patterns includes certain aspects of the audience and content, as well as the communicators.

> Not only is the basis for the network already established, but the responses to the communication media have come to assume common patterns. There are certain segments in society that have greater access to communications than others. The various mass media seem characteristically to have accepted a division of labour in the spread of information that crosses national and cultural boundaries.

> Necessarily, all of these phenomena occur in conjunction with a standardization of the content of communication so that there is neither the variety not the unique flavour in subject matter that would be expected from the immense diversity of peoples. Partly because of the history of the professional training in mass media techniques, and partly because of the organization and interrelationships of the great news agencies, what is news in London seems also to be news in Buenos Aires (pp. 151–52).

If the above is true, it is not surprising that we found far more similarities than differences in the mass communication system operations in disasters in Japan and the United States. There are undoubtedly many sociocultural differences between the two societies, but both mass media systems — as one of the more newly evolved and culturally independent social institutions — transcend those differences. If our study had been of the social institution of religion, we would have expected the reverse finding.

Of course, our general hypothesis needs considerable testing. We need to build on the handful of cross-societal studies in the disaster area done so far (these are summarized in Dynes, 1988). Cross-societal research is difficult and fraught with problems and difficulties (see Quarantelli, 1979), but, as our study has shown, it not only can be done, but the findings can be significant.

We would also suggest that the study of the mass media in disasters ought to be better integrated with research on other disaster topics. For example, a number of the problems of mass media groups in disasters seem to be quite similar to the problems faced by most other emergency organizations (see Dynes, De Marchi, and Pelanda, 1987). There very well may also be unique or distinctive aspects to the mass media area, and these too will have to be empirically established. These kinds of possible similarities and differences cannot be determined by speculations or popular beliefs but only by research. It is perhaps not unimportant to note that when we started the research reported in this paper, our speculative feeling was that we would find more differences than similarities. However, as we have indicated, the study findings strongly point in the opposite direction.

SOME OTHER IMPLICATIONS

While a number of the implications of our work have already been noted, we want to make explicit three major ones ragarding policy. They have to do with the consequences of common mythologies around the world about human and social behavior in disasters, which are partly rooted in news reporting; how institutionalized social structural and cultural arrangements make any changes in disaster reporting very difficult; and why disaster reporting in developing societies, as well as those in non-Western industrialized and urbanized societies, is likely to develop in the same direction as we found in Japan and the United States.

Researchers outside of the United States and Canada have arrived independently at similar conclusions about popular, and to some extent official, beliefs about disaster behavior. (Some of the studies are reported in Drabek, 1986.) For example, in almost all societies it is widely believed that human beings do not react well in the face of major disasters, and that they will panic, engage in antisocial behavior like looting, break down psychologically, abandon work roles in favor of helping family members, and so forth. Systematic social science research everywhere has found these and similar beliefs to be primarily myths, that is, widely and strongly held beliefs that have little standing in the empirical data brought to bear on the matter by social science disaster researchers.

From whence come the myths? Among obvious major candidates are mass media accounts of disasters (Kreps, 1980). While the relationship is a complex one, and disaster reporting is far from being totally inconsistent with research findings, it does appear that the media do perpetuate the myths. (For disasters in American society, see Wenger and Friedman, 1985 and Fischer, 1989, and for those elsewhere see Blong, 1985 and Bolduc, 1987.) This tendency stems partly from the use of a command post perspective, the diminution of the gatekeeping process, and the other findings reported. To the extent that mass communication systems elsewhere are similar to those in Japan and the United States in their reporting of disasters, they reinforce the myths.

However, it is important to note, as anthropologists have long noted, that myths are not necessarily or always dysfunctional with negative consequences. Our point is not that mass communication systems are somehow responsible for negative consequences as a result of their reporting, but only that they do reinforce mythological beliefs about disaster behavior. The question of the functionality or dysfunctionality of myths is another matter, and it is possible to suggest instances of the former as well as the latter. But, from a policy viewpoint, it is first necessary to establish whether mass communication systems do support mythological beliefs; we think this has now been done. It follows that the consequences should be examined, so the next step is to see in what ways the myths are functional or dysfunctional (Quarantelli, 1985). We might hypothesize that the consequences are more negative than positive, but this should be systematically and empirically established, as has been done partly for everyday television news by Altheide (1976; see also Fishman, 1980).

Another policy implication of our research is that it will be very difficult to quickly institute any significant changes in mass media reporting about disasters — assuming it would be desirable to do so in some degree. The reason is simple: the reporting process in disasters is mostly a reflection of the very social structure of mass media organizations and of the subculture of the world of journalism, as is also true of everyday reporting (see Epstein, 1973; Tuchman, 1978; Ettema and Whitney, 1982). The reporters, editors, and other staff members involved in news gathering have been socialized into a work world and occupational subculture. They are not operating outside of some social setting, but just the opposite. They are following the framework of their world, which they have learned as a result of being members of mass communication organizations.

Social structures and subcultures are of course not static, and changes can be brought about in both. But the disaster reporting of journalists in the field today will not be significantly altered just by telling them about disaster myths or the different procedures they should follow in their coverage of disasters. Journalists will change only if they are socialized or resocialized into different behavior patterns.

This in turn requires structural alterations in mass communication organizations and journalistic subcultures. For example, changes in disaster reporting could follow if, as a result of preimpact planning, there is stronger rather than weaker organizational gatekeeping during the emergency time period. Similarly, there might be alterations in emergency time reporting if, in the curricula of journalism schools, some negative consequences of disaster myths were systematically taught, such as officials failing to issue warnings about threats because of a mistaken concern about generating panic. Likewise, changes in reporting could result if journalistic norms and values stressing speed of reporting and beating the competition were downplayed for those emphasizing accuracy and gaining a reputation as a legitimate source — in more popular terms, a New York *Times* rather than a *National Inquirer* approach. Without such changes the existing institutionalized social and cultural patterns will continue to guide reporters and editors in their reporting of disasters.

Finally, to the extent that what we have seen in Japan and the United States is typical of Western ideas about mass media operations generally and disasters specifically, the future could bring a more worldwide standard. We might anticipate that disaster reporting in developing countries will more and more resemble that which we have observed in our study, based on the assumption that the mass communication systems in Western developed countries will provide the model for societies elsewhere.

The role a national mass communication system should play in the transmission of news is, of course, a highly controversial matter at the international level. It is currently the basis of considerable dispute between many developed countries, primarily Western democracies, and developing countries, and was also at the heart of sharp divisions regarding mass communications issues, as these have been dealt with by UNESCO in the last two decades (for some of the issues see McPhail, 1981). This chapter has no intention of addressing this divisive issue or forecasting how it might be resolved, but if for purposes of discussion we assume the mass communication systems of developing societies continue to develop toward a Western model, it follows their disaster news reporting will come to resemble that of the West. This has the same implication for non-Western urbanized and industrialized societies, such as in Eastern Europe, as their mass communication system is likely to become freer of governmental control in the 1990s.

NOTE

Part of the research reported was supported by a grant from the NHK Foundation in Japan. However, all statements made are the views of the authors and do not necessarily represent the position of the NHK Foundation. We also want to thank our Japanese colleagues headed by Prof. Okabe, at that time at the University of Tokyo, for allowing us to use the research findings obtained in Japan. A volume detailing many aspects of the study not reported in this paper is being jointly prepared for later publication by some of the Japanese and American researchers who collaborated in gathering and analyzing the field data.

8

Organizational Communication and Technological Risks

Phillip K. Tompkins

INTRODUCTION

As students of risks and hazards find it increasingly necessary to shift their attention from the traditional concern for natural disasters (floods, earthquakes, hurricanes) to the modern perils of technological disasters (oil spills, nuclear accidents, industrial pollution) they will also find it necessary to come to terms with organizational behavior in general and organizational communication in particular. The Greek root of the word technology, *techne,* is defined by Runes (1962, p. 314) in a way that could also apply to the concept of organization: "The set of principles, or rational method, involved in the production of an object or the accomplishment of an end." Since Weber's (1978) formulation of the "ideal type" of bureaucracy in the early twentieth century, organizational theory has sought to describe the cooperative and rational accomplishment of ends.

The close connection between technology and organization is more than etymological in nature, however. As technology becomes more complex, those who must control it have had to create organizations of increasing complexity to do so. The Law of Requisite Variety would suggest that the organizations built around modern technology need to be at least as complex as the technology itself (Weick, 1979). This relationship was clearly understood by Charles Perrow, whose *Complex Organizations: A Critical Essay* (1979) established his reputation in part by means of a devastating critique of the psychological approach to organizations and a spirited defense of Weber's ideal type of bureaucracy.

Perrow's later book, *Normal Accidents: Living with High-Risk Technologies* (1984), placed organizations at the center of risk analysis. In this influential work Perrow argues that modern technology is too much for Weber's rational, calculating, and efficient bureaucracy to control. Requisite variety has not been achieved. The problem, according to Perrow, is the unanticipated complexity of the technologies modern bureaucracies must master before those technologies — nuclear power production, nuclear weapons production, petrochemical production, air and marine transportation and genetic engineering — master the globe.

The title of Perrow's book is a trope or rhetorical figure, called perspective by incongruity by Kenneth Burke, directing attention to his conclusion that in complex, tightly coupled systems, the inevitable failures of components will one day interact with each other in ways that are incomprehensible to the operators. The result is catastrophe, the "normal," or expected, accident. The accident can be called normal because it is inevitable. Indeed, some have said that Perrow's book in a sense predicted the disasters of Challenger, Chernobyl, and Bhopal, India. A close reading would not support that claim. For example, his chapter on petrochemical plants, written before the Bhopal incident, says the industry is "quite safe" (Perrow, 1984, p. 101).

My general evaluation of Perrow's book is that it is admirable in many ways and too important to be ignored. Nonetheless, it is a contentious book that can be called neither true nor false. It is an argument by probability that arrives at certainties. The probabilities are most likely on his side, but at the same time there is a deformity in his analysis of human nature that is regrettable in the work of a social scientist.

Consider his implicit model of humans. Perrow regards human managers and workers in technological bureaucracies as "components" little different from the machines they watch. He took Weber's (1978) metaphor for bureaucrats — "cogs" — too literally. When nonhuman components fail, they interact to produce "system" errors; the human components, like so many robots, inevitably find the situation incomprehensible. No doubt the situation looked so dark to Perrow because his workers are speechless, bereft of the capacity for language.

One of Perrow's key terms, interaction, does not seem in context to mean human conversation, dialogue, debate, deliberation, or communication. From its context it suggests an analogy to physical or chemical reactions. The word communication appears in neither his extensive index nor his analysis. Perrow's human is stripped of any apparent method of communication — the social skill that is for most humanists and social scientists a defining characteristic of the animal. Communication did not enter into his analysis and is not recognized as having the ability either to create or solve problems — with one curious exception I shall consider later in this chapter.

ORGANIZATIONAL COMMUNICATION

In the 1950s, a new movement was launched into the pluralistic world of organizational studies: organizational communication. This is no place to narrate the history of this field; two histories have recently been published (Redding, 1985; Redding and Tompkins, 1988). Nonetheless, it should be obvious that the assumptions of this growing area of organizational studies stand in sharp contrast if not opposition to Perrow's silent, deaf and dumb bureaucracy. Organizational communication assumes that organizations are created and maintained in the very act of communication. However, organizational communication does not, or ought not, promise that it can eliminate failures and disasters. It does promise that to ignore organizational communication is to increase the risk of disaster.

As one of the earliest theorists in organizational communication, Chester I. Barnard, put it: "In an exhaustive theory of organization, communication would occupy a central place, because the structure, extensiveness, and scope of organization are almost entirely determined by communication techniques" (1968, p. 91). It is perhaps no coincidence that in his earlier book on organizational theory, Perrow submitted Barnard and his communication-based theory to a savage and unfair critique, even quoting Barnard out of context.[1]

PARTITION OF THE CHAPTER

The rest of this chapter will show the relevance of the methods and hypotheses of organizational communication to both the creation and control of technological hazards. Two case studies will be considered: the National Aeronautic and Space Administration (NASA) during the Apollo Project, and the Aviation Safety Reporting System (ASRS). Finally, tentative extrapolations will be made from these two case studies to other relevant organizations and industries.

NASA

On January 28, 1986, at 11:38 A.M., when the Challenger experienced a "major malfunction," the reputation of NASA as an organization of excellence collapsed. The loss of life was tragic, but had the Challenger been carrying the casket of plutonium as originally scheduled, the world might have experienced an unprecedented disaster. The Rogers Commission declared that this was an accident rooted in history, and that problems of communication plagued NASA and its relationships with the contractors.

Marshall Space Flight Center and the Apollo Project

I propose a longer view of history than the one adopted by the Rogers Commission in order to show that in the days of the Apollo Project, NASA provided an exemplar of organizational communication. I first arrived at NASA's Marshall Space Flight Center (MSFC) in 1967 as a summer faculty consultant in organizational communication. Located in Huntsville, Alabama, MSFC was and is the largest of NASA's field centers; its director in 1967 was Wernher von Braun. Von Braun gave me a number of assignments for the summer, the largest being the responsibility for a diagnostic study of the center's management structure, the management communication system.

As a participant and observer in the organization, I attended briefings for the director and his top management and, in addition, interviewed the top 50 managers at the center. The interview notes were organized into categories of successes, problems, and proposed solutions (see Tompkins, 1977, 1978 for a more complete discussion of methods and results). All interviews but one were anonymous; only the director's remarks were for attribution.

A journalist would two years later write that "NASA has probably the most communication-conscious management in history" (Alexander, 1980, pp. 156), but I had already discovered that to be truer of MSFC than of the agency as a whole. Von Braun spelled out during our interviews his philosophy of management by communication. Because of the magnitude of developing the Saturn V or moon rocket — more than 100,000 people were involved in the project — von Braun believed that disaster could best be averted by cultivating upwardly-directed communication channels. As he put it in one of his characteristic analogies, "This is like being in the earthquake prediction business. You put out your sensors. You want them to be sensitive enough, but you don't want to get drowned in noise. We have enough sensors, even in industry. There are a lot of inputs about trouble. . . . You need balance in the system — to react to the critical things" (Tompkins, 1977, p. 7).

Monday Notes

Von Braun then described in theoretical terms "open and closed communication loops," a simple technique he had designed to supplement the traditional hierarchical reporting relationships. The technique was called the "Monday notes." He asked two dozen of his managers at the third level from the top of the hierarchy to send him a weekly one-page note summarizing the previous week's problems and progress. There was no form to be filled out. The simple requirements were to put the data and the name of the contributor at the top, and no more than one page of comments. The 24 notes by-passed the second level of the hierarchy in the sense that managers at that level could read but not in any way edit the notes flowing through them. They were due in the director's office each Monday; hence, Monday notes.

As the director read each note he initialed it with his "B" and noted the date in the top right corner. He also added a considerable amount of marginalia in his own handwriting, posing questions, making suggestions, even handing out praise. The 24 annotated notes were then reproduced as a package for each of the original contributors. That package was the most diligently read document at the center. The benefits for the organization were obvious: the boss was kept informed about potential problems; the notes performed a crucial horizontal or lateral function because each contributor could read the notes of the other 23 contributors, not unimportant in an organization with high subunit competition and perhaps the ultimate in subunit interdependence; the feedback function — how the boss responded to each note — was a benefit to all of the contributors; the notes kept channels open, despite the director's frequent trips to Washington, D.C., California, the Cape, and other locations, when face-to-face communication was impossible; and the notes provided redundant channels for assuring that, despite "noise" or "distortion" in the system, potential problems did get the attention of the director.

This simple technique provided still other benefits. They served as an antidote to the sterile, formalized procedures that dominated their communicative activities. Instead of a code-numbered, official MSFC-NASA form used for every other occasion designating the lab, division, or office, each note was headed simply by the contributor's name and date. The informality, frankness, and quickness were appreciated. Fierce battles were fought on those pages, and each contributor knew the notes could serve as a court of last resort in case of emergency.

In my interviews with the contributors and, in 1968, in interviews with their subordinates, I discovered that this simple technique had a more profound impact on the organization than had been realized by the director. In almost every case, the contributors turned to their several subordinates and asked for a Friday note, many of whom in turn required a similar note from their subordinates, and so on. Von Braun's simple request for a Monday note had produced a powerful discipline of communication in which, at least once a week, nearly everyone at the center paused to consider what should be communicated up the line.

Automatic Responsibility

Coupled with the Monday notes was another practice that encouraged upward-directed communication: automatic responsibility. This concept had long been part of the organization's operations. Its underlying premise was that in a highly differentiated or specialized organization, there is always the threat that an important problem might fall through the cracks and not gain the attention of top management. In practice it meant that, for example, mechanical engineers working in the labs on assignments related to disciplinary competence assumed automatic responsibility for any problem that they perceived fell within their area of competence, regardless of whether or not their laboratory had been given official responsibility for it. If the engineer who spotted the problem lacked the technical competence to see it through to its solution, he or she assumed responsibility for communicating the problem up the line. Top management, thus alerted, could direct specialists to give attention to the problem.

Both the Monday notes and automatic responsibility depart from typical bureaucratic practice; each gave communicative license to by-pass hierarchical levels. Automatic responsibility also runs contrary to the tidy, efficient, and rational division of labor; together, these practices allow for necessary redundancy, overlapping, and criss-crossing communication channels. Both address the central problem in organizational communication as practiced in large organizations: the inhibition of upward-directed communication because of status differences separating managers at the top from the ultimate contributors at the bottom, because of the fear of acknowledging problems and failures to one's superiors, and because of the powerful inhibiting effect of "mystery" in the hierarchy (see Tompkins et al., 1975).

Penetration

Because there are profits to be made from space and defense systems, the development of rockets and weapons are not left up to NASA and the Defense Department. Private contractor organizations must enter the analysis. Historically, private contractors have not performed well for the U.S. government, particularly after World War II. Cost over-runs and unworkable weapons were too often the consequences of the contract system. Nieburg (1966) documented a catalog of economic and technological atrocities committed by what he called the "contract state." In a review of "systematic waste and profiteering," of technical failures, of cost over-runs and ineptitude, Nieburg described a congressional inquiry into how a particular contractor, General Dynamics Astronautics, could have made such basic mistakes in developing the Centaur rocket for the air force. Von Braun was called to testify because the Centaur had been shifted from supervision by the air force to NASA. As he testified, "I think what we felt was lack of depth of *penetration* [emphasis added] of the program on the part of government personnel, in very general terms. We believed that this staff of eight people . . . [was] inadequate coverage on the part of the government, no matter whether it is NASA or the Air Force" (Nieburg, 1966, p. 275). Von Braun went on to say that when NASA took over Centaur from the air force, he assigned 140 technical people, as compared to the air force's eight, to supervise and "penetrate" the contractor.

Here is how penetration worked. MSFC, as the customer, had a sufficiently deep technical competence to know and evaluate what it was buying from the contractor. Penetration involved sending MSFC personnel into contractor plants in order to observe the work and talk to contractor personnel. Contractor personnel were willing to tell the NASA and MSFC representatives about problems they knew could not be communicated up corporate lines for the reasons just given: messengers with bad news got killed. Penetration explains von Braun's interview remark about the need for having earthquake prediction "sensors" located in "industry." Penetration helped improve a contractor's performance when its management realized MSFC knew as much, perhaps even more, about the contractor's problems than the contractor did.

There were other innovative communication principles and practices at work in MSFC with which the Monday notes, automatic responsibility, and penetration combined to produce the most communication conscious management in history. NASA, during an era of war, assassinations, scandal, cost over-runs and technological failures, provided the United States with its most spectacular technological success — the Apollo Project. The success of the Apollo Project provided our culture with one of its more hackneyed questions: "If we can put a man on the moon, why can't we . . .?"

Challenger's "Major Malfunction"

How did the successful organization MSFC, also a central player in the development of the space shuttle, contribute to the disaster of Challenger? The first answer is that MSFC had always fought against the development of solid rocket fuels. Its long-term experience with missiles and rockets, whose propulsion is achieved by controlled explosions, taught them that liquid fuels could be more easily controlled than solid fuels. Once ignited, solid fuels cannot be shut down. Liquid fuels, by contrast, can be extinguished by simply closing a valve. Nonetheless, it was decided at the highest levels in Washington, D.C., to fly the shuttle with solid fuels, award the prime contract to Morton Thiokol, and assign the responsibility for the research and development of the propulsion systems to the outraged and skeptical members of MSFC (see McConnell, 1987, for an analysis of the Utah connections of James C. Fletcher, then recently appointed administrator of NASA, who made the decision to award the solid rocket booster contract to Morton Thiokol, a Utah-based contractor).

In addition, my reading of the primary and secondary documents dealing with the Challenger disaster has convinced me that many of the innovative communication practices pioneered by MSFC during the Apollo Project had disappeared by the time of the catastrophe. Von Braun had long since left MSFC and had died in 1976. William Lucas, his successor as director of the center, had been a lab director under von Braun, but after taking the top job he demonstrated much less concern for communication than his mentor had. McConnell (1987) paints these contrasting portraits:

> Dr. Lucas had a certain authoritarian manner; the Washington *Post* called him "strong-willed;" reporters from other newspapers were far less charitable, privately describing him as a "tyrant." But everyone who knew him did agree that the sprawling, complex operation at Huntsville bore the stamp of Dr.

Lucas's personal leadership. Ironically and contrary to popular press myth, Lucas had not acquired his "Teutonic" management style from Wernher von Braun and the "Hunsville" Germans; in fact many observers saw Lucas's leadership style as the exact opposite of von Braun's. Where von Braun had been a charismatic visionary who instilled loyalty through personal magnetism, Lucas was a coldly distant (and often rigid) master bureaucrat. He believed in doing things according to regulations. Interpreting the regulations was his personal prerogative (pp. 106–7).

Reconsider penetration, a practice that guarantees contractors assume the burden of proof about the ability of their hardware to perform as expected. During the infamous Monday night (January 27, 1986) teleconference involving MSFC and Thiokol personnel in which a decision to launch was recommended by Thiokol managers, the burden of proof was reversed. Thiokol engineers were being asked to prove, despite their convictions to the contrary, that the Challenger could fly. This was a reversal of the presumption of penetration. In fairness to MSFC personnel, another communicative rule of long standing was violated by Morton Thiokol during the teleconference, a departure from past norms that would have a profound impact on the group dynamics of the discussion. A Marshall manager would later learn and note with

bitterness that Morton Thiokol's senior executives, Jerald Mason and Calvin Wiggins, did not even acknowledge their presence in the Thiokol conference room. This was absolutely contrary to established NASA procedure, which required all persons present in a teleconference to identify themselves, whether they took an active role or not. Because Mason and Wiggins's presence was not known to the NASA officials ... it was assumed that all the recommendations and conclusions emanating from Thiokol were based on engineering criteria, just as Al McDonald had earlier requested. Although the Rogers Commission did not stress this point, it seems clear that this was an important aspect of the group dynamics at work that night (McConnell, 1987, p. 194).

The teleconference was interrupted by a caucus in which Thiokol personnel met to reconsider their reservations about the O rings. Mason, the unannounced manager from Thiokol, turned to an engineer and said, "Take off your engineering hat and put on your management hat" (McConnell, 1987, p. 199). In this way, the Thiokol managers persuaded their engineers, against their technical judgment, to accept a management decision to launch in accord with the presumed wishes of the MSFC personnel. Thus, the presumption of penetration and the burden of proof was reversed.

Summary

In summary, this analysis strongly suggests that the scrupulous and innovative practices of organizational communication at MSFC during the Apollo Project contributed significantly to the success of the organization and its historic missions. By contrast, that communication consciousness, in an egregious example of institutional amnesia, seems to have been forgotten during the research, development, and operation of the space shuttle and no doubt contributed to the organizational and technological failure.

ASRS

As indicated above, Charles Perrow (1984) eschewed any consideration of organizational communication with one exception. On pages 168–69, Perrow provides a note on the ASRS. This, as we shall soon see, is an excellent communication system. After briefly explaining the system, Perrow piled on the praise: "The fruits of the program seem to be substantial. Reports pour in about unsafe airport conditions which are then quickly corrected. Changes in ATC [air traffic control] and other types of procedures have been made on the basis of analysis of the ASRS reports" (Perrow, 1984, p. 169).

Origins

The origin of ASRS is rooted in tragedy. On Sunday, December 1, 1974, at 11:09 A.M., Trans World Airlines (TWA) Flight 514 was headed toward Dulles Airport in turbulent weather. The aircraft descended below the minimum safe altitude and slammed into a Virginia mountain top. Nearly 100 people were killed. As required by law, the National Transportation Safety Board (NTSB) investigated the accident as usual.

Two significant findings emerged from the investigation. The first was that a United Airlines plane had narrowly escaped the same fate in the same approach only six weeks before the crash of TWA 514. If the incident involving the United flight had taken place one year earlier, the result would only have been a troublesome memory for the crew; there would have been no institutional memory of the event. Eleven months earlier, however, United had created an internal reporting system called the "Flight Safety Awareness Program," in which crew members were strongly encouraged to report anonymously any incident they felt was a potential threat to safety. The United pilots reported the incident at Dulles, and other United pilots were informed of the trap. Unfortunately, no established channels of communication were then available for spreading the word to other airlines. The TWA crew was unable to benefit from the report filed by the United crew.

The second fact that emerged from the NTSB investigation was that both the United and TWA incidents were caused by the "ambiguous nature of the charted approach procedure and the differences in its interpretation between pilots and controllers" (Reynard et al., 1986, p. 3). There were two different meanings for the word clearance — one intended by controllers (the approach plan was approved) and a second assigned by the pilots (the actual landing may begin). In short, a misunderstanding between controllers and pilots contributed to both incidents. The drama of the two flights illustrates the potential importance of communication in both creating (by breakdowns and misunder- standings) and mitigating or removing (by alerts and corrective actions) risks and hazards.

The Federal Aviation Administration (FAA) established in May of 1975 the ill-conceived Aviation Safety Reporting Program (ASRP) to encourage members of the aviation industry to provide the FAA with timely reports about critical incidents. As an incentive, the FAA offered a limited waiver of disciplinary action in case the person making the report had broken any laws. The ASRP did not work. The FAA, as both the maker and enforcer of the rules in the industry, was not viewed as a disinterested party. NASA still enjoyed an incomparable reputation at the time, and was asked to serve as a broker, an honest third party, in receiving and processing the reports of the ASRS process which began on April 15, 1976. The actual operations have been handled by a contractor, the Battelle Memorial Institute's office in Mountain View, California.

Input

The ASRS is an interorganizational communication system for an entire industry. Input is provided by controllers, pilots, other crew members, and occasionally by other observers. Those who file reports are promised both anonymity and immunity from prosecution. The reports are filed with a strip identifying the reporter. (The analysts sometimes need to call the reporter for clarification of the text.) Once the analysts believe they understand the incident well enough to code and store the entire report in the computer, the identification strip is mailed to the reporter. Possession of the identification strip provides the reporter with immunity from prosecution (except for criminal acts that may have been performed during the incident) and assures anonymity.

The analysts, by virtue of their previous experience as pilots or controllers or sometimes both, have "been there and seen it." Their coding of the incidents is checked independently by another analyst, but no reliability studies have been conducted. The total input for the system as of the summer of 1987, when I visited the Battelle operation, was staggering: 70,000 reports concerning 50,000 incidents (a single incident is sometimes reported by more than one person). All of these reports have been received and processed without a single breach of the promise of anonymity and immunity.

Output

The output of the ASRS has been voluminous and, between 1976 and 1987, took the following forms:

More than 835 alert bulletins, time-critical notices about ongoing hazards such as overgrown trees blocking approaches to a runway, faulty navigational lights, and runway markings, were issued.

Over 900 special data requests from the FAA, NTSB, and other organizations were honored. These involved searches of the computerized data base for reports about recurring problems and hazards.

Fifteen program reports, originally issued on a quarterly basis and now issued on an irregular basis, were published. These contain samples of the reports thought to be instructive to the aviation community or illustrative of trends, as well as summaries of corrective actions taken in response to the alert bulletins.

Thirty-four research reports and technical papers were produced, dealing primarily with such human factors as fatigue, cockpit distraction, altitude deviations, and, as we shall see, problems involving human communication.

Callback, a highly readable, one-page monthly newsletter devoted to timely safety issues, became available to every member of the aviation community.

Effects

There can be no quantitative measure of the ASRS's impact on the nation's aviation safety record. It is impossible to count nonevents. Nor is it possible to find an adequate comparison condition, or to study the record of ASRS without being convinced that the system has reduced risks, eliminated hazards, and saved countless lives. Reading the alert bulletins and the corrective actions taken in response to them will convince any reasonable reader of this conclusion.

In addition, the ASRS has improved communication between and among all elements of the aviation community. Its data base has been used to reach a better understanding of risks and hazards and of ways to eliminate them. ASRS materials are used by flight instructors, flight schools, and both military and private training facilities. ASRS data are used as the basis of moral suasion to support a legitimate safety improvement. The act of composing a report is in itself a valuable learning experience; reporters often go beyond the recitation of mere facts to probe their own levels of competence, concentration, knowledge, and motivation.

The ASRS, then, is a successful industrywide system of communication that has demonstrated beneficial effects on the aviation system. (Deregulation seems to have increased not only the volume of traffic, but also the number of incidents reported to ASRS.) Before considering the applicability of the ASRS system's principles to other industries facing significant risks, it remains to be shown how recurring problems in communication increase the risk of accidents in the aviation industry.

Nature and Frequency of Communication Problems

In the summer of 1987 I interrogated the ASRS data base about human factors. ASRS had already reported that communication problems, or "information transfer" as it is sometimes called, were noted "in over 70 percent of 28,000 reports submitted . . . during a five-year period 1976–1981" (Billings and Cheaney, 1981, p. 1). After I specified that the incidents had to involve a "message sent from one person to another," the computer was able to find this factor in 61 percent of the reports filed in the data base between 1978 and 1987. The analysts helping me with the search believed this was a conservative figure. My conclusion is that 60 to 70 percent of the reports in the data base included a reference to human communication as a contributing factor to the incidents regarded as serious threats to aviation safety. (Any given incident may have several such factors.)

The analysts are neither social scientists nor communication experts, but they have provided rough categories for this frequently recurring problem. More than one-third of these problems in communication involved the absence of information transfer in situations where, in the opinion of the analysts, the transfer of the information could have prevented a potentially hazardous occurrence. In another third, information transfer took place, but it was adjudged incomplete or inaccurate, leading in many cases to incorrect actions in flying or controlling aircraft. One-eighth of the reports involved information transfer that was correct but untimely, usually too late to be of assistance, in forestalling a potentially hazardous chain of events. In one-tenth of the reports, the information was transferred but was not perceived or was misperceived by the intended recipients. The remainder of the reports involved equipment problems and a variety of miscellaneous conditions (Billings and Cheaney, 1981, p. 85).

Additional research into the data base by experts in communication would no doubt yield additional insights. For example, do communication problems occur in diachronic or temporal patterns across incidents? Examination of a small sample of incidents tentatively suggests that the communication problem may occur after, and interact with, an initial contributing factor, such as mechanical problems, to produce a high-risk situation. Do communication problems interact with other factors in regular and recurring ways? The answers to these and other research questions could well lead to the development of training materials on communication for aviation personnel to reduce the probability of accidents associated with these human factors.

Application to Other Industries

As indicated above, Perrow concluded that "it would be extremely beneficial if such a virtually anonymous system were in operation for the nuclear power industry and the marine transport industry" (1984, p. 169). That is, Perrow thought it desirable to consider the possibilities of applying the concept of anonymous, "immunized" reports to an honest third party empowered to call for corrective action in those other high-risk industries enumerated above. Those possibilities were being considered at the time Perrow wrote those words, and other applications have since been attempted. Reynard et al. (1986, p. 79) discuss extrapolation of the concept as "technology transfer," and report that similar systems are either in place or are being pursued in Great Britain, Canada, Ireland, and Japan. Interdisciplinary technology transfers are being considered in a variety of activities that are "labor intensive and rely heavily on humans interacting with increasingly sophisticated automation" (p. 79). The interdisciplinary examples reported include the U.S. Nuclear Regulatory Commission (NRC), Institute of Nuclear Power Operators (INPO), Electric Power Research Institute (EPRI), Nassau County (New York) Criminal Justice Commission, University of Washington/U.S. Coast Guard, and the Swedish Department of Labor.

In a lengthy interview with Battelle's project manager I learned more about these technology transfers or spin-offs of ASRS principles. The results are at best mixed. The Department of Transportation and Battelle, who together tried to initiate the ASRS concept in the marine transport industry, were beset with problems from the beginning. The potential reporters — ship captains and masters — have a distrust of government that inhibits reporting. The marine unions did not endorse the concept. At the moment when a critical mass of participants was persuaded to participate, the Office of Management and Budget cut the funding for the program.

Application to the nuclear energy industry faced a different set of problems when it advanced on two fronts as indicated in the list above. The NRC was on the brink of adopting the ASRS concept when the INPO announced that it was implementing a program. Unfortunately, an industry association does not have the distance from the activities being monitored that NASA and Battelle achieved in the aviation system, and the concept of transactional immunity was not adopted. Even if transactional immunity is adopted, there is a theoretical and practical problem that would have to be addressed in the nuclear power industry. Suppose a serious problem develops in a plant and a report to that effect is received; how could an alert bulletin concerning that specific plant be issued without identifying or at least pointing in the direction of the reporter? Therefore, I am convinced that the ASRS concept has not yet been fairly tested in the nuclear power industry because of the absence of two factors: transactional immunity and a third party to serve as an honest or disinterested broker. The concept should be tested fairly in the future.

There are additional prospects for application. The General Accounting Office has become interested in incident-reporting systems for decentralized industries such as pharmaceuticals and medical equipment, and, ironically, the ASRS concept is being imposed on NASA itself. After the Rogers Commission investigated the Challenger accident it concluded that NASA had paid insufficient attention to safety. In response to the commission report, NASA has appointed a new guru for safety and instituted a program called the Protected Reporting System, which is still in a trial stage.

CONCLUSION

This chapter completed the loop from NASA's practices during the Apollo Project — Monday notes, automatic responsibility, and penetration, all upward-directed communication practices that, although not promising legal immunity, did resemble the ASRS concept — to the failure of Challenger, to ASRS, and, finally, back to the imposition of NASA's own original principles and techniques of communication to its own current practices. Communication consciousness constitutes a powerful factor to be considered in the analysis of high-risk organizations and technology.

Are there any policy lessons from these historically based analyses? At least two come to mind. The first is to correct Perrow's error. Communication, particularly organizational and interorganizational communication, must become part of the analysis of risky systems. Failures of human communication must be considered as possible causes for system failures. The successful enactment of communication has to be conceived as a way of reducing, if not eliminating, risks.

Second, there are three principles that need to be accepted if high-risk systems are to operate more successfully. First is the principle of a broker, an honest third party to act as a trusted agent of communication on an industrywide level. This broker must regard safety or reliability as its most important premise. Second is that family or constellation of principles at the heart of MSFC's pre-Challenger practices and ASRS's recent practices: redundant channels, open and closed feedback loops, and the communication empowerment of employees at the very bottom levels of risky organizations, which means they automatically accept responsibility for communicating perceived problems to the proper authorities. Von Braun's model or metaphor of organizational communication as an earthquake prediction system needs to be extended to all organizations capable of producing environmental disasters — if not all organizations without qualification. The third principle is immunity from retaliation for exercising or enacting the concept of communication empowerment. The field of organizational communication would teach that inertia ails the organization that discourages disturbing reports and kills the messengers, an inertia that must be consciously and formally reversed if high-risk system failures are to be decreased.

NOTE

The author expresses his gratitude to two esteemed colleagues, John Waite Bowers and George Cheney, for the close reading of, and excellent suggestions made in response to, the first draft of this chapter.

1. Among many rather specious criticisms, Perrow faults Barnard because "the uncritical emphasis upon communication as a manipulative device is maintained" (1979, p. 89). Although Barnard's discussion of communication cannot fairly be called "manipulative," it does include analyses of "propaganda" and "persuasion." These analyses are remarkably similar to the modern concept of "hegemony," and provide insights into how a capitalist society and its network of organizations "inculcate" materialistic and patriotic motives in its members. Perrow has trouble distinguishing between description and prescription. Perrow even misquotes Barnard in an effort to disparage his treatment of the individual's cognitive capacity: "Only in organization can we have the 'deliberate adoption of means and ends' since this is the 'essence of organization'" (1979, p. 76). Perrow's footnote for the quoted material in that sentence is to page 186 in Barnard's *Functions of the Executive*. Here are the exact words Barnard uses on that page: "It is the deliberate adoption of means to ends which is the essence of formal organization" (1968, p. 186). The mistake in the quotation is unfortunate and misleading. Perrow's overall aim is to coopt Barnard's successor, Herbert A. Simon, into his own "Neo-Weberian" model of organization. The absurdity of this move, which necessitates the attack on Barnard, is illustrated by the fact that Simon clearly and openly indicates in his *Administrative Behavior* (1976) that it is Barnard, not Weber, upon whom he drew heavily. He invited Barnard to compose an introduction to his book and cites him frequently. Both Barnard and Simon are properly classified in the communication and decision-making school of organizational studies.

9

The Security of Secrecy

DAVID M. RUBIN

Even before the momentous political events of 1989 and 1990 were played out in Eastern Europe, American journalists had begun to acknowledge that the great organizing principle of foreign and national security reporting for the past 45 years was about to change ("The 'End' of the Cold War?" 1989). The Cold War in Europe was over. A new political order was replacing it. Although it was potentially no less dangerous to American interests, this new order would pose significantly different threats to U.S. security. Deterring nuclear war and checking Soviet expansionism no longer seemed urgent or relevant. In the years ahead neither of these touchstones would be quite so useful to government officials and journalists in explaining foreign and military policy to the American public.

A new conceptual scheme, or frame, to interpret the news from abroad would have to be created (Gans, 1979, pp. 40–45). This would require recognizing not only new power relationships but also adopting a whole new journalistic vocabulary to replace the anti-Soviet model (Kress, 1985, p. 85). The Soviet Union of Mikhail Gorbachev would no longer serve either logically or emotionally as the Evil Empire, the significant "other" in all national security reporting.

Enemies of the state, however, are fungible. Even as the immediate military threats from Moscow, East Berlin, and Prague were fading, some American officials were using the news media to float the specter of Iraq, Libya, and other states gaining the ability to deliver chemical and nuclear weapons on ballistic missiles (Engelberg, 1990, p. A12; "The Iraqi Breakout," 1989, p. A14). Others were busily reminding the public that, contrary to logic, East bloc spying against the West would not only continue, but perhaps even increase as the Warsaw Pact unraveled (Wines, 1989, p. A15).

Such news stories served as sober reminders that the intimate relationship between news media and government in the United States is more stable and resistant to change than even East-West relations. As new threats queued up to replace the old, hopes that an end to the Cold War would also produce a significant change in the way the media report on national security issues were disappointed. A weakened Soviet Union, democracy in Eastern Europe, the bankruptcy of communism — these events by themselves would not shock American journalists into adopting a genuinely independent and adversarial posture.

Such a fundamental change cannot occur until reporters and officials interact in a wholly new environment, free of the suffocating secrecy and the simplistic superpower view of the world accompanying journalism in the nuclear era. Government has come to rely heavily on secrecy to obscure and manipulate information, thereby eliminating the public from effective participation in foreign policy and national security decision making. Government has also used the regime of secrecy to discipline the news media. Rather than fight this trend, journalists have come to embrace secrecy as the normal milieu for the practice of national security journalism. With the acquiescence of the media, government uses secrecy to define the news, establish the truth, create legitimate news sources, and raise the value of the information it chooses to release. Those journalists disinclined to cooperate with the regime of secrecy find it difficult, if not impossible, to practice their profession.

If secrecy and the reverence journalists have for secrets continue to thrive in the post-Cold War era — and there is every indication that it will — then journalism will remain utterly subservient to government in its coverage of national security affairs. Unless secrecy is drastically curtailed as a legal tool of statecraft, journalists will remain unable, even unwilling, to present a more accurate picture of American foreign policy, the employment of American military power, and the options available to the American electorate.

THE LEGAL ROOTS OF SECRECY

Far from providing the press with a strong weapon to attack the regime of secrecy, the First Amendment, as interpreted judicially, does not interfere with government's effort to keep information out of the public realm. If the courts interpreted the First Amendment as providing a Constitutional right of access to government information to satisfy the public's right to know, then government would bear the burden of demonstrating why that right should be frustrated. However, as Justice Potter Stewart wrote in the case of *Pell v. Procunier* (1974, p. 2386), which concerns whether journalists have a First Amendment right to interview prisoners,

> The Constitution does not ... require government to accord the press special access to information not shared by members of the public generally. It is one thing to say that a journalist is free to seek out sources of information not available to members of the general public.... It is quite another thing to suggest that the Constitution imposes upon government the affirmative duty to make available to journalists sources of information not available to members of the public generally. That proposition finds no support in the words of the Constitution or in any decision of this Court.

In the absence of a Constitutional right to challenge government secrecy, the news media and public must rely on statute, specifically, the federal Freedom of Information Act of 1966 (FOIA). This act established a right of access to records held by the federal government, but it was passed with a number of important exemptions. The first of these protects the confidentiality of records "specifically authorized under criteria established by Executive order to be kept secret in the interest of national defense or foreign policy." This national security exemption seriously weakens the FOIA as a tool of access to classified data. As long as the document requested has been properly classified under a current executive order as either confidential, secret, or top secret, it need not be released by the government agency in control of it, and no judge is likely to second guess that decision.[1] This exemption recognizes the legitimacy of the executive branch's classification system, the cornerstone of government secrecy.

Additional statutes and judicial rulings support the government's regime of secrecy. For example, the Atomic Energy Act of 1954 punishes the communication of information about nuclear weapons design and manufacture. It was used to prohibit publication of an article in *The Progressive* about H-bomb design (*United States v. The Progressive, Inc.,* 1979). The Espionage Act of 1917 led to the prosecution and conviction of a U.S. government employee who sold a classified picture of a Soviet aircraft carrier to a British magazine, which subsequently published it (*United States v. Morison,* 1988). As a condition of employment, government workers with access to classified information have been asked to sign an agreement that obliges them to submit their speeches and writings to a government censor for vetting (Demac, 1984, pp. 19–25, 88, 92–95). Those who comply have, on occasion, been censored (*United States v. Marchetti,* 1972). Those who have not complied with this condition of employment have been administratively disciplined or fired, or suffered the loss of all income from the prohibited speech (*Snepp v. United States,* 1980).

Perhaps intimidated by these legal precedents, journalists have been unwilling to explore the potential boundaries of their freedom in the national security area. On only two occasions since World War II has the government found it necessary to restrain publication of arguably secret information: the aforementioned *Progressive* case, and the so-called Pentagon Papers case (*New York Times Co. v. United States,* 1971), in which a group of newspapers and wire services sought to publish a secret study of the origins of the Vietnam War.

This is a remarkably small number of legal showdowns for a period marked by growing government secrecy, massive military spending, and the constant threat of nuclear annihilation. Nevertheless, the press has preferred to pay for its freedom by foregoing its exercise. The price of a theoretically free press has become the press's own willingness to steer clear of national security secrets.

Journalists who do challenge the regime of secrecy are often greeted not only with an injunction stopping publication, but with the scorn of fellow journalists. When Howard Morland, author of the enjoined *Progressive* article, showed one of his H-bomb diagrams to Walter Pincus, the national security reporter of the Washington *Post,* the latter was uninterested in it.[2] "I think there are some legitimate military secrets," he told Morland. "I don't know why anybody would want to know this kind of information" (Morland, 1981 p. 133). Pincus's boss, executive editor Benjamin Bradlee, wouldn't even meet with Morland when he visited the *Post* during the legal fight. He supported him legally, Bradlee admitted, "with as much enthusiasm as I would Larry Flynt and *Hustler*" (Mooney, 1980, p. 38).

Nor was Bradlee alone. The *Atlanta Constitution* attacked *The Progressive*'s "arrogance and mindlessness." The *Los Angeles Times* said this was "the wrong issue, in the wrong time, in the wrong place."

Editors of the *Charlotte News* called the magazine "reckless in the extreme" (Hentoff, 1979, p. 31).

Supreme Court Justice Antonin Scalia recognizes, and applauds, the press's unwillingness to, as he puts it, "spit in the street" of national security by pushing hard for broader rights of access and publication:

> I suspect that the average journalist would not feel free to disregard governmental protestations of compromise of the national security by simply saying, "We can't trust the government." If I didn't believe that, I'd be worried. . . . Society is the freest which is the most responsible. If you don't have a lot of people in your town spitting in the street, you don't need a non-spitting ordinance. The occasional individual who feels he must spit in the street can be free to do so. But when you have a lot of people who go around spitting, you enact an ordinance. In other words, the First Amendment is a very liberal amendment as it is now applied and interpreted by the courts and implemented by statutes. The liberality depends to a large extent upon the responsibility with which the freedom that it confers is exercised. Since the ultimate law of any society is going to be survival, if that responsibility disappears, other statutes will be passed ("The Pentagon vs. The Press," 1985, p. 52).

This brief summary of the legal underpinnings of government secrecy in the United States demonstrates that those who would challenge the government's prerogative face an uphill battle, harsh penalties, and uncertain support from their colleagues.[3] Under both the First Amendment and a variety of federal statutes, the government has more than enough weapons to severely limit publication of national security information.

THE SWADDLED PRESS

It will be argued later in this chapter that secrecy — and the way in which journalists have reacted to secrecy — is by far the most significant reason for the historically inadequate coverage of national security issues provided by the American media. But it would be misleading not to first take note of other factors that have contributed to the lack of aggressiveness by journalists on this beat.

When Howard Morland was asked by *Newsweek* to contribute a "My Turn" column about the *Progressive* case, he included two strong paragraphs attacking the logic and morality of nuclear deterrence theory. Both were edited out of the piece (Morland, 1981, p. 182). While Morland was outraged, *Newsweek*'s decision is not surprising. Journalists identify quite closely with government policy makers on how to manage the nuclear arsenal. They are not about to challenge that logic and agitate the public. They have grown almost comfortable with the balance of nuclear terror.

The possibility of achieving a nuclear free world is now beyond the journalistic imagination. When Presidents Ronald Reagan and Mikhail Gorbachev briefly explored that possibility at the Reykjavik summit in 1986, journalists declined to place it on the public's agenda. It was dismissed as foolish and unrealistic. National security journalists quoted a variety of military and political leaders who, predictably, labeled the idea utopian, even dangerous. Among major news media, only the *Christian Science Monitor* chose to present a series of articles (November 18 to 24, 1986) examining what such a nuclear-free world would be like ("Thinking about the Unthinkable," 1987, p. 6).

With some notable exceptions, most journalists who work for the major print and broadcast media share the views of those they cover. They have adopted the logic of the arms race and deterrence strategy. When researchers at the Center for War, Peace, and the News Media at New York University surveyed 23 national security reporters for their opinions on arms control and nuclear strategy, they found that, as a group, their views were not far from those of Georgia Senator Sam Nunn, the Democratic chairperson of the Senate Armed Services Committee. They favored a strong defense, were suspicious of the Soviets, and supported nuclear disarmament (Bram, 1987, pp. 1–2, 7–9; Bram, 1988, pp. 8–9). In such a political and intellectual climate, why would journalists attempt to dig up secrets at the Pentagon that might embarrass the military or, worse, aid the Soviets?

Journalists determined to challenge conventional thinking and place the nuclear arms race squarely on the public's agenda find it is a story that does not fit comfortably within the time-honored definition of news. Journalism is event centered (Hess, 1981, p. 15), but there have been few publicly acknowledged news "events" to report over the years. Those that have occurred, such as the so-called "Broken Arrows," or military accidents involving nuclear weapons, have been so carefully wrapped in secrecy that the reporters have often been unaware of them (Hanauer, 1981, pp. 23–28, 52–59).

Not using the bomb is not a news story. The gradual evolution of deterrence strategy is not a news story. The month-by-month production of nuclear warheads is not a news story, until environmental and health hazards at the manufacturing sites force the Department of Energy and Congress to investigate, thereby providing the national media in New York and Washington with the news peg they need to publicize the scandal. The training and deployment of military personnel to manage the nuclear arsenal is not a news story. The ongoing opposition of a small peace movement is not a news story. Low-level angst about the presence of the bomb is not a news story. Indeed, it is difficult for journalists to find a way to report the arms race that fits the traditional definition of news and does not raise potential legal problems.

And when an event, such as the signing of an arms control treaty, provides the necessary news peg, sustained coverage is undermined by the press's unwillingness to stick with any story for the long haul. Interest in exploring the consequences of dropping the atomic bomb on Hiroshima waned quickly (Boyer, 1985a, p. 285), as did concern about the public health effects of radioactive fallout after the "Bravo" series of H-bomb tests in the early 1950s (Divine, 1978, pp. 26–27). More recently, the pernicious effects of this "issue attention cycle" (Rourke, 1977, p. 113) could be seen in the press's disinterest in following up implementation of the INF Treaty (Manoff, 1988, pp. 1–2, 11). In addition to secrecy, therefore, the processes and traditions of journalism make the nuclear story, and military policy in general, difficult to cover.

SECRECY TAKES ROOT

The media have been the willing keepers of nuclear secrets from the beginning of the atomic age, and journalists have accepted the principle that legitimate national security secrets do indeed exist.[4] One scholar who studied how carefully the press avoided mention of atomic energy during World War II found that

> The press revealed virtually no technical details about the bomb, and few stories connected its development with the three principal project sites in Tennessee, Washington, and New Mexico. What was run on almost every occasion was simply that the U.S. or Germany, or both of them, were working on the bomb.
>
> . . .
>
> Not one instance occurred where the press deliberately violated the Office of Censorship's voluntary regulations concerning atomic energy. Instead, violations usually occurred because publications did not know about the regulations or, even if they were aware of them, they did not think they applied to their specific story (Washburn, 1990).

Nor was the press any more zealous in challenging the government's desire to protect non-nuclear military secrets during World War II. Theodore Koop quotes the following view of Byron Price, who coordinated the voluntary censorship program during the war:

There is abundant evidence that newspapers and radio stations are suppressing news for no valid reason. . . . Many of you have been led to overzealousness to withhold information having no security value. . . . I solicit your continued cooperation to see . . . that a dangerous psychology of over-censorship is not created throughout the land (cited in Heise, 1979, p. 265).

Cold war conditions have been sufficient to maintain this "dangerous psychology of over-censorship." Immediately after the war, secrecy misled the press and public into believing there actually was an atomic bomb secret that could be kept from the Soviets, and this set the stage for the spy scares that effectively made international control of nuclear weapons impossible. Secrecy, and the atmosphere created by the spy scares, diminished the quality of public debate over civilian control of the Atomic Energy Commission. Secrecy concealed the misguided plan of General Leslie Groves to corner the world market on uranium ore, a strategy that produced the wildly incorrect estimates of how quickly the Soviets would develop their own bomb. Secrecy about the true size of the American nuclear arsenal not only misled the public about the ability of the United States to cripple Soviet society, but also made it difficult for the air force itself to develop a plan of attack. So pervasive was secrecy during the Truman administration that Secretary of Defense Louis Johnson did not want to tell other members of the administration about detection of the Soviet atomic bomb, and even the president did not want to know the details of the nuclear arsenal (Herken, 1980).

Nor have assumptions about the necessity for secrecy changed. Indeed, the power of government to censor may now be stronger than ever. Day Thorpe, one of nine censors in the Office of Censorship during World War II, commented to the *Washington Star* that if a reporter had brought the Pentagon Papers to him and asked for clearance to publish them, he would have granted it "without a thought." The papers would have been, he said, "of no interest to Censorship" (cited in Heise, 1979, p. 114). Yet, publication of the papers in 1971 required a mighty First Amendment struggle in the courts.

Significant challenges to the secrecy regime have been so rare that, when they occur, they are immediately converted to discussions of the appropriate limits on a free and responsible press. The secrets themselves are ignored, or rather overwhelmed by the First Amendment debate. While Morland and Daniel Ellsberg, who leaked the Pentagon Papers to the press, both succeeded in reaching the marketplace with their information, neither made an impact on policy. Neither achieved what he hoped to achieve. Publishing the Pentagon Papers did not shorten the

Vietnam War, and revealing the secret of the H-bomb did not end, or even call into question, nuclear secrecy.

The press shows vastly more interest in protecting a particular legal interpretation of its freedom than in actually expanding that freedom. As a result, the government has discovered that exercising prior restraint of the press is a can't lose proposition. After a restraining order has been judged unconstitutional and the press has been permitted to publish, the secrets — the original purpose for publishing — have long since been lost to public view in a fog of rights and responsibilities. From the Manhattan Project forward, government has made the media so reverential of secrecy that even when they win the freedom to publish secrets, they have little stomach to do so. Secrets are dropped demurely — apologetically — into the marketplace, with no effort by the media to politicize the information or attack the principle of secrecy itself.

GOVERNMENT'S USE OF SECRECY TO TAME THE PRESS

A truly adversarial press, one that, in Justice Scalia's words, would be constantly spitting in the street, is a frightening thing for any government to contemplate. Secrecy is one way for government to discipline the news media so that they do not spit.

On the most basic level, secrecy limits what journalists know. What they don't know they can't publish. But to conclude that national security issues are poorly reported simply because the classification system keeps journalists in the dark is an oversimplification. Secrecy works in other ways to tame the press.

Often when government acts aggressively to protect secrets, either by taking legal action against the media or by mounting a public campaign of criticism (often referred to as "jawboning" the media), it is difficult to believe that the contested information has any real security value. Government seems to be playing a different game.

How else can one explain the government's decision to enjoin publication of the H-bomb secret? What sort of secret was this? All the information in Morland's article was publicly available, some in encyclopedia articles, or readily deducible from public sources. Morland had no special scientific background and no access to classified data. Potential builders of the bomb would need much more than Morland's diagram to produce one, such as a well-developed industrial base and the ability to support a testing program, which could be easily detected by the other nuclear nations.

Surely the government did not believe there is a country in search of the H-bomb so foolish and bereft of other resources as to rely on a recipe in an American political magazine. In this era of disinformation, no such country, even if it did exist, could accept the diagram as accurate. Indeed, the U.S. government could have stated that the diagrams were incorrect, thereby hopelessly confusing the picture for any potential user.[5]

The *Progressive* case can best be understood as a periodic reminder to the press that it must not fly too close to the sun. "The idea of secrecy is terribly important to them," Erwin Knoll, editor of the *Progressive,* told the *Columbia Journalism Review* at the time:

> The mystique of secrecy is something they protect more jealously than the secrets themselves. So long as we have that mystique, it is possible for a tight little group — the guardians of the secrets — to make policy in this terribly important area and to exclude all the rest of us from having a say in that policy. To say the secrets aren't secret is to say the emperor has no clothes (Friedman, 1979, p. 34).

On many other occasions the government has attacked the release of information that seems far removed from national security considerations. In December 1984, for example, Defense Secretary Weinberger, invoking the language of treason, said the Washington *Post* may have given "aid and comfort to the enemy" by publishing the information that an upcoming shuttle flight would be used to launch an intelligence gathering satellite. The *Post*'s executive editor, Benjamin Bradlee, responded that virtually all the information in the article was public knowledge (Hiatt, 1984, p. 1).

In his study of the Pentagon press corps, Stephen Hess documented a number of leaks that upset the government on national security grounds, but he concluded that none posed a clear threat to national security (Hess, 1984, pp. 91–92). "Government," Hess contends, "is quite good at keeping its real secrets."

For government, secrecy serves a number of purposes. It shields information from public view, thereby permitting the executive branch to form policy in a vacuum, without the sobering effects of public debate. It provides a structure for government censorship of the news media despite the protections of the First Amendment. It encourages self-censorship by journalists, which further limits the marketplace of ideas. Finally, it provides a needed rationale for the occasional extralegal attacks on journalists by the executive branch. This reminds journalists that spitting in the street of national security, however defined by government, will not be tolerated.

JOURNALISM'S ACCOMMODATION
TO SECRECY

Now and then journalists prevail over government in the struggle to publish a national security secret. In 1975, for example, the CIA tried to convince the press not to report its effort to raise a sunken Soviet submarine using the Glomar Explorer salvage ship. With columnist Jack Anderson leading the way, the news media did publicize the story, although to this day it is not clear if any salvage effort was actually made, or if the CIA genuinely preferred that the salvage effort be kept secret (Kondracke, 1975, p. 10; Arnold, 1975, p. 31).

Providing the press with an occasional triumph is a necessary public relations tactic for government to sustain the impression that First Amendment freedoms also operate in the realm of national security. Although such victories are often hollow, the media seem not to be discomfited by them. After living with cold war secrecy for 45 years, journalists have so thoroughly integrated its requirements into their own procedures and assumptions that secrecy now defines the news.

Journalists make three important assumptions about secret information: that it is true, that it is about serious matters, and that it is specific in content. These three assumptions are central to any definition of newsworthiness and to maintaining the ideology of objectivity. Since journalists have chosen to make themselves so dependent on government officials for information, it is in their interest to assume that these officials have important, authoritative knowledge to impart. By declaring information secret, government can be certain that, if leaked, it will be a hot property in the marketplace.

The keepers of the secrets have become invaluable, not to say irresistible, sources for national security reporters. Those potential sources, often from the public sector, with no access to the secrets have almost no claim on the attention of journalists. The degree to which these officials in the executive branch command the news channels is demonstrated by a study of the sourcing patterns of 23 journalists on the national security beat who report for seven major American newspapers. An analysis of the sourcing patterns in 678 stories written by this group during 1988 reveals that Pentagon sources were cited most frequently, and that Pentagon, congressional, and State Department sources represent fully 50 percent of all source citations. The top 5 percent (38 individuals) account for 44.7 percent of all citations. This included such sources as Secretary of Defense Frank Carlucci, Secretary of State George Shultz, President Reagan, Congressperson Les Aspin, and

Senator Sam Nunn. The purely civil or nongovernment voice, as opposed to the statist voice, was heard in these stories a scant 2.7 percent of the time (Hallin, Manoff, and Weddle, 1989).

On the national security beat, at least, secret data is the coin of the realm. By contrast, when information is no longer secret, it often loses its journalistic cachet, such as happened with coverage of the INF Treaty, signed in December 1987. Early reports focused on classified leaks about the numbers of such missiles that both sides possessed. As classified data, these numbers were taken most seriously.

The INF Treaty, however, ended the necessity of relying on leaks by including a quite specific and highly authoritative memorandum of the missile count. It was public and available for examination by all. Some of the numbers in the memorandum were quite different from the leaked data. Yet, the press largely ignored the memorandum. Few detailed analyses appeared (Arkin, 1988, pp. 1–2, 9–11). The numbers were no longer secret and were therefore considerably less interesting to journalists.

Dependent as it has become on the keepers of the secrets, the national security press corps often functions as little more than a bulletin board for authorized leaks from government officials (Fromm, 1983, p. 32). This role, far from the concept of the press as fourth branch of government, seems not to concern the journalists themselves. One of the most experienced is Leslie Gelb, a reporter and editorial writer on national security affairs for the New York *Times,* who formerly worked for the State Department and headed the task force that compiled the Pentagon Papers. Gelb admits that "any half-way competent and disciplined administration can get its story published pretty much the way it wants," a problem in the coverage of government not limited to national security issues (Fromm, 1983, p. 33).

Gelb returned to this theme in a revealing New York *Times* editorial bemoaning how little his pack of government experts knew about the historic events occurring in Eastern Europe in late 1989 or their implications for U.S. foreign and defense policy. Yet, Gelb was unwilling to expand his network of sources. In explaining why, Gelb confesses to the power these official sources exercise over his reporting:

> Reporters seem to think they have nowhere to turn but to the old experts to help them interpret and design the new order. It matters little that the experts . . . are busily expounding on the very same realities they insisted would never come to pass. . . . Why, then, do statesmen and reporters continue to rely on them? In part it's because the experts know how to play the game. . . . They set the boundaries of the debate, shape agendas and define

what is and is not considered possible. Inevitably their vision will be severely circumscribed by now-obsolete security considerations. Almost invariably, they will translate unimagined opportunities for cooperation into geopolitics as usual (Gelb, 1989, P. A20).

Barring that rare instance when the national security establishment is seriously and publicly at war with itself and employs the selective release of classified information as a tool in this war (such as occurred between the CIA and the Defense Department in assessing the Soviet threat to Western Europe in early 1990), a press that depends on secrets can only function as a source for conventional wisdom. The keepers of the secrets are not those persons likely to challenge the accepted realities of nuclear deterrence or the cold war view of the world. To the extent that journalists rely on these sources — which, as has been shown, is almost exclusively American — journalism will be a conservative force for maintaining the status quo in foreign relations and defining national security along traditional military lines.

SECRECY, PUBLIC IGNORANCE, AND ITS CONSEQUENCES

Nearly 50 years of such journalism has produced an American public ignorant of, or misinformed about, virtually every important aspect of American nuclear policy. As a result, the most far-reaching decisions of the nuclear age have been made by a small circle of officials unencumbered by public input or debate.

Whenever polling organizations have included public knowledge questions in their surveys, the results have been sobering. For example, a 1985 survey by Marttila and Kiley found that three out of four Americans believe, incorrectly, that the United States subscribes to a no first use policy for nuclear weapons in Europe (Rosen, 1988, p. 7). In fact, the United States has always been willing to use nuclear weapons to halt a Soviet conventional advance.

Thirty years earlier, at the height of the debate over atmospheric testing of nuclear weapons, a Gallup poll (March 1955) revealed that only 17 percent of Americans could correctly state a definition for fallout (Divine, 1978, p. 43). The polling literature is filled with similar examples. Three-quarters or more of the public does not know:

that an antiballistic missile shield could protect at best only 10 percent of
the population (November 1985);
that there is an ABM Treaty (February 1983);

the approximate percentage of the defense budget spent on nuclear
    weapons (April 1984); and

the identities of the two countries engaged in the SALT process (January
    1979) (Rosen, 1988, p. 3).

Dozens of other examples could be offered.

Such findings should be profoundly unsettling for the journalists who
report on these issues. In defense of the media, it has been argued that the
public simply does not want to know about national security issues and is
not educable (DeVolpi et al., 1981, p. 240). Others argue that the
refinements in nuclear strategy of the Robert McNamara years were too
complicated for the public. It was one thing to understand a doctrine of
massive retaliation, in which the United States would rain bombs down
on Soviet cities. But the public lost interest in, and was no doubt chilled
and confused by, a targeting strategy to permit nuclear war fighting at
various levels of intensity. The public simply tuned out (Boyer, 1985a,
p., 358).

Others wonder if the task is beyond journalists, even the very best.
John Hersey's classic *Hiroshima,* which appeared first in the *New
Yorker,* was unable to spark a debate about the use of nuclear weapons,
despite the impact of his word pictures (Boyer, 1985a, p. 205). Are
newspaper and television journalists better equipped than Hersey?

In the face of such odds, many journalists on the national security
beat make no attempt to appeal to the general public and write only for
their peers and members of the national security community. Stephen
Hess, who has observed the working habits of the Washington press
corps, believes that, as a rule, journalists do write for one another and not
for the audience back home (Hess, 1981, p. 12).

While secrecy is not the only cause of public ignorance, it has
seriously encouraged it. Its impact on American foreign and defense
policy and the management of the nuclear deterrent is beyond calculation.
If one were to compile a list of the major decisions made in secret in this
realm it would be encyclopedic, beginning with the Manhattan Project
and the decision to drop the A-bomb through virtually every twist and
turn in the strategy of deterrence (DeVolpi et al., 1981, pp. 47–48, 55,
84–112).

Year by year this ignorance is compounded, and the ability of the
public to ever take control of decision making in the national security
realm slips deeper into the blackness of secrecy. Even if the press were to
make a commitment to address this problem, where would it start? On
what common base of information? In connection with what events?

THE WANING OF SECRECY?

In the fall and winter of 1989, when the press was filled with stories of the collapse of Communist governments in Eastern Europe, a handful of related stories appeared offering the barest possibility that the regime of secrecy itself may begin to crumble.

The most startling state-sanctioned breach of secrecy came from the Soviet side. On October 23, 1989, Foreign Minister Eduard Shevardnadze admitted that a radar station built at Krasnoyarsk in Siberia was, as the Reagan administration had repeatedly charged since 1983, a serious violation of the ABM Treaty. That treaty permits early warning radar installations to be constructed only on the nation's perimeter, where they cannot be used to coordinate a defensive attack against an incoming missile barrage. The purpose is to leave the two superpowers naked to each other's ICBMs, one of the principles of deterrence strategy. By outlawing ABM systems, the treaty was also intended to head off what most experts believed would be a fruitless and expensive mutual effort to develop and deploy such systems.

The Reagan administration had used classified data on the Krasnoyarsk violation to brand the Soviets as cheaters on arms control agreements, thereby hoping to reduce public pressure for negotiating additional agreements. Other critics of the Soviets, both in and out of the administration, went a step further, charging that the Soviets were secretly constructing a whole network of battle management radars. Krasnoyarsk was just one of them, the only one we had publicly admitted locating with our spy satellites. According to this scenario, the Soviets were intending to break out of the limitations imposed by the ABM Treaty and gain a strategic military advantage. This might include the possibility of launching a first strike, employing their illegal ABM system in reserve to mop up whatever second strike response a devastated United States might muster.

With so much at stake, it is not surprising that the Krasnoyarsk radar became a highly emotional issue that represented different things to different constituencies. Anti-Soviet supporters of the Reagan administration saw it as further proof of Soviet perfidy and confirmation of the administration's early position against negotiating arms cuts with the Soviets. They also used it as an argument for the United States to develop its own ABM system, called the Strategic Defense Initiative(SDI). Critics of the administration put their faith in Soviet denials that the radar was a violation, and they were skeptical of the administration's motives for releasing this intelligence data, if indeed it was "intelligent." They saw Krasnoyarsk as a bogeyman for avoiding negotiations, heightening superpower tensions, and whipping up public support for SDI research.

One's position on Krasnoyarsk had less to do with the data, which was of course all classified and doled out by partisans, than with long-held beliefs about Soviet performance as a negotiating partner and Soviet goals with respect to nuclear parity or superiority. Those unwilling to believe that the Soviets would ever launch a first strike could hardly accept the administration's charge that this illegal radar had been built to allow for just such an eventuality. Similarly, those who suspected the worst about the Soviets had no reason to believe their denials.

Secrecy made it possible for both sides to stick to their positions. The two governments had a monopoly on the relevant information, and they were saying quite different things. National security journalists, without intelligence data of their own, were in no position to settle the dispute. Getting the truth about Krasnoyarsk would have required gaining access to even more secrets about nuclear strategy, the capabilities of other Soviet radar sites, the quality of American intelligence collection, and more. Indeed, Krasnoyarsk was the typical intelligence secret that cannot be understood or verified without access to additional secrets, which also cannot be understood or verified without additional access, and so on *ad infinitum*. Such secrets can only be rebutted by the enemy and so are not capable of rebuttal at all. Therefore, such secrets can be manipulated by a government to suit its own purposes.

Shevardnadze's surprise admission of guilt thus brought closure to the sort of national security dispute that is usually never resolved but rather lives on in the rhetoric of ideological opponents. In his candid confession Shevardnadze said,

> The power of perestroika does not in itself insure us against mistakes. It's important not to hide them and correct them.
> We were charged with violation of the ABM Treaty because of the [Krasnoyarsk] station. It took the Government quite a while to learn all the truth of the project. Finally, we say it clearly: The station had been built on the wrong site, not where it should have been.
> All these years, we have been working hard to keep up the ABM Treaty as a foundation for strategic stability.
> · · ·
> And all the while, there stood the station, the size of an Egyptian pyramid, representing, to put it bluntly, a violation of the ABM Treaty ("The Kremlin Apology," 1989, p. A12).

An end to secrecy between the nuclear superpowers was undoubtedly not Shevardnadze's chief motive. The Soviets were hoping the United States would abide by the treaty and stop work on its SDI program. This admission would make it harder for the U.S. to violate other terms of the treaty at some future point. Nevertheless, although Shevardnadze may not have been motivated by concern for the people's right to know, when governments admit they have been cheating on international agreements, the publics in both countries can decide the significance for themselves without relying almost wholly on propaganda from the opposition.

Other slight tears in the fabric of secrecy occurred during this period, also chiefly at Soviet instigation. In what the New York *Times* described as "an unusual twist," the Soviets announced they would be willing to make public data from two underground nuclear testing experiments designed to demonstrate the reliability of on-site techniques, to verify treaties that would limit the size of underground nuclear explosions. But the United States was opposed to the public release of the data (Gordon, 1989, p. A7), even though it has been shared with the Soviets. Given that one of the presumed virtues of a free and democratic system is a commitment to openness, this disappointing response by the United States suggested at least to the *Times* readership that the American government may, at this point in history, be no less committed to secrecy than the Soviets.

The Soviets also opened their secret laser research center at Sary-Shagun to a group of ten Americans, including three members of Congress, to help support their claim that no powerful beam weapon was being developed at the site (Keller, 1989, p. A1). The complex proved to be considerably less threatening militarily than the Pentagon public relations machine had promised. The visit prompted Princeton University physicist Frank Von Hippel to remark ruefully, "It's incredible to think that the Pentagon SDI folks probably got an extra $10 billion because of this place." Major General Yevgeny V. Tarasov admitted to New York *Times* reporter Bill Keller that excessive secrecy at the site had hurt the Soviets, as well as the American taxpayer, because it had contributed to a mood in the USSR of public skepticism about the military.

Secrecy as a consistent policy will ultimately damage the people it is supposed to protect. This is Tarasov's point, and it is slowly being acknowledged by policy makers in the United States. The air force lost support in Congress for its $530 million stealth bomber in part because of excessive secrecy about its mission and capabilities (Halloran, 1989, p. A14). Under the cloak of secrecy legislated by the 1954 Atomic Energy Act, the nation's nuclear weapons laboratories were able to operate in such a cavalier fashion that environmental safety and health problems eventually brought their bomb-making capacity to a halt in 1988 and 1989. "If openness had occurred in the past," said Under Secretary of Energy Joseph F. Salgado, "we wouldn't have been in the shape we're in now" (Schneider, 1988, IV, p. D7). Similarly, Communist Party control over information in Eastern Europe has, in the absence of public debate and accountability, produced a highly polluted environment.

As the 1990s approached, those cultivating the regime of secrecy were, for the first time, on the defensive as they attempted to justify the benefits of secrecy in the face of serious public health problems at weapons manufacturing sites. Whether this proves to be a significant development in the attack on secrecy or only a minor embarrassment depends on the willingness of American journalists to demand changes in their own profession to match a changing world order.

SECRECY AND NATIONAL SECURITY

"Out of [the Manhattan Project] there grew a conviction that secrecy was an essential prerequisite for national security, and this view was to become firmly fixed as part of the dominant political consensus of the cold war. The opposite viewpoint — that secrecy can sometimes be damaging to national security — was hard-pressed to make itself heard" (Rourke, 1977, pp. 114–15).

Now, for the first time since 1946, the United States is being forced by events in the Soviet Union, Eastern Europe, and Japan to "rethink the definition of national security in a basic way" (Barnet, 1990, pp. 65–66). Past definitions of national security have been entirely the creation of government, based on information kept secret from the press and public. These definitions have been rooted in the fear of a single enemy and focused almost exclusively on military challenges. The news media, against their true calling, have supported the government's view of national security, even though the government has used that view to strike legally against First Amendment freedom (in prior restraint cases) and informally (through jawboning and other extralegal efforts at intimidation).

The new political order, and the seeming disappearance of the Soviet Union as The Enemy, should stimulate new thinking in American journalism on how to wrest its constitutional freedom from the prison of national security.

First, journalists should lobby as aggressively for substantive changes in the classification system as they have for relief in other areas bearing on press freedom, such as elimination of the fairness doctrine, shield laws to protect confidential sources, and judicial permission to take cameras into courtrooms. These are comparatively trivial issues when weighed against the ability to report accurately on the nuclear arms race, yet journalists have been much more vocal and successful arguing for relaxation of legal restrictions in these areas than they have on the subjects of classification and secrecy. The time is ripe for a reassessment of the classification system and the proper exemptions to the Freedom of Information Act.

Second, journalists and their legal advisors should be more willing to test the limits of their freedom in the courts. Judges are also aware of the end of the Cold War, and this cannot but affect their view of the definition of national security. The burden on government to demonstrate the need to enjoin publication of secret information should now be more difficult to meet. In light of the revelations about health risks at nuclear plants where bombs are manufactured, judges may also look less charitably at enforcement of the Atomic Energy Act.

Third, journalists must wean themselves from their reliance on anonymous sources. Public officials must be held accountable for their words. In a less tense world, journalists should not permit officials to use them as a conveyor belt for inaccurate and politically motivated information.

Fourth, journalists should resist passing on to the public only those secrets leaked to them by government officials. The result of this practice has been to produce a highly distorted marketplace of ideas, one skewed toward the government's view of the world. It also keeps much essential information away from the public, thereby discouraging informed public debate.

Last, journalists must make an effort to open up the airwaves and newspapers to voices other than those of government officials. The people of Eastern Europe demonstrated that much political activity can occur in the civil realm, beyond the reach of the state. This civil activity helped prepare the way for the collapse of the Communist regimes and the move toward democracy. Somewhat belatedly, American journalists recognized that the end of the Cold War could not be reported only at the state and military levels. The same holds true in the United States. Journalists ought not cede to government the sole right to debate the establishment of a new world order.

If the media do not accept this challenge, the Cold War will be replaced by new political realities (or seeming realities) that are just as threatening as the old. The media will continue to find their security in secrecy, at great peril to First Amendment values and democratic self-government.

NOTES

1. For an historical overview of the classification system, see Demac (1984, pp. 13–18). For a discussion of the Reagan administration's executive order on classified information and the national security exemption to the FOIA, see Watkins (1990, pp. 231–33).

2. For another view of Washington *Post* national security reporter Walter Pincus, see Whitman, 1986, for a description of how he broke the neutron bomb story during the Carter administration.

3. Official secrecy is an even more serious problem for British journalists. The Official Secrets Act constrains public servants from revealing any government information to persons unauthorized to receive it, regardless of whether such information impinges on the security of the state. Journalists can be prosecuted under the act for receiving such information. The D Notice system serves to advise British journalists about defense-related information that ought not be published. It has no legal effect by itself, but journalists who contravene the wishes of government and publish such information may run afoul of the Official Secrets Act. For an overview of the D Notice system and the Official Secrets Act, see Supperstone (1985).

4. McGeorge Bundy, special assistant to President Kennedy for National Security Affairs, has said that, having been both inside and outside of government, he now believes there are no real secrets that cannot be found out by aggressive journalists. While journalists may genuinely believe such secrets exist and ought to be protected, Bundy is more skeptical of this partnership of silence between press and government (personal communication, March 6, 1990).

5. For a view from the scientific community of the *Progressive* case, which nicely compliments Morland's first-person account (1981), see DeVolpi et al. (1981).

6. For a comprehensive discussion of secrecy in American society, with special attention to the effects of secrecy on public officials and journalists, see Bok (1982).

10

A Case of Need: Media Coverage of Organ Transplants

DENI ELLIOTT

THE CASE

The call came into Portland, Maine, newsrooms on a snowy day in early February 1988.[1] Norma Lynn Peterson, a seven-year-old from the neighboring town of Windham, had end-stage liver disease. Doctors said that, without a liver transplant, Norma would be dead within a year.

She was a candidate for a liver transplant at the well-respected Pittsburgh transplant center. Until her donor organ was allocated, there was little for Norma and her family and friends to do but worry about money. Norma's illness was a financial burden for the working class Peterson family. Her father's health insurance would cover 80 percent of the $200,000 surgery and associated medical costs, but that left at least $40,000 that the Petersons needed to save their little girl's life. And those were just initial costs. Cyclosporine, the drug that Norma would take to stave off rejection of the transplanted organ, would run at least $3,000 a year for the rest of her life.

That's what the phone calls to the *Portland Press-Telegram* and the ABC, NBC, and CBS affiliate stations were all about. A Valentine's Day potluck dinner had been planned in support of the Norma Lynn Fund. Ed Jandreau, the volunteer fundraiser, suggested to news directors and reporters that the community effort would make good news.

News media agreed. Stories on Norma Lynn appeared from mid-February through her triumphant return home from transplant surgery in August. Nearly all carried information on where contributions could be sent, although few let the audience know that medical insurance would cover the lion's share of the bill. In all, Norma Lynn commanded more than 200 column inches and more than two and one-half hours of airtime. "Every time something happened to Norma Lynn," said Jandreau, "the news media were there."

In the months before her transplant, Norma Lynn's need became public drama as well-wishers waited to see if a liver would be found in time. Cards, letters, and testimonies to her bravery poured in from fans across the state. Local merchants donated various items including a video camera, carloads of stuffed toys, and almost anything that would make the child happy or the waiting easier.

"Norma Lynn wanted a puppy," her mother said. "So I went to the pet store, but it was like $425. I figured I could pay $50 a week. So, I asked the manager and she said, 'Norma, do you want this puppy?' and she says, 'It's yours.'"

Norma Lynn's fund topped $100,000 by the end of 1988. The little girl's classic good looks and her family's willingness to let television cameras bring their medical crisis into homes across the state paid off.

Cameras stayed close by during her surgery on May 20 and at her "press conference" at the transplant center a few weeks after her operation. News media stood watch as she recovered from two complications: a leaking bile duct and a viral infection. They documented her triumphant return home. She shared the donated private jet ride from Pittsburgh to Portland with a television reporter and videographer, whose stations had paid $900 in jet fuel to get this exclusive coverage.

On the surface, the Norma Lynn coverage seems like a media success story. Media critics would argue that, for a change, the news underscored the positive — the community rallying around Norma Lynn — instead of the negative elements that so often command media attention. Journalists find stories like this satisfying. The family welcomes them; sources are eager to talk; there is no hidden agenda; everyone has the child's best interests at heart. But, there are difficult ethical problems just below the surface of this typical human interest story. Here I will raise some of those questions, discuss how the principals in the Norma Lynn case responded to those issues, and then provide suggestions for a style of medial coverage that would avoid the problems identified.

THE NEWSWORTHINESS OF
TRANSPLANT CANDIDATES

The first obvious question is: What made Norma Lynn news? Many children and adults have life-threatening illnesses. Many are in financial need. It's unlikely that Norma Lynn was the first liver transplant recipient in the state, or the youngest.[2]

While journalists cited Norma's exceptional good looks as helping her get coverage, the news directors in the Portland market credited community spirit with creating the news story. Peter Wyle, news director for WMTW, the ABC affiliate, said, "It was more than the story of a little girl who needed a transplant. It was about how her neighbors and friends got a lot of support for her."

Jim Sanders, news director for WGME, a CBS affiliate, agreed. "We covered Norma Lynn so that this community would know that there was something some people in this community care enough about to give up their time, their energy to do something for this little girl. That's the story for us."

But, family and friends talk about the news coverage in a different way. "The whole thing with the media was to get some money for Norma because she's always going to need money," said Louis Peterson, Norma's father.

Her mother said that parents of other transplant candidates should get news attention as quickly as they can. "We knew a couple of families in Pittsburgh. . . . The transplant's done and they don't have the funds they need because they didn't have the media involved to help them out."

While the news directors said that they covered Norma Lynn because of the community's participation in fundraising, Jandreau, who coordinated activities for the Norma Lynn Fund, said attracting media coverage was the primary fundraising activity. Jandreau said that they planned a potluck supper at the local church on Valentine's Day for the initial event and then called newsrooms: "I said I've got a story in Windham, a human interest story. There's a little child in Windham who needs a liver transplant."

News media arrived and made the story their own. News coverage then became the primary fundraising tool. "Every time Norma Lynn's face appeared on TV," Jandreau said, "we received oodles of money more. If it weren't for the media, the Norma Lynn Peterson fund would not be where it is. We would have $5,000–$6,000. . . . The more coverage we got, the better off we were."

Jeff Marks, news director for television station WCSH, conceded that the news coverage certainly helped Norma Lynn, although that was not the station's intent. "As long as our driving purpose was not to raise money for Norma Lynn's surgery, and we kept the arm's length we need to keep, we cannot help that there were some good outcomes from our coverage. I would say that the people who were behind the Norma Lynn case did skillfully use the media opportunity." However, WCSH sometimes closed stories on Norma Lynn by providing the address of the fund for viewers who wished to make donations.

What made Norma Lynn news seems to be her family and friends' ability to manipulate the local news media. No one can blame the fundraiser for attempting to enlist the media's support, but one can question the media response. The news directors, in this case, claim they covered bona fide events of community interest. The fundraiser and family maintain that there were no bona fide events and little community interest until news media turned the public eye in their direction. It's disturbing to think and difficult to believe that journalists could be fooled so easily.

The television stations and newspaper published the address of the Norma Lynn Fund at the end of news stories. The journalists were blatantly participating in the fundraising effort. But, if they admitted to doing so, they would have new problems. If they are encouraging people to send money to a particular cause, don't they the incur some responsibility to make sure that those funds are used appropriately? And, as a matter of fairness, shouldn't they give the same effort to others in similar situations? It's far easier to say that some people are news and some are not. The clear implication of what some called the media circus for Norma Lynn is that other needy people would not profit in the same way.

WHO GETS COVERED?

From a cynical perspective, we could say that what made Norma Lynn news is that another child's need hadn't been news the week before. One news director said, "If we tried to do every transplant, we'd be doing the transplant hour."

In every news market, there are more people in need than those who receive publicity. In Maine that summer of 1988, at least one of those was a 24-year-old wife and mother.

While Norma Lynn was recovering from surgery, Cindy Short traveled to Pittsburgh to become Maine's first heart and lung transplant recipient. Unlike the Petersons, the Shorts had no health insurance; the cost of the surgery was picked up through Medicaid. Unlike the Petersons, the Shorts didn't know how to ask for or receive media attention. Steven Short, Cindy's husband, said that they knew about Norma Lynn from watching television and from seeing the media coverage in the hospital in Pittsburgh. "It's sad that they do so much for one and nothing for another one," Short said.

Cindy did not survive her surgery. "She died in the hospital and it was kind of rough," said Steve. "I had to find my own way back. The state won't pay for your lodging, your food down there or for flying back."

Short said that the day his wife died, he got ready to hitchhike back to his four-year-old daughter. Someone at the hospital became aware of his need and paid for an airline ticket for his return home. No news media were aware of the Shorts at the time, but it doesn't follow that they would have received coverage if their need had been known. Marks from WCSH said, "It is not the job of news media to apply attention equally to all people who may be in the same situation. Just because Norma Lynn was an interesting story doesn't mean that all transplants should be featured in news coverage."

From a media relations viewpoint, it's clear that news organizations who make decisions like this without a policy are heading for trouble. The father who calls the newsroom a week after a media blitz on one child and is told that his son's need isn't news isn't likely to understand "that's just the way news is." When editors and news directors decide who gets media attention and who does not, they are literally playing God.

Although not listed as clinical criteria, transplant surgeons will talk off-the-record about the financial requirements for transplant recipients. Potential transplant candidates will often not be put on the list to be matched with a donor organ until they show proof of insurance, Medicaid reimbursement, or a minimum of $50,000. For some people, the kind of boost that the news media bring to fundraising can be a matter of life or death.

RESPONSIBLE COVERAGE OF ORGAN TRANSPLANTATION

No one can deny that, at least within the United States, the news media can cover whatever they choose. That is, a news organization isn't legally accountable to anyone for what they do or do not cover. But, it doesn't follow that all coverage is responsible coverage. The hallmarks of responsible coverage can be found in understanding the social function of the press.

The news industry and individual media representatives are awarded special privileges and constitutional protection in this society. This wasn't an arbitrary gesture on the part of the framers, and it certainly isn't accidental that these privileges and protections still continue. Representatives of the news media warrant special treatment because they fulfill a particular and needed social function. It's primarily up to the news media to provide people with the information that they need to be self-governing citizens in a participatory democracy (Elliott, 1986). A responsible news organization will fulfill this duty while avoiding causing harm unless reporters and editors have adequate justification for doing otherwise (Gert, 1989). The technicalities of how this is possible is an interesting discussion but not necessary to explicate the issue at hand. The relevant question for the coverage of organ transplants is what constitutes responsible media attention to the issues and, by extension, what does not. What do people need to know about organ transplantation, so that they have the information necessary to be self-governing citizens in a participatory democracy?

Technological Advances

News coverage of experimental transplantation — xenographs, artificial organ substitutes, new and multi organ attempts — is legitimate, even though that means focusing on individual cases. These cases are unique. Interestingly enough, the potential for manipulation of news media for fundraising is not an issue here. Because of the experimental nature of the procedure, clinical costs to the patient are absorbed as research expenditures. The patient incurs the costs in a procedure which is not experimental.

The Real Costs of Extraordinary Medical Procedures

Why does transplant surgery cost hundreds of thousands of dollars? The common answer is that the talent and equipment necessary to complete the complicated procedures is very expensive. If so, then why are there so many transplant centers? Why is it necessary to fund more than one transplant center in a region when the result is competition between transplant teams for the same donors and candidates? Why does it cost so much and how is the health care dollar being allocated to meet those costs?

Access

Who are the candidates for extraordinary medical treatments such as transplantation, and who are the recipients? Beyond clinical considerations, how are determinations made about who should receive organs? Ability to pay is an important criterion, as is the perceived worthiness of the candidate. How often is a white child with medical insurance given a liver transplant; how often is a black adult alcoholic with a cirrhotic liver and no medical insurance denied?

Dilemmas

It's important for people to know that they and their families can designate that their organs and tissue be donated at death. But it's also important that the more subtle issues find their way into the public dialogue. If one's organs are one's property, as they evidently are if people can choose to donate them or not, then why can't people sell them? We allow blood products to be sold. Why not kidneys or bone marrow? On the other hand, since there are clearly not enough organs available for people who need them, why not declare citizens' organs a national resource and distribute what can be harvested from cadavers as needed?

Informed Decisions about Health Care Policy

Organ transplantation, particularly if funded through state Medicaid programs, uses a portion of the health care dollar not available for other items like prenatal health care. And, while we've decided that some services, such as police protection and public education, should be universal we have made different decisions about health care. However, since these decisions are rarely juxtaposed in news stories, it's not surprising that the public would consider individual aspects in isolation.

CONCLUSION

So what does this mean for the coverage of Norma Lynn and other individual transplant candidates? It doesn't mean that individual cases cannot be covered, but that they should be covered differently.

The larger issues listed were not addressed in the story of Norma Lynn's transplant. Marks, the news director from WCSH said, "It was easy TV journalism. It could have used some probing and depth. The question of whether this is a good way to raise money for critical surgery is a good question. We didn't deal with that." Upon reflection, he said, "I think we should have stepped back and said, 'Why is it that they should come to the media? Why is it that they have to have bake sales?'"

Individual cases can be used to illustrate the larger issues, but the societal issues should not be lost in the drama of covering an individual case. A child in need of community assistance so that she can get life-saving medical treatment is not episodic, it is a vivid symptom of a health care system in need of attention. When news organizations cover the child in need without turning the public's attention to why the child is in such need, they become part of a system that exploits sick children to finance health care.

NOTES

1. This synopsis and all quotes are taken from the 1988–89 research and production of *A Case of Need,* a documentary film distributed by Fanlight Productions and produced by Deni Elliott and Bill Fitz in 1989.

2. It's also not known how many there have been. Each of the more than 70 liver transplantation centers in the United States keeps separate lists of candidates. Since a person can become a candidate at as many transplant centers as is financially and clinically feasible, the focus of the tracking is by procedure and center rather than by the candidate's state of origin. UNOS, the National Organ Procurement and Transplantation Network, may have this information available sometime soon. And, due to patient confidentiality, identities of transplant donors, candidates, and recipients are not released by the medical community without permission.

11

Science as Symbol: The Media Chills the Greenhouse Effect

LEE WILKINS AND
PHILIP PATTERSON

THE ROLE OF THE POLITICAL SYMBOL

How Americans come to regard an issue as important enough to demand political action remains a crucial question in the study of politics. Events in the twentieth century, however, have indicated that the process of deciding what is politically important is a rich one, a symbiotic relationship among elites, interest groups, and the electorate, where different members can either lead or follow as circumstances dictate (Burns, 1978).

The emergence of the mass media has added yet another voice to this dialogue. While historically it was assumed that the media acted as a conduit of information, informing the public about political issues and providing a mechanism for the public to respond, that role was later expanded when studies indicated that the mass media also performed an agenda-setting function, selecting and elevating certain issues to public awareness (see, for example, McCombs and Shaw, 1972; Rogers and Dearing, 1988). More recent studies indicate that the media, particularly television, have an even more subtle effect, priming the electorate to believe that one issue from among the many on the agenda is particularly salient (Iyengar and Kinder, 1987). Media coverage of specific issues also has become a way of communicating about policy options within the federal government (Linsky, 1986). Scholars of political communication now understand that media coverage of political issues is not a one-way street, but influences both the public and decision-making elites in obvious and subtle ways.

One subtlety is the transforming of a political issue into a political symbol. "The parade of 'news' about political acts reported to us by the mass media and drunk up by the public as drama is the raw material of such symbolization" (Edelman, 1964, p. 8). For an issue to become politically meaningful and capable of generating debate, it must move from the realm of something that is important to the realm of political symbol — a person or event that enables people to link political choices to specific issues. "Political symbols bring out in concentrated form those particular meanings and emotions which the members of a group create and reinforce in each other. There is nothing about any symbol that requires that it stand for only one thing" (Edelman, 1964, p. 11). Such political symbols may be embodied in individual leaders such as Martin Luther King, or in what scholars have called critical events, those events "which will produce the most useful explanation and predictions of social change" (Kraus et al., 1975, p. 99).

These symbols can have important ramifications throughout the political process. They can promote a range of political understanding, from increasing public awareness to the enactment of specific legislation. Political symbols enable citizens of a democracy, both elites and the voting public, to understand the relationship between abstract decisions and their concrete results.

Symbolic events are easy to spot — with hindsight. Less well understood is how an issue or event becomes transformed from an agenda item into a meaningful political symbol. Whether the media is even capable of aiding in this transformation of the complexities of scientific problems into political symbols is a valid concern.

This chapter examines the media coverage of one issue, the greenhouse effect, to document whether the issue acquired symbolic political power. In the process, media coverage itself is examined, as is the interplay between scientists, who have studied the problem, and members of Congress, who are proposing and enacting legislation on the issue. The interaction between these two elite groups is one signal of the growing conviction among some members of the scientific community that the greenhouse effect is the single most important political issue facing the planet, with the possible exception of nuclear war. But, an examination of media coverage of the issue indicates that this sense of urgency has been incompletely translated into public opinion and policy options. The inability of the greenhouse effect to achieve a mediated symbolic threshold has ramifications for political decision making.

In order to understand the role that media coverage of the greenhouse effect played in its framing as a political issue, it is important to understand both the science of the concept as well as its political ramifications. What follows is a brief introduction to those issues.

LIFE IN THE GREENHOUSE

The greenhouse effect is arguably the best accepted theory in climatology. In its simplest terms, the greenhouse effect describes how gases in the atmosphere trap heat from the earth's surface that would otherwise escape into space. These trapped gases warm the planet, making life on earth possible. In the total absence of the greenhouse effect, the mean temperature of the earth would be about 33 degrees centigrade colder (one degree centigrade equals about 1.8 degrees Fahrenheit), rendering the earth, like Mars, uninhabitable for life as we know it.

What has made the greenhouse effect scientifically contentious is that the amount of warming it provides has not been historically stable. In previous geologic eras, the age of the dinosaurs, for example, some greenhouse gases were more plentiful and the earth was apparently warmer. The reverse of this relationship existed during the ice ages. The current debate centers on whether the greenhouse itself is heating up again, and what role humans play in the process.

Contemporary academic study of the effect began in 1958 at Hawaii's Moano Loa volcano. Until recent years, carbon dioxide, CO_2, was thought to be the sole greenhouse gas, but in 1985 researchers from the National Center for Atmospheric Research in Boulder found other gases were contributing to global warming and could potentially surpass the impact of carbon dioxide. Together these gases constitute roughly 12.6 percent of the earth's atmosphere and are annually increasing in concentration. Current research has isolated the following greenhouse gases:

Carbon dioxide, the largest component of the greenhouse gases, is chiefly the result of burning fossil fuels. About 170 billion metric tons of carbon dioxide have been released into the atmosphere since 1850, and another 6 billion metric tons are added each year (Ciborowski, 1989). The amount of carbon dioxide in the air has increased by about 30 percent each year in the past 100 years (From and Keeling, 1986) and is increasing at a rate of about 4 percent each year.

Methane, CH_4, a more efficient greenhouse gas than carbon dioxide, may potentially be the most difficult of the gases to control because it is created naturally in agriculture, particularly in rice paddies, and is emitted from wetlands and the intestines of animals. Tons of methane are also trapped beneath ice that could melt in future years should global warming go unchecked. Atmospheric methane is increasing at a rate of 2 percent per year (Kahlil and Rassmusen, 1985).

Tropospheric ozone, produced photochemically as a result of the oxidation of carbon monoxide, methane, or other hydrocarbons, has increased between 20 and 50 percent in the last 100 years. Tropospheric ozone is a by-product of, for example, automobile exhaust, and is currently increasing at a rate of about 1 percent per year. This gas is similar to, but is in a different atmospheric layer from, stratospheric ozone, one of nature's filters of harmful ultraviolet rays.

Nitrous oxide, or NO_2, is largely a by-product of the breakdown of nitrogen-based fertilizers. Although it is a minor greenhouse gas in terms of quantity, when released into the air it has a lifetime of about 150 years. It is increasing at the rate of .2 percent per year (Weiss, 1981).

Finally, the *chlorofluorocarbons,* CF_2C_{12} and CFC_1, commonly occurring as freons and styrofoam, constitute the rarest of the greenhouse gases. However, their totally synthetic make-up means one molecule of either gas in the atmosphere can have the same radiative effect as adding 10,000 molecules of carbon dioxide (Ramanathan, 1989). The number of molecules of the gases in the atmosphere is expanding at the rate of 5.1 percent per year (Cunnold et al., 1986).

All the greenhouse gases are closely, and in some cases exclusively, related to human activity, thus allowing climatologists to characterize global warming as a human-created hazard. Furthermore, the greenhouse effect is an interactive problem. The burning of rain forests in Brazil, fast-food packaging, the depletion of the ozone layer, and an expanding human population all contribute to the greenhouse effect but seldom in a linear fashion.

Humanity's impact on global warming dates to the Industrial Revolution, and most scientists believe our contribution to global warming since that time has been between .5 and .7 degrees centigrade. While the amount seems small, studies indicate the rate of increase is accelerating. As global warming becomes a reality, scientists project the following scenario.

The earth's ambient temperature will rise. The number of 100-degree Fahrenheit days in Dallas, Texas, for example, is expected to increase from a current average of 19 per year to an average of 78. Similar increases are forecast for the Midwest. Each one degree centigrade of global warming will shift temperature zones north by about 100 miles (Abrahamson, 1989). With this warming, plant species will be forced to migrate to survive. A worst case scenario projects such a significant ambient temperature increase in as little as two decades, yet many species of trees are capable of migrating only one to 20 kilometers per century (Peters, 1989). Precipitation patterns will shift. Most climatic models agree substantial decreases in rainfall could occur on the American Great Plains, while the lower latitudes may see seasonal increases. Local, national, and international economies will have to adjust.

As the air warms, scientists believe the oceans will rise. Already, the global average sea level has risen 10 to 15 centimeters in the past century. Current estimates call for a rise of 10 to 20 centimeters by 2025, and 50 to 200 centimeters by 2100 (Titus, 1989). The rising ocean levels will cause the loss of virtually all recreational beaches. The cost of rebuilding a beach to compensate for a 30-centimeter rise in ocean level is estimated by the Army Corps of Engineers to be $1million to $3 million per kilometer. In the United States the states of Louisiana and Florida would be the largest economic losers, along with isolated coastal cities such as Charleston, South Carolina, and Galveston, Texas. Worldwide, scenarios project a loss of up to 20 percent of the total land in Bangladesh and the Nile delta.

A rising sea level adds salinity to the fresh water of surrounding communities and increases the possibility of flooding. Increasing salinity will influence both the cost and the quality of water purification and treatment. Warming ocean temperatures would also mean longer hurricane seasons and hurricanes at higher latitudes.

Human health also will be affected. As summer temperatures escalate, heat-related mortality also is expected to increase, particularly among the young, the elderly and the disadvantaged. Increasing lower atmospheric ozone concentrations will magnify respiratory distress and disease. Plant-related diseases once checked by climatic variations may spread, as may some insect-born diseases.

The severity and the details of these scenarios are poorly articulated by current scientific models and requires a blend of social science and hard science that makes scholars in both areas uncomfortable. Nonetheless, the scenarios agree enough in general outline for both scientists and policy makers to assert that the greenhouse effect raises important political questions.

However, because most greenhouse research is based on computer models or projections from the earth's past, scientists cannot be precise about either the degree of warming or of site-specific climatic responses. The continuing scientific analysis of the problem, with conclusions that are often hotly debated, has obscured the fact that the theory is widely accepted, even by those who disagree with the specifics.

Recent climate events, which may or may not be caused by the greenhouse effect, have focused attention on the problem. Five of the nine warmest years in the 134 years of worldwide temperature monitoring have occurred since 1980. Floods, droughts, stronger than normal hurricanes, and forest fires in the western United States all fit the greenhouse scenario, leading some scientists to assert that humanity has already entered the greenhouse century (Schneider, 1989a).

Scientific and political response to the problem also appears to be accelerating. Since 1985, major greenhouse studies in the United States have been conducted by the National Center for Atmospheric Research, National Aeronautic and Space Administration (NASA), the Environmental Protection Agency (EPA), and the Department of Energy. Senate committees have held hearings on several occasions, and one bill, the Global Climate Protection Act, was signed into law by former president Ronald Reagan. In addition, the United States is a signee to the Montreal Protocol, agreeing to a 50 percent cut in the consumption of fluorocarbons (commonly found in refrigerants and urethane foams) by the year 1999, and an October 1989 agreement to cooperate with other industrialized nations to limit the dispersion of chemicals known to attack the earth's ozone layer.

THE POLITICS OF THE GREENHOUSE: UPSTAIRS, DOWNSTAIRS

For some Americans, the greenhouse effect has become a political issue. According to a June 1989 Gallup poll, 76 percent of the public identified themselves as environmentalists. Thirty-five percent say they worry "a great deal" about the greenhouse effect or global warming; 28 percent say they worry about it "a fair amount." The amount of worry increases with income and education. However, the same survey showed that only 4 percent of the public listed the environment and pollution as the "most important problem facing this country today," rating the environment behind the economy, drugs, poverty, unemployment and crime. Even among a list of environmental problems, such as pollution, toxic waste, soil contamination, and so forth, the greenhouse effect ranked tenth in a list of ten serious environmental concerns (Gallup, 1989).

If the statistics are correct, what Americans probably don't yet comprehend is the impact the greenhouse effect will have on problems they view as more important. At its most stark, mitigating the greenhouse will depend on national wealth, a commodity that is unevenly distributed within countries and among nations.

The developed world, as it copes with the greenhouse century, will face decisions that are politically divisive and economically disruptive. Spending literally billions of dollars for dykes to protect property along the coastal United States, for example, may demand a shift in resources away from military and social programs. Deciding how the country is going to fuel its economy, while abandoning coal and substituting natural gas as an energy source, pits politically entrenched interest groups against each other. Public sentiment is likely to be in for a severe shock as the "N" word — nuclear energy — surfaces as a potentially less greenhouse intensive energy source.

While most of the models predict a developed world that will continue to be able to feed itself, almost all agree that short-term disruption is likely and that food will eventually become more expensive. There will also be less of it, which will affect the balance of trade for nations such as the United States, the Soviet Union, and Japan.

The onset of these problems will bring a major challenge to the leadership of the developed world. Remedies such as an energy tax, new planning and zoning laws, and more spending on research have been suggested to allow market forces to begin the work of reallocation. But few believe the market alone will be successful in mitigating the greenhouse effect without substantial disruption. While little about the specifics of the greenhouse effect is certain, policy makers and scientists alike agree that even developed nations will be strapped to meet the demands of the greenhouse. The more rapidly the globe warms, the more Draconian the political choices will become.

But, while the developed world can take minimal comfort in viewing the greenhouse effect as a terribly expensive but nonetheless fixable problem, the developing world can be far less sanguine. The poorer countries of the planet have fewer resources to reallocate, and they face problems the developed nations have already handled with varying degrees of success.

The greenhouse effect for the developing world may bring decreased national economic security. Burning fossil fuels has historically meant the development of wealth, just as the planting of rice paddies and the harvesting of cattle, the principal contributors of methane to the atmosphere, have meant sustaining an increasing human population. For the developing world, the politics of the greenhouse becomes the politics of food and of jobs. It is the politics, literally, of survival, and as such is fraught with a potential for political and social disruption on a scale probably not seen since the convulsions of the Industrial Revolution in Europe.

The central political and economic question facing the developing world is whether development can be accomplished at all without an industrial revolution dependent on the burning of some sort of fuel. Human history suggests that less developed countries become developed by replicating the development processes that have gone before. In the greenhouse century such a replication is perilous, yet the south possesses the moral right to develop just as surely as does the north. The north's willingness to sacrifice the south for its own survival will be unacceptable to the developing world, but those nations may lack the political muscle to assert their own views.

As intractable as the problems of the developing nations appear to be, they by themselves do not capture the total political difficulty because, like the gases in the atmosphere, the politics of the greenhouse are global and interactive.

Take for example the issue of the burning of the Brazilian rain forest. In order to develop economically and feed an expanding population, Brazil needs more arable land. Creating of such wealth by destroying the rain forest also helps the country pay its national debt, which in turn helps sustain a worldwide banking industry, much of it located in the United States. But, burning the rain forest contributes to the greenhouse: it adds carbon dioxide to the atmosphere, leaves fewer trees to take the gas from the atmosphere and trap it temporarily, and destroys ecosystems containing important genetic material scientists might use to help mitigate the impact of the greenhouse effect.

But, as the Brazilians well know, people need to eat. Burning the rain forests of the Amazon lessens the potential of food riots in the barrios of Rio. Deforestation places a political premium on short-term security while depleting a long-term resource important to the entire planet.

The ramifications of political decisions made about the greenhouse effect have been likened to ripples in a pond. Perhaps the better metaphor is the storm surge before the hurricane. Knowing the surge is imminent provides some opportunity for mitigation, but not without cost to even the richest of nations. Global mitigation demands global cooperation, a proposition that has always been politically difficult. It is difficult to talk about political solutions, particularly more global ones, without seeming like Pollyanna. The heat of the greenhouse has the potential to temper a new national and international political ethic, if the heat itself doesn't shatter the process into its competing component constituencies.

ANALYZING MEDIA COVERAGE OF THE GREENHOUSE EFFECT

To obtain media coverage of the greenhouse effect for 1987 and 1988, all the stories mentioning the term greenhouse effect were gathered from the New York *Times, Christian Science Monitor,* Washington *Post,* and *Los Angeles Times* using the NEXIS data base. Book and restaurant reviews, one sports story, gardening stories, and stories that mentioned the greenhouse effect only in a tangential fashion were culled. Those stories constituted less than 10 percent of the total sample.

To gather coverage of the greenhouse effect by the three U.S. television networks, stories were obtained from the Vanderbilt Television University archives using a variety of descriptor terms, such as environment, drought, heat wave, forest fires and hurricanes. The Vanderbilt index currently does not categorize stories under the descriptors global warming or greenhouse effect, so synonyms had to be used. From these descriptors, it is assumed that the vast majority of network news stories mentioning the greenhouse effect during 1987 and 1988 were recovered. More than 100 separate stories, almost six hours of television time, were examined. A total of 11 broadcast stories used the term greenhouse effect during those two years.

The unit of analysis in the print media was the individual story, and the content analysis examined the type of story, news peg, general subject matter, harms and benefits associated with the greenhouse effect, number and type of sources cited, and verbal metaphors used. Three coders analyzed the stories in two separate waves and achieved an intercoder reliability of .81 (Holsti, 1969).

In television news coverage the items analyzed were type of story, news peg, harms and benefits, political solutions proposed, use of visual and spoken metaphor, sources used, and story length. Two coders analyzed the broadcast stories, achieving an intercoder reliability of .92 (Holsti, 1969). Because of the small number of television stories, no statistical analysis of television was conducted.

THE GREENHOUSE IN THE MEDIA: 1987

The story of the greenhouse effect in 1987 was a story of science. Of the 71 articles that appeared in the four print publications studied, more than 46 percent were feature stories focusing on the science of the greenhouse effect or the release of the report or study on the topic. Among those issues that received media coverage were studies of the climate on Venus and Mars, particularly those examining the presence or absence of carbon dioxide on the planets' atmospheres as an analogue for climate on earth. Climatologists have dubbed such work "the Goldilocks effect": earth is the only planet where atmospheric carbon dioxide appears to be "just right." Of the remaining stories printed in 1987, 35 percent were news stories, primarily reports of a first in science or the release of a report, while 18 percent were opinion pieces. No analysis pieces appeared in the sample.

This focus on the science of the event also carried over into sourcing patterns. Because the greenhouse stories emphasized science, the top three sources in the 1987 stories were U.S. scientists. This sourcing pattern contrasts significantly with other sorts of environmental stories, where the top sources tend to be government officials (Wilkins, 1987; Wilkins and Patterson, 1990).

The 1987 print coverage of the greenhouse effect also was harm-oriented. More than three-fourths of the stories included a mention of specific harm. Of those, more than 56 percent of the stories included a mention of global warming as a harm resulting from the problem, with an additional 7 percent of the articles including a more general reference to widespread climatic warming. Furthermore, the harms mentioned clustered among those that are dreaded or uncontrollable (Fischhoff et al., 1981).

Coverage of the harms dwelt on the hazards while ignoring the benefits derived from the technology that produced the problem. Air conditioning, refrigeration, automobiles, and industrial production were benefits seldom linked to the problem. As might be expected from such an orientation, any potential benefits of the greenhouse were de-emphasized. Almost two-fifths of the 1987 stories did not include mention of any benefit from the greenhouse, and the benefits most frequently mentioned were the coding categories "spur to international cooperation" and "opportunity for scientific discovery." These more abstract concepts, or the discussion of a more comfortable life style, could not match harms associated with the problem in applicability to individual readers. In short, in the coverage of the greenhouse effect, the risks were dreaded while the benefits were drab.

In 1987 the network news provided only one story about the greenhouse effect. The "Special Segment," which aired April 15 on NBC, was just under five minutes in length and part of a week long series on the environment. The segment was set entirely in the coastal city of Lakeland, Florida, to explain what would happen if the greenhouse scenario became reality. The scenario included temperature increases and the flooding of much of Florida.

Like the print media coverage, the story focused on the science of the greenhouse and included two scientists as sources: one government official and one citizen who said he wasn't worried about the greenhouse effect because he "would be dead then anyway." The greenhouse effect was compared to the changes expected from nuclear war, a metaphor that would surface again in television coverage the next year.

THE WARMING OF THE COVERAGE: 1988

In 1988 the media began to warm to the greenhouse story, sometimes in curious ways. The first evidence of increased attention was in the sheer number of stories that used the term. In 1987 only 71 stories dealt with the issue; 268 stories appeared in 1988 — an increase of 377 percent. In the four publications studied, the New York *Times* printed 84 stories about the greenhouse effect, the *Los Angeles Times* 92 stories, the *Christian Science Monitor* 35 stories, and the Washington *Post* 57. These numbers also reflect a statistically significant shift ($p < .001$), as the *Los Angeles Times* provided more mentions of the greenhouse effect than the New York *Times,* the paper that had dominated greenhouse coverage in 1987.

In addition to the sheer increase in volume, the kind of coverage the issue received also changed. In 1987 the greenhouse story appeared slotted for feature treatment. It wasn't hard news and was seldom opinion. But in 1988 more than 35 percent of the greenhouse stories printed were opinion pieces — many letters to the editor, editorials, and columns. The shift in the type of coverage the issue received was statistically significant at the $p < .001$ level. About 31 percent of the stories were hard news, focusing on the presidential election or the release of a massive EPA study of the greenhouse and its potential political and social impacts. Almost as many stories — about 30 percent — fell into the feature category, many dealing with new scientific findings about the issue. Finally, about 2 percent of the stories were labeled analysis pieces.

In 1988 a debate on policy alternatives replaced science as the dominant news peg for greenhouse stories, a change that was significant at the $p < .001$ level. Only 1.5 percent of the greenhouse stories used scientific discoveries about the greenhouse or a first in science as a peg.

Mention of the issue in the presidential campaign or commentaries about the campaign was the news peg for an additional 11.5 percent of the print stories; debate in Congress or international bodies was the news peg for 10.4 percent of the reports. Stories that focused on the politics of the issue, usually revolving around local or national debates about a variety of potential regulations, were news pegs for 24.6 percent of the stories.

By far the largest percentage of the news accounts, 31.7 percent, fell into the miscellaneous news peg category, in part the result of the large number of letters to the editor. However, certain interest groups, such as foresters and the automobile and coal industries also contributed a substantial number of op ed pieces to the total. These articles generally promoted a certain view of the greenhouse effect and possible mitigation strategies. The foresters, for example, urged Americans to plant millions of trees to cope with the problem, while the auto and coal industries took pains to convince readers that more stringent emissions standards for their industries would not alleviate the problem and, as stated in some more extreme arguments, might actually make things worse.

However, the top three sources in the greenhouse stories did not reflect this gravitation away from the science of the issue. Scientists remained the top source for greenhouse information, followed by U.S. government officials.

The 1988 print coverage continued the harm orientation of the 1987 stories. About 75 percent of the stories mentioned at least one harm associated with the greenhouse effect. The most frequently mentioned harm was global warming (47 percent of the stories), followed by widespread climatic change and pollution. Of those stories that listed two or more harms associated with the problem — 18 percent — global warming was again the most frequently mentioned second order harm, followed by widespread climatic change and drought. Nine percent of the stories listed three or more harms for the greenhouse effect, with a rise in ocean levels and drought the most popular of the third order harms. More than 22 percent of the 1988 stories listed four or more harms associated with the greenhouse effect. A relatively small number of stories, 46, mentioned drought as one problem associated with the greenhouse effect, but almost none of those stories linked the 1988 drought specifically to the greenhouse effect.

Television's coverage reflected shifts similar to those found in the print media. In 1988 the three networks broadcast ten stories, totaling 23 minutes and 10 seconds of air time, focused on or mentioning the greenhouse effect. Six of these were on NBC; CBS and ABC aired two each. All were pegged to either political events — a June 23 congressional hearing on the greenhouse effect, an October 20 EPA report, a presidential campaign story focusing on the environmental challenges that either contender would face if elected, and a late November meeting between President-elect Bush and environmental groups — or the summer heat wave, a peg for six of the ten stories.

The stories themselves were of average length — 2 minutes, 20 seconds — and none ran 5 minutes in length. Only one story led a newscast. By comparison, Patterson (1989) found that more than half of all Chernobyl stories ran more than five minutes in length, and Wilkins (1987) found that the Bhopal, India, disaster was one of the top three stories in network newscasts 70.8 percent of the time a Bhopal story aired.

Common metaphors in television coverage included comparing the greenhouse effect with nuclear war and the dust bowl. Visually, the stories relied heavily on direct shots of the sun, shots of haze and smokestacks, shots of endangered nature and wildlife, and frequent graphic schematics illustrating the physical impact of greenhouse gases on the planet.

Television coverage, like that provided by the print media, was harm oriented. The harms that were most frequently mentioned, such as global warming, a change in ecosystems, drought, and flooding, were dread harms. Unlike print coverage, television reports were pessimistic about the role international agreements might play in alleviating some of the more serious greenhouse problems.

The sourcing patterns in television coverage also reflected those of the print media. Scientists dominated the news reports, followed by government officials and interest group representatives.

MEDIA LOGIC: THE NUANCES OF NORMS

There were some additional subtleties in the media coverage of the greenhouse effect as the story moved from 1987 through 1988.

Because in 1987 the greenhouse issue was almost exclusively a science story, it was reported and written primarily by science writers. Their coverage was far from perfect. For example, most of the stories failed to describe the greenhouse effect as an interactive phenomenon. Almost all failed to make the centrally important point that the problem is largely one of humanity's making. And, a group of stories focused on the debate within the scientific community — the dueling scientists scenario (Friedman, Dunwoody, and Rogers, 1986) — while obscuring the fact that the greenhouse theory itself is well accepted and that the vast bulk of scientific debate centers not on whether the greenhouse effect itself is real, but the precise extent of future disruption.

But while these were important failures of depth and analysis, the print greenhouse coverage in 1987 did a good job of recounting the science of the issue as it was known and being discussed by scientists. The story seldom strayed from a strictly scientific focus, and as such it was handled well.

However, by the early months of 1988 the national context had changed, a result of elite influence in at least two specific areas. The first was political. Albert Gore, Jr., who ran an unsuccessful campaign for the Democratic party's nomination to the presidency, had made the environment and specifically the greenhouse effect a part of his political platform. His campaign took the issue from among the myriad of environmental causes and attempted to place it squarely in the political spotlight. Gore had support in the Senate from Colorado Democrat Tim Wirth, and several other senators also became involved with the issue. By the end of that year, 32 separate bills that dealt in some way with global warming had been introduced in either the House or the Senate. While only some minor acts became law, for example, a bill resolving land disputes for a Washington Indian tribe, the greenhouse issue had at least become a minor part of the congressional agenda.

But Congress wasn't working alone. While the scientific community continued to refine computer models to produce more geographically accurate long-range forecasts, certain scientists began to assert that the greenhouse was at least as political as it was scientific. These visible scientists testified before congressional committees and spoke to the media. For example, Steve Schneider of Boulder's National Center for Atmospheric Research testified before eight congressional committees between August 1988 and May 1989 (Schneider, 1989b). What had once been an arcane scientific debate was now being championed by articulate politicians and scientists. The result was that the story moved out of the science columns and into areas of political and economic policy. Science writers no longer controlled the majority of greenhouse coverage, and the change in authorship was evident in how the story was written and reported.

When the greenhouse stories weren't written by science writers, they lost much of their scientific depth, and the chances to link specific scientific findings to policy options were lost. The greenhouse effect was often explained too simplistically as the result of burning fossil fuels, but the burning was seldom linked to a high-energy life style. In addition, the other greenhouse gases, with their links to food and certain types of industrial production, were seldom mentioned. When nonscience writers covered the stories, they lost much of their potential political edge and depth.

Furthermore, when the interest groups got hold of the story on the op ed pages, they often offered a technological fix — planting trees, nuclear power, refusing to stringently regulate auto emissions — as a mitigation strategy without first identifying the tangled roots of the problem.

Television, much more so than the print media, tied the greenhouse effect directly to humanity's burning of fossil fuels. Other components of the problem —indeed greenhouse gases other than carbon dioxide — were mentioned only once in television news reports. Television offered conflicting visual symbols. The common visual metaphor of polluted skies, industrial smokestacks, and parched crop land was unequivocally bad news. But other shots common in greenhouse coverage, for example, people sunbathing on the beach, the sun, and apparently healthy plant life, are generally thought of as pleasant and desirable. Television's words made it plain that these desirable things were in danger, but the visual information presented a mixed message. Television's pictures could not always sustain its words, and it is reasonable to question how the average viewer might have interpreted these stories, particularly when they appeared relatively late in the newscast.

However, in the summer of 1988 the small screen provided viewers with a wonderful insight into the potential of the greenhouse century. There was the summer drought. There was Hurricane Gilbert, an unusually intense storm. And there were the Yellowstone forest fires. In all, network television devoted more than 150 separate stories, more than seven hours of total air time, to these events. But only five stories pegged the greenhouse effect directly to the drought and heat wave. None linked the greenhouse to Gilbert or to the forest fires. Television explained what the greenhouse century might bring, but it aired the concept itself only ten times.

WHAT SHOULD WE EXPECT FROM THE NEWS?

The greenhouse effect definitely became news in 1988, but it had not yet been transformed into a political symbol capable of generating choices among options and establishing relative importance. The lack of symbolic power was due, in part, to journalistic and scientific norms — to the political detriment of the issue.

Due to its interdisciplinary nature, the greenhouse effect ran into the same problems with reporters and editors as it had years before with traditional scientists. It fell between the cracks. It was too much a part of somebody else's beat or area of scientific expertise for one group of journalists or scientists to cover all the angles well.

The science writers knew the science, and in both 1987 and 1988 they reported that science accurately. In fact, although some 1988 coverage reported scientists questioning the greenhouse theory itself, the 1988 coverage by science writers no longer focused on dueling scientists disputing the theory but rather on the detailed working out of the greenhouse scenario. The tone was one of scientific certainty, although details continued to remain clouded.

But, the science writers either didn't understand the politics of the greenhouse, believed politics was not pertinent to what they were reporting, or were unwilling to tread on some other reporter's turf to get the political side of the story. This unwillingness to grapple with political questions came despite the fact that at least some scientists were insisting that the greenhouse has important political ramifications.

The political and economic writers' stories reflected the same problem. Because the science was not covered, the politics lost its edge. Indeed, in 1988 an in-depth discussion of the political potential of the greenhouse seldom appeared in news columns but it became the province of editorial writers, who did an adequate job with the political story but who reach a relatively limited, elite audience. The fact that congressional and scientific elites also appeared to warm to the issue in 1988 may indicate that the editorial writers were talking to, or at least reinforcing, other elites. But, the average reader, viewer, and voter may well have been left out of that conversation, at least if public opinion polls taken in mid-1989 are accurate.

In 1988 the greenhouse story became a victim of the specialized journalistic beat system. Environmental reporting requires a grasp of both science and politics and an ability to report well about an array of interconnected issues. Few journalists made the attempt, which left the door open for interest groups to provide their own slant on the issue, a slant frequently incomplete and often misleading. But, if the greenhouse coverage was undermined by traditional journalistic ways of operating, it was equally devastated by the norms of doing careful science. The drought of 1988 is a perfect example.

The drought provided perhaps the best opportunity for the media to find an event with which to link the greenhouse effect with Congress and the White House. The drought could have become a critical event in much the same way that the Three Mile Island accident and the Bhopal disaster became critical events for nuclear and chemical industries, policy makers, and the public. But, the media did not link the drought and the greenhouse effect, and that failure wasn't the result of bad reporting but, in fact, of its opposite.

Schneider, who fielded many calls from reporters wanting to know if the greenhouse effect caused the drought, explained that one particular drought could not be linked to the greenhouse effect, that the effect itself would make things a little hotter than normal, that the throw of the dice indicated the probabilities were good that more droughts would occur, but that this particular drought, or any particular drought, could not be specifically linked to the greenhouse effect (Schneider, 1989b).

Schneider, and other scientists around the country who answered similar questions, were doing good science. Journalists, at least those who worked for the print and broadcast outlets examined in this study, responded by doing good journalism.

Not only had the greenhouse fallen through the cracks in the journalistic beat system, but caution of the scientific sources for the story, the sources that dominated coverage in 1987 and 1988, precluded asking some important political questions because a factual linkage was never a certainty. It was only about six months later, when NASA's Jim Hansen raised the ire of his scientific colleagues by asserting that he was 99 percent certain that the drought of 1988 had been caused by the greenhouse, that journalists got the link they needed. But by that time the warm summer was a memory, and the summer of 1989, because it was generally cooler, never provided the event necessary to fire a mediated debate. Not all scientists involved in the debate believe the media have been intentionally remiss.

"The problems with most press coverage, I believe, reflect the demands of their audience for entertainment or brevity more than a conscious conspiracy of journalists to reduce the complexity of modern life to slogans that will fit on bumper stickers" (Schneider, 1989a, pp. 217–18).

However, the problems with media coverage of the greenhouse run deeper than the audience's admittedly limited attention span and poor understanding of science. The norms of careful science and the norms of journalistic accuracy gutted the story of most of its political meaning in 1987 and 1988. The demands of the various mediums studied — television's need for visuals and print's commitment to a separation of its analytic and reportorial roles — compounded the problem.

American society expects much from the mass media, and when the subject was the greenhouse effect, many of those expectations were fulfilled. News accounts were generally accurate and restrained, although there were predictable failures of depth and analysis. Editorials and commentary attempted to place the issue in political perspective. The resulting impact on public perception and policy appears to have been negligible. In the absence of intense media attention the greenhouse effect failed to advance beyond the agenda-setting stage, either for the public or for policy-making elites. It has not come near the priming stage, where it must arrive before serious policy making involving the public can begin.

Many of society's problems such as the homeless, world hunger, and the like come with built-in symbols. However, such symbols are not readily available for many ecological problems such as global warming, desertification, soil erosion, and ozone depletion. The lack of this symbol is keeping the newest player in the political process — the media — from helping political and scientific elites as well as the public become involved in policy making. In the absence of a symbol for the greenhouse effect, the media, particularly network television, is limited in its interest and its impact.

Symbol formation is not a function usually ascribed to the mass media. When the media do manage to aid that process, scholarly evaluations tend to be at least as critical as they are laudatory. But the greenhouse effect continues to remain an issue in search of a mediated political symbol. Until it can find one, the question of whether political and scientific elites will be willing to act, particularly considering the complexity of the short-term problems facing both groups, will remain open. And that reluctance means political trouble for all of the earth's inhabitants in the greenhouse century.

12

Disasters and the Making of Political Careers

SUE O'BRIEN

"There's a fire in Malibu. It's perfect!"

In the 1972 film *The Candidate,* this announcement from an aide propels a U.S. Senate challenger played by Robert Redford into a breathless visit to the scene of a wildfire, where he hopes to grab votes and visuals to fuel his campaign. Thus, filmmakers freeze in time the image the Kennedys added to the visual vocabulary of American politics: the energetic candidate, suit jacket slung carelessly over one shoulder, swinging down from a helicopter to inspect the disaster scene.

In addition to providing dramatic photo opportunities, natural disasters offer citizens the chance to scrutinize the character and capacity of elected leaders. An everyday local politician can take on a larger than life dimension, whether as hero or hapless victim, as reporters spin their stories of crisis and response.

The belief that disasters open windows into politicians' souls often shapes voter decisions. "People think they can read character or fundamental intention" in times of crisis, said *Almanac of Politics* co-author Grant Ujifusa (personal communication, July 13, 1989). Unlike routine events, which can be manipulated by their principals, accidental events are beyond the players' control and can reveal more than the actors want to show (Molotch and Lester, 1974):

For people in everyday life, the accident is an important resource for learning about the routines of those who ordinarily possess the psychic and physical resources to shield their private lives from public view. The Ted Kennedy car accident gave the public access to that individual's private activities and dispositions (p. 109).

Similarly, presidential scholar Tom Cronin identifies the paradoxical public expectation that a leader will reassure but accentuate a sense of crisis: "Although a president is expected to exude hope, reassurance, and an I'm OK we're OK sense of confidence, the public nevertheless likes to see presidents visibly wrestling with crises" (1980, p. 16).

The official faced with crisis or disaster, then, enters a period of real political risk. "The wrong move or a misspoken word at a crucial moment can damage a career," wrote *Los Angeles Times* Sacramento bureau chief George Skelton (1989), citing former California governors Edmund G. (Pat) Brown and his son, Jerry:

The senior Brown, touring a catastrophic North Coast flood during his second term, proclaimed to the news media that "this is the worst disaster since I was elected governor." Everybody got a good laugh except Brown and his advisers.

Two decades later, his governor son became the subject of ridicule and criticism for not taking the Med fly seriously and delaying spraying until the tiny fruit pest had spread almost out of control. His career suffered severely and he lost a Senate bid in 1982 (p. A3).

Unforeseen catastrophes often serve as internal triggers for issue formation and help shape the domestic agenda (Cobb and Elder, 1983). Problems move onto the public agenda only when they are perceived as being amenable to human action. To win support, one side in a political battle may portray a difficulty as within reach of human intervention while rival political actors seek "to push it away from intent toward the realm of nature or to show that the problem was intentionally caused by someone else" (Stone, 1989, p. 293).

Abney and Hill (1966) observe that a political crisis created by natural disaster can "test whether a government's output capabilities can accommodate the resulting strain or will fail, causing one regime to replace another" (p. 980). But the researchers' Hurricane Betsy study also found that officials are not automatically harmed by natural disasters.

Indeed, disasters can create winners. The 1989 northern California earthquake, for instance, provided what the *New Republic* called a rare opportunity "for politicians to show their stuff." Art Agnos, mayor of San Francisco, was clearly a winner: "His take-charge manner when the real disaster struck made people think even a liberal politician can be strong, composed, and in control" (Bradley, 1989, p. 15).

Although relatively few emergencies can conclusively be said to have conferred lasting harm or help on politicians, a significant handful have had the power to make or break public careers. This chapter will explore why public officials have been held accountable for the response to some disasters but permitted to escape responsibility in others.

RESEARCH FINDINGS

Finding Someone to Blame

Scholarly findings on the political impact of disasters have been mixed. In general, politicians with highly visible involvement have gained electoral support, but results are not consistent. Although several officials seen as failing to secure adequate federal aid were punished at the polls, other leaders perceived as performing well also suffered setbacks. "These anomalies suggest voter reactions to politicians' involvement are not simply rewards for good intentions" (May 1985, 120).

Nor are they simply punishments for presumed bad intentions; there is no scholarly consensus on the mechanisms voters use to assess blame. Rank-and-file citizen reactions to disasters range from "docile dependency" to "aggressive irritability," which Janis characterizes as a "readiness to give vent to angry resentment, and heated condemnation, particularly of local officials" (1954, p. 19). Studying the Coconut Grove fire, Veltfort and Lee found that by blaming club owners and public officials — scapegoating — citizens may have been able to enhance their own self esteem (p. 150).

Other scholars, however, say intense anger develops only when the office holder is shown to have been culpable. Bucher (1957) argues that the primary purpose in assigning blame is to prevent reoccurrence, and that the assignment of responsibility tends to be shifted upward in the authority hierarchy. But once responsibility is attributed, she contends, two additional elements are necessary for blame to be cast: first, those who cast blame must be convinced the responsible agents will not take remedial action on their own; second, the responsible agents must be seen as having a reprehensible character or motive.

This tendency to blame "our problems on the inadequacies or guilt of individuals rather than on systems or institutions" is deeply imbedded in society (Drabek and Quarantelli, 1967, p. 17). But although the motive may be to prevent future disasters, the result may distract from corrective action: "A spotlighting by the mass media may give the appearance of action and actually drain off the energy and time that might have led to action" (p. 16).

Courting Political Credit

In a variation of scapegoating, several state and local officials have managed to sidestep blame by passing the buck to Washington. In the Hurricane Agnes aftermath, Pennsylvania Governor Milton Schapp became an outspoken critic of federal recovery policies. The resignation of federal Housing and Urban Development Secretary George A. Romney was widely believed to have been precipitated by a nationally publicized news conference shouting match. Romney urged "pull yourself up by your bootstraps" solutions; Schapp and leaders of the victims' flood recovery task force disagreed (Wolensky, 1984; Wolensky and Miller, 1983).

Although she was ultimately to lose her 1980 primary, Washington Governor Dixy Lee Ray apparently gained points with voters through her efforts to increase the level of federal assistance to Mount St. Helens victims. Senator Warren Magnuson, who was perceived as controlling the federal aid spigot, saw his standing decline (May 1985). During the Three Mile Island nuclear power plant emergency in 1979, then-Pennsylvania Governor Richard Thornburg, reflecting reporters' and residents' frustration with confusing messages from the Nuclear Regulatory Commission, finally persuaded the White House to centralize all federal communications on the accident (Friedman, 1989; Sandman and Paden, 1984).

Voters appear to expect some political jockeying — it's important for office holders to deliver the aid their constituents expect — but attempts to exploit emergencies evoke suspicion. The suggestion that Illinois Attorney General Tyrone Fahner might have been using the Tylenol poisonings investigation to aid his flagging re-election campaign (Nimmo, 1985) probably neutralized any advantage the publicity might have brought him. New Orleans voters saw challenger James Fitzmorris's attempt to use the floods from Hurricane Betsy against embattled Mayor Victor Schiro as a subversion of the process (Abney and Hill, 1966, p. 980).

The Politics of Disaster Relief and Preparedness

Emergency management has essentially no continuing political constituency. Elected officials can rarely commit to any mitigation or relief promises that extend beyond the next election. They are likely to invest their political capital only in projects that offer significant short-term benefit and to avoid steps that carry more risk than benefit, such as efforts to decrease hazards through stringent land use or zoning codes (Waugh, 1990).

The low probability of disasters also reduces the salience public officials accord emergency planning (Cigler, 1988; Cigler and Burby, 1990). Local government respondents are much less inclined than federal and state officials to rank natural hazards as likely risks; the odds of any single municipality suffering disaster are too low. Thus, the "intergovernmental paradox" arises to bedevil emergency management specialists: "The government officials least likely to perceive emergency management as a key priority — local officials — are at center stage in terms of responsibility for dealing with emergencies" (Cigler and Burby, 1990, p. 59).

Just as important, local government has a lot of other things to worry about (Rossi, Wright, and Weber-Burdin, 1982, pp. 45–46):

> First, they [natural hazards problems] are but a handful among a very large set of problems clamoring for attention and resources, and second, they are not seen to be, in general, among the most serious problems (see also Wolensky, 1984).

Very little publicly accessible polling has studied the link between disaster management and political approval. Analysts are therefore left to speculate. Mayor Agnos suddenly appeared on the California poll's recognition scales with a 55 percent positive rating in late 1989. He was so little known, he hadn't been included in previous image polls, said Mark DiCamillo of the Field Institute. "But the [October 1989] earthquake vaulted him in high prominence in California and around the nation" ("Agnos Now," 1989). The continuing decline in Vice President Dan Quayle's showing on the California survey, however, could only be speculatively linked to his highly publicized spat with Agnos in the aftermath of the earthquake (Barabak, 1989).

Politics is considered the art of the possible, and the existing research indicates that voters base their decisions on what is and what is not possible. They clearly make distinctions between appropriate and inappropriate responses to various sorts of disasters. When voters believe politicians can do something to lessen the impact of a disaster or prevent a reoccurrence, they expect that action. But when events are literally out of human control, voters appear willing to forgive and forget come election time.

ILLUSTRATIVE CASES

Observers have attributed political impact to a broad array of natural and human-caused disasters, including hurricanes, earthquakes, the Med fly, prison riots, Three Mile Island, tornados, and volcanic eruptions. This chapter will concentrate on snowstorms, which have relatively mild consequences to life and property but grievous political impact, and floods, which are generally conceded to be the most serious of the frequently occurring natural disasters.

Snow

"As natural disasters go, snow storms don't rank very high," the Washington *Post* editorialized in 1979. "As political disasters, however, they rank considerably higher" ("Snow and Politics").

Perhaps the nation's two most prominent mayoral victims of snowstorms are Chicago Mayor Michael Bilandic, who was stunned by political novice Jane Byrne in his 1979 primary, and Denver Mayor Bill McNichols, who didn't make the run-off in his 1983 re-election bid.

Chicago

The seven feet of snow that landed on Chicago in January 1979 buried the city for weeks and started to smother the political machine that had been struggling since Mayor Richard B. Daley died in 1976. Chicago's proud "the city that works" boast suffered as Bilandic, the machine's new mayor, failed to collect the garbage, get the transit system running, and clear the snow. But voters' patience snapped when the *Chicago Tribune* revealed that Bilandic had paid a former city hall crony $90,000 to prepare an ineffectual snow removal plan ("Lady," 1979; Peirce and Hagstrom, 1983). In the February 27 primary, angry Democrats snatched their mayoral nomination from Bilandic and gave it to Byrne, who Bilandic had fired as city consumer affairs commissioner when she charged him with "greasing" a taxi fare increase (Blumenthal, 1982; "Lady," 1979).

Had the snow not wreaked such havoc, Byrne probably could not have beaten Bilandic. In his postelection analysis, New York *Times* reporter Douglas Kneeland concluded, "It was widely acknowledged by both Byrne and Bilandic supporters that this would not have been much of a race if voters had not been angered by City Hall's inability to keep the streets cleared" (February 28, 1979 p. A1). Public opinion polls of the time confirmed this view. A CBS poll taken immediately after the storm showed Byrne ahead of Bilandic 50 to 38 percent with 12 percent undecided, "a sharp reversal from a similar poll taken three weeks earlier" (Kneeland, February 25, 1979, p. A1).

Byrne's campaign could not have asked for a more graphic example than the snow to show voters the problems, corruption, and inefficiencies in the Bilandic administration. "When things stopped working it was everything people feared when Daley died," said Byrne campaign manager Don Rose. "We capitalized on that anxiety" (Blumenthal, 1982, p. 126).

While Byrne played up Bilandic's snow-handling problems, the embattled mayor did not help his own cause. One mistake was making nightly television appearances to tout his nonexistent "snow command" and proclaim everything to be fine ("Lady," 1979; "Snow and Politics," 1979). Another was claiming to have been crucified by the media. "It's our turn," he told a group of supporters, "to see if we are made of the same stuff as the early Christians, the persecuted Jews, the proud Poles, the blacks and Latinos" (Coyne, 1979). Perhaps his biggest mistake, however, was repeatedly lashing out at his critics: "'Many citizens have responded well but unfortunately many have not,' the Mayor said angrily on Tuesday" (Sheppard, 1979). "There is no such thing as a perfect plan . . . no matter what you read in Pravda," he said in another outburst (Kneeland, January 31, 1979).

It is unclear whether Chicagoans would have blamed Bilandic so harshly for the city's snow problems had Byrne not turned them into campaign sound bites and photo opportunities. Most commentators agree that Byrne would not have won without the snow (see Barone and Ujifusa, 1981; Coyne, 1979; Kneeland, March 2, 1979; and Peirce and Hagstrom, 1983 among others).

Byrne, however, contends she could have won without the snow, using issues like health care and transportation to illustrate her gibe that "the city that works" didn't. "To me, had it not been the snow, it would have been something else" (personal communication, March 1, 1990).

"It was not the snow which defeated Bilandic but his conduct toward the snow," Rose told United Press International (UPI) (Smothers, 1981). "He was arrogant, trying to pretend everything was just wonderful. . . . I'd have had him out shoveling his walk and helping his neighbors shovel."

Denver

Seventy-two-year-old Bill McNichols was in his fourteenth year as mayor of Denver and facing another re-election bid when a storm dropped more than two feet of snow on the city on Christmas Eve, 1982. Denver and much of the surrounding suburban area was paralyzed. Stapleton Airport, one of the nation's busiest air terminals, was closed, stranding thousands of holiday travelers. Streets and highways were snow blocked. Neither the Denver *Post* nor the *Rocky Mountain News* was published on December 25 because of concern for their employees' safety in getting to work and distributing the paper.

When the *Post* published again on December 26, its front page headline was prophetic: "Snow Removal Expected to Take Days." By December 27 — "Chaos Feared in Downtown Parking" — the first negative comments on the city administration's response to the storm appeared in print.

For the next several weeks, negative coverage of snow removal predominated. City officials denied early rumors that some snow removal equipment was not used or functioning. When a reporter asked why more roads had not been cleared by December 26, McNichols sounded almost like Bilandic: "If we'd have had 400 plows, they wouldn't have done any good. You can't plow automobiles" (Denver *Post,* December 27).

And when McNichols promised performance, he had to backtrack. On December 27 he predicted all residential streets would be cleared by December 31 if there were no setbacks. The next day, he pushed his target "well into next week." The city eventually stopped plowing January 2. "His attitude is 'Who the hell cares,'" one voter told the *Post.* "'He'll find out'" (January 3).

Asked early in the clean-up if snow problems might hurt his re-election chances, McNichols said snow removal was outside the realm of politics: "If you're going to judge politics by what nature does, we better change the system" ("If that's not," 1982).

But politics entered in earnest December 30, when the *Post* surveyed the mayor's rivals. Challengers' criticisms focused on the snow removal plan or the alleged lack of a plan, mismanagement, a failure to lead, a 36-hour delay in opening the emergency storm center, and the use of city crews to plow private parking lots. The mayor's defense, as summarized, was that there was an emergency plan, but this was a 100-year storm. On December 31, the front pages featured reports that the city had violated its storm plan by ignoring the weather forecast as the holiday approached. Other city officials — not the mayor — responded to this new round of criticism.

And the crisis dragged on. A January 5 *Post* editorial cartoon showed a woman pushing a car out of a snowbank while the befuddled male driver listened to a radio newscaster: "The mayor announced today that the streets are clear. The snow has blown away to Seattle, he explained." On January 6, the city was still logging more than 1,000 complaints a day about snow removal.

Of 1,366 storm stories printed or broadcast during the 31 days from December 21, 1982, to January 21, 1983, researcher Lee Wilkins (1985) found that about 25 percent advanced the theme that individuals could do little to reduce the impact of the crisis; 11 percent suggested local officials could and should be taking action. "The majority of the stories," Wilkins wrote, "portrayed the individual, even local government, as helpless against the onslaught of nature." Even the "heartening" number of stories — 148 — that addressed rehabilitation actually "concerned the impact Denver's snow-clogged streets would have on the upcoming city mayoral election" (pp. 62–63).

The snowstorm was prominent in stories reporting McNichols's February 28 announcement that he was running for a fourth term:

> Like Mr. Daley when he was Mayor of Chicago, Mr. McNichols has sought to project an image of Denver as a city that works. And, like Chicago in 1979, lingering public resentment over the city's failure to deal with the effects of a major snowstorm Christmas Eve poses one of the most serious threats to Mr. McNichols's re-election (Schmidt, March 1, 1983).

During the campaign, however, the issue was relatively quiet, although it lurked in the background of many stories. As in Chicago, the piled-up snow had come to symbolize a mountain of complaints about city hall's ineptitude, including a police bingo scandal. Like Bilandic, McNichols never made it to the general election. He finished a distant third in a seven-candidate field in the May 7 mayoral primary.

In the face of the other scandals and complaints that hit the McNichols administration in its last months, there will never be consensus on whether the snow caused his defeat. There's little dispute that it cinched his downfall. "After the paralysis of the Christmas blizzard," the New York *Times* later wrote, "it was not the snow but Mayor McNichols' springtime re-election bid that melted away" (Schmidt, November 30, 1983).

McNichols attributes his re-election problems more to a "hostile" media environment than to the storm itself. If the newspapers hadn't been able to criticize him for the clean-up, he suggests, "they could have found anything they wanted to" (personal communication, May 1, 1990).

Other Snow Victims

It isn't hard to make political mistakes during a blizzard. At least two other big city mayors have felt winter's nip. Washington, D.C., Mayor Marion Barry's first troubles with snow were with God's kind. The Washington storm began on Thursday, January 22, 1987, while Barry was in southern California at the Super Bowl. He was still at the Beverly Hills Hilton the next Tuesday, when he confided to reporters that he'd been working too hard and planned to take more time off in the future (Barone and Ujifusa, 1987; Sherwood, 1987). The mayor came home to a barrage of local and national media criticism.

> USA Today, complete with a color photograph of Barry on the front page, headlined, "D.C. Mayor Takes Heat in Cold Snap," and The New York Times made the city out to be an inept hick southern town. Jack Nelson, bureau chief here for The Los Angeles Times, held aloft an "Impeach Barry" bumper sticker at the close of "Washington Week in Review" (Sherwood, 1987).

Finally, a week after the storm hit, Barry moved to curb the political damage, but the effectiveness of that effort was never tested. His campaign for an unprecedented fourth term was permanently altered with his January 18, 1990, arrest on charges of cocaine possession (Ayres, 1990; see also Washington Post, January 1–22, 1987).

New York City Mayor John Lindsay, long associated with the upscale residents of Manhattan and the blacks and Hispanics of the city's ghettos, wasn't popular with the middle class residents of the outer boroughs to begin with. When the mayor appeared unable to clear 15 inches of snow from their streets in February 1969, "Queens homeowners screamed bloody murder" (Barone, Ujifusa, and Matthews, 1974, p. 648; see also Hentoff, 1969).

And Queens voters showed their anger during the Republican primary that June, denying Lindsay the GOP nomination in his race for a second term. Although he eventually won re-election running on the Liberal party ticket, "snow was a political liability which, some say, dogged him to his defeat in 1973" (Kidder, 1981; "New York," 1969).

Snowstorm Winners

At least as instructive are the stories of those few political officeholders who have had neutral or beneficial exposure to winter storms. The once in a century Great Blizzard that ravaged New England in February 1978 could have been ordered especially to help the second term re-election campaign of Massachusetts Governor Michael Dukakis. The governor donned a crew neck sweater and set up a full-time storm command center. "He came across on television as calm, understanding, and in charge," report biographers Charles Kenney and Robert Turner. "It was the kind of sustained positive publicity that politicians dream about" (1988, pp. 107–9).

But the snow-inspired popularity melted away. Conservative Democrat Edward J. King defeated the governor 51 percent to 42 percent in the primary and went on to win the governorship in November (Barone and Ujifusa, 1981, 1983). Why didn't Dukakis's popularity stick? Biographer Turner speculates that the take-charge behavior may, in retrospect, have seemed heavy-handed. Whatever seeds had been planted during the blizzard may not have been cultivated: "To the extent to which he showed leadership then, I don't think that they reinforced that and reminded people of it" (personal communication, March 15, 1990).

What Nebraskans were to call the "storm of the century" hit on January 10, 1975. With 60-mile-per-hour winds and 19 inches of new snow, the storm buried Omaha beneath snow drifts that rose to 10 feet (Omaha City Planning Department, 1977). Coupled with a tornado that hit the city on May 6, the blizzard is widely given credit for propelling Omaha's popular mayor Edward Zorinsky into the U.S. Senate (Ehrenhalt, 1981; Kotok, 1987).

The mayor's activities ranged from apologizing in advance for the exigencies of snow removal ("We hope citizens will bear with us, because snow is going to be plowed right onto private property and will block driveways") to urging citizens to establish a buddy system to get to work through snow-clogged streets (Omaha *World-Herald,* 1975).

The *World-Herald* summed up Zorinsky's accomplishments in a May 16 editorial:

> Zorinsky's method of operation has let it be shown that someone competent is in charge — a vital consideration in a time of confusion and crisis when people look for the symbolism as well as the substance of leadership and direction.
>
> The mayor has asked that Sunday be a day of rest for those who have labored so hard in the funnels' path. We suggest he take the day off, too — he

has earned it, as well as the respect of the community for a chief executive who has lived up to the title.

Flood

Snow did not make the list when Rossi and colleagues (1982) set out to study the political salience of natural disasters. Even flooding, ranked as the most serious of the emergencies measured, made it only to twelfth place when rated nationally. In communities with a recent history of flooding or hurricane-caused flooding, however, the story was different. Hurricanes ranked as the number one problem in Louisiana; floods came in second in Pennsylvania, where tropical storm Agnes's 1972 flooding was heavy, and fourth in Colorado, where the Big Thompson Canyon flash flood hit in 1976.

Coleman (1957) argued that, in addition to higher salience, floods also have the ability to unify communities. In contrast to drought, for example, which can drive a community into despair, defeat, and controversy, a flood "seldom divides a community," Coleman wrote. "It affects all men much the same, pits them all against a common enemy" (p. 4).

In snowstorms, heroes are rare and scapegoats common. In crises cause by floods, however, many officials have consolidated their relationships with constituents.

Rapid City

The June 9, 1972, flash flood roared down Rapid Creek, burst an earthen dam, and crashed through Rapid City, killing 238 people and destroying or damaging from 1,500 to 2,100 homes (Federal Emergency Management Agency, 1987; Toman, 1972). Mayor Donald B. Barnett had been on the job for only 14 months.

Barnett, then 29 years old, later told reporters that a man 18 miles west of the city had telephoned to tell him a wall of water was headed downstream. Subsequent reports depict the mayor springing into action, issuing warnings by radio and television, sending police and guardsmen to alert threatened neighborhoods, and going house to house himself, urging residents to flee.

As the floodwater finally began to seep away, Barnett faced reporters "at the east edge of Canyon Lake, on what was left of an earthen dam":

> "We've only been out of the life-saving racket for about 10 hours," Barnett said. "Now the body search is under way. Then we'll do what we have to do next.

"I'm proud to be the mayor of this city," Barnett said. "I'm proud to show the strength we've shown here. I'm proud of the wonderful character of the citizens and their willingness to help others. . . . And, God, am I tired!" (Denver *Post,* June 12, 1972).

Meanwhile, South Dakota Senator George McGovern interrupted his presidential campaign to visit the "incredible destruction" at home. McGovern, who was about to lock down the Democratic presidential nomination, brought a full national press contingent trailing in his wake. As reported by the *Los Angeles Times,* the symbolism was familiar: "In a subsequent walking tour of the flood site, McGovern stripped off his jacket and loosened his tie in the June heat that was rapidly turning the endless mud to dust" (Cooper, 1972).

At the same time in Washington, President Richard Nixon ordered expedited aid for the flood-stricken city, dispatching advisor Robert Finch to represent him at the scene and First Lady Pat Nixon to attend a June 19 memorial service for the victims (Denver *Post,* June 11, 12, 1972; *Sioux Falls Argus Leader,* June 12, 19, 1972; see also the *Rapid City Journal,* June 11, 13, 19, 20).

Within a week after the flood, Barnet recalls, "politicians and politics were starting to raise their heads" (personal communication, May 12, 1990). South Dakota Democrats were beginning to criticize the Republican administration's aid effort, so the mayor issued a press statement: "And I told the politicians of South Dakota to keep their mouths shut, that we had too much grief and too many people on the missing list and if this got to be political the only losers were going to be the flood victims."

As the recovery progressed, Barnett and Governor Richard Kneip appealed for private contributions to aid the victims and raised a new theme: preserving Black Hills tourism (Denver *Post,* June 22, 1972). Barnett used an appearance on NBC'S "Today" show to encourage tourist visits:

I went five minutes on how the bridges are open and Mount Rushmore's there and, God, the nation's been wonderful to send all the donations and now you gotta take your vacation here. And boy, my stock just went through the roof all over South Dakota, but I wasn't running for anything (personal communication, May 12, 1990).

When Barnett went for a second mayoral term in April 1973, he won in a walk: no Republican candidate emerged to oppose him. "That's significant impact," says political consultant Jody Severson, a former aide to Senator James Abourezk. "He was the town hero. So it's not surprising he wouldn't have any opposition" (personal communication, May 13, 1990).

Barnett, however, balks at claiming the flood response as a political plus and points instead to a booming postflood economy, fueled by $170 million in federal reconstruction aid. "I don't want to say that the flood *per se* made me a hero and got me re-elected without an opponent, but the economy was pretty damn good" (personal communication, May 12, 1990).

By 1978, when Barnett got only 33 percent of the vote in a Senate race against Republican Larry Pressler (Barone and Ujifusa, 1981), most observers agree the flood was no longer relevant to voter decisions. Further, Barnett had specifically instructed his campaign staff not to raise the flood as an issue (Barnett and Severson, personal communication, May 8, 1990; J. Harrington, personal communication, May 11, 1990).

Other Flood Beneficiaries

The literature of floods is rich with heroes. But, although floods have stimulated institutional change, relatively few individuals have been punished by press or public for contributing to a flood disaster or mismanaging community response. Among those who appear to have gained credit with constituents for their response to floods are two governors from the west.

Bruce Babbitt was Arizona's third governor in less than five months. He followed Raul Castro, who resigned, and Castro's successor, Wesley Bolin, who died March 4, 1978, of a sudden heart attack. Before Bolin died he had declared a state of emergency and activated the National Guard to evacuate flooded areas of Phoenix, where there were two deaths (Scott, 1978).

"It was in the midst of a flood, in the midst of a crisis, that the transition took place," said Fred DuVal, manager of what had started out to be Babbitt's campaign for re-election as attorney general. "Governor Bolin was spending lots of time, long hours . . . and he wore himself down to the point where he had a heart attack" (personal communication, March 29, 1990).

Babbitt spent the first two days of his term dealing with the flood and the gubernatorial death. He was up all night the first night monitoring the flooding, regularly appearing on television in sweat shirt and sweat pants to report on the situation.

DuVal is one of many who believe that the crisis helped Babbitt take hold in his new role: "It was a situation where people's panic greatly outstripped the reality of risk and so any reassuring words had political upside." The momentum established in that first week, DuVal said, "was then the new benchmark for measuring him for the balance of his term."

Ratcheting his attorney general campaign into a full-fledged gubernatorial campaign, the "governor by accident" (Reid, 1986) won a full term as governor with 52 percent of the vote in November 1978. Four years later, he was re-elected with 62 percent (Barone and Ujifusa, 1983).

Governor Dick Lamm of Colorado, first elected in 1974, was badly wounded in feuds with the legislature and press during his first two years in office (Barone and Ujifusa, 1981). But as the state responded to the July 31, 1976, Big Thompson Canyon flood, Lamm says, his governorship began to come together. "I think the Big Thompson gave me a chance to show that I was in charge and doing things" (Lamm, personal communication, March 29, 1990).

The scenic canyon, a primary route into Rocky Mountain National Park, had been filled with tourists and summer residents when the late afternoon thunderheads socked in above. The 12 inches of rain that fell between 6:30 and 11:00 P.M. turned the normally benign river into a raging killer. At least 139 people died in the flood (Gruntfest, 1987; Smith, 1986).

News of the disaster under way was slow getting out. The Associated Press bureau closed at midnight Saturday, staffers aware only of vague warnings of flash flooding (Ritz, 1980; Wright, 1987). Lamm learned of the situation when he returned from a late supper (personal communication, March 29, 1990): "I was out there at 7 in the morning and we were the first helicopter up the canyon. It was both symbol and substance for people. . . . We really had a full-scale rescue operation going."

Lamm was still wearing faded blue denim when he returned to Denver that night. He'd missed the rehearsal, but he got there in time to narrate Aaron Copland's "Portrait of Lincoln." The emotions of the canyon crept into the recitation, and symphony-goers responded with a standing ovation. "And you know," Lamm said, "I just feel that the whole tide turned at that time" (personal communication, March 29, 1990).

The governor came back from the nadir of his first two years to win re-election in 1978 with 59 percent of the vote and, in 1982, with 66 percent (Barone and Ujifusa, 1981, 1983).

Mixed Messages

Voters send mixed messages in response to flood mitigation and recovery. Individual politicians may escape unscathed, but floods sometimes create momentum for systemic political reform.

Abney and Hill's (1966) study of the 1965 New Orleans mayoral race in the aftermath of Hurricane Betsy found that voters resented efforts to make hurricane damage a campaign issue. Many believed the hurricane and flooding were "the action of an inscrutable God" and felt that any effort "to blame mortal politicians . . . was largely futile and seemed irreverent" (p. 980).

Wolensky (1984) has documented three cases in which perceived mismanagement of hurricane-caused floods led to true institutional changes in the form of city governments in Galveston, Texas; Dayton, Ohio; and Wilkes-Barre, Pennsylvania. Those reform drives were fueled by powerful political symbols of local officials essentially helpless in the midst of disaster.

Although some of the conditions that beget reform existed in each city, however, Wolensky argues that the pre-storm governments were operating adequately. In the absence of any true revolutionary ferment, he suggests, "the disasters presented politically ambitious groups with an opportunity to attain pre-existing goals" (Wolensky, 1984, pp. 110–11).

WHAT THE VOTERS SEEM TO KNOW

Paradoxically, political risk is most extreme when actual risk is least. The politician who seems to hide is more likely to be criticized than the one who makes his mistakes in public. And although a plea of helplessness may divert blame, the official who is perceived as helpless is more likely to be punished.

Furthermore, the snowstorm is more likely than the much more disastrous flood to bring down an office holder.

Observers — press or public — operate on two levels during a disaster. First, they genuinely want to see the people in charge succeed. Second, they believe that the stark light of disaster will illumine character and intention and that the stress of the moment will bring out the best and the worst in the central players.

Voters watch carefully for exploitation and showboating; McGovern may have been more harmed than helped by his quick media tour to Rapid City. In most cases, however, the glare of television lights serves more to enhance than reduce credibility. "The American public," Cronin writes, "has become conditioned by the media not to believe in the reality of a public act until it has been transformed into a dramatic or theatrical gesture before the cameras" (1980, p. 104).

And in this revealing light, observers test their hunches. If a mayor is already seen as strong, his decisive behavior in crisis will resonate strength. But woe betide the politician whose crisis behavior validates suspicions of indecisiveness, ineptitude, insincerity, rashness or incompetence.

The most common cause of citizen anger in the cases studied was the perception that officials weren't doing enough to help or, worse still, didn't have the power to help. Local officials are more vulnerable here. The degree to which power is concentrated or diffused among government agencies can directly affect the speed and efficiency of response (Stallings, 1983). There is also a significant mismatch between the citizens' need for an activist local government, at least in times of disaster, and the custodial role local officials define as their principal responsibility (Wolensky and Miller, 1981).

"The biggest problem is not doing something," says veteran political consultant Stuart K. Spencer. "You do something, even if it's wrong. The real peril is getting frozen in inaction — being afraid to make a mistake" (Skelton, 1989).

The difference between snow and flood is night and day. One is an extension of normalcy, a difference only in degree; the other is a paradigm shift. We have snowplows to remove snow from streets. We have nothing to pull bodies from rivers.

Voters are willing to be tolerant, even forgiving, of conduct in true act of God crises. Unless actual fault can be assessed — the dam bursts, for instance, because inferior cement was used — most citizens believe natural disasters are beyond the realm of human control.

The more serious crises, therefore, are more likely to produce heroes. The mayor or governor standing against the implacable power of nature takes on a David-versus-Goliath quality. Rarely are individuals called to account for their behavior in the most serious crises. Collective authority — a commission or council charged with relief and relocation, for instance — may be criticized in the aftermath, but individual scapegoats are rare. Fundamental fairness is part of this. Most major disasters — floods, earthquakes, avalanches — are quick, like a Nolan Ryan fast-ball. There's no time for second guessing. Only during the recovery phase, as long-term policy decisions are made, is there time to call balls and strikes.

However, in lesser emergencies like snowstorms, where annoyance and inconvenience are at stake rather than life and livelihood, voters are far less charitable. Two elements — money and public awareness — combine to make the politics of snow so difficult, according to the

Christian Science Monitor's Rushworth Kidder (1981). The cost of snow clearance can be immense, and there is virtually no cost benefit justification for buying the fleet needed to cope with a major storm. One choice is to let millions of dollars worth of equipment sit idle as mild winters breeze past. The alternative is to take the heat when a major storm finds the city unprepared and ill-equipped. No one will fail to notice: snow falls without regard to riches, race, or creed. The entire public is instantly aware of uncleared snow. "Few things," Kidder concludes, "rivet such intense attention on a city's political leadership as an uncleared snowfall" (p. 6).

And few things generate such anger. Snow offers an all-purpose symbol for all the annoyance and frustration of urban life. Already beset by nature, citizens feel betrayed and angry if they discover their leaders are helpless, too. Yet media reports regularly emphasize the helplessness or powerlessness of individuals and local governments.

SUGGESTIONS

Fairly or unfairly, journalists often assign the hero and villain roles in disasters. Most often they designate the goat — the official who simply fails to measure up and becomes a figure of disrespect, ridicule, or contempt.

It is not the reporters' job to build respect for government. Nor is it their job to throw sand in the wheels of government. Reporters are responsible, however, for giving readers and viewers the information and insights they need to make sound judgments and live effectively. The following suggestions may be useful to the reporter or editor charged with assessing politicians' conduct in the face of natural disaster.

Avoid adding uncritically to the demands on an officeholder's time. Another trip to the disaster scene may shore up morale, but it may also divert energy from actual recovery efforts. Make sure there's more to be gained than fresh video and new quotes.

Don't try too hard to find someone to blame. Instead, concentrate on keeping the problem in context. Does your audience understand what it would cost to prepare adequately for a 100-year storm? In terms of costs and benefits, local decisions may have been sound. Similarly, a technological accident such as Three Mile Island can be depicted as a disaster or "a predictable malfunction of a complicated system" (Wilkins 1989, p. 172; see also Burkhart, 1987). The tendency to wrest disasters from their causal contexts contributes to the need to find villains when things go awry.

Be sure your quest for immediacy and human interest isn't shaping a message of helplessness instead of helping the public understand hazard mitigation. Back off from event-oriented coverage and consider broader issues: Where is help available? How can the community assist in its own recovery? How can this work better next time?

Stay with the story after the edge is off the disaster and be prepared to demand ongoing political accountability. Politicians rarely experience sustained public interest in efforts to use zoning and land use powers to mitigate future hazards. Attentive journalists can keep the spotlight on the mitigation debate. Disaster coverage shouldn't stop when all the bodies are identified.

Don't be afraid to admit what you don't know. "Acknowledged uncertainty makes for better reporting than the reporting of erroneous facts," writes Deni Elliott. "The most accurate media message may be the assessment that no one is really sure of the situation at the moment" (1988, p. 170).

Journalists, of course, are not solely responsible for the effectiveness of political communication during a community crisis. Office-holders, too, need to protect their flanks.

Be visible. Don't try to hide while you figure out what to do next. Your best protection may be your willingness to make your mistakes in public and to admit what you don't know. Unguarded moments such as Don Barnett's "God, I'm tired" contribute immensely to officeholders' credibility with press and public.

Unless you're dealing with a prison riot, you belong at the scene of the disaster, but make your "tourist" visits judiciously. Although some emergency management specialists disdain site visits as blatant bids for media attention, others defend them as a way to build citizen morale, shore up a damaged tourist industry, and focus attention on relief needs. The National Governors' Association discourages on-site visits only in civil disturbances where a governor or mayor's position could be compromised (1985, p. 17).

Don't try to downplay the problem or make promises you can't keep.

Be willing to take public policy risks. In the crisis atmosphere, both winners and losers may be more willing to consider painful alternatives that otherwise might not reach the table (Benjamin, 1985). Don Barnet can lay claim to lots of heroics during the immediate Rapid City flood fight, but the real pride comes into his voice when he speaks of the fight to keep new development out of the flood plain: "We wouldn't even give people a building permit to repair their house. That's how firm we were. We were bold and daring and the scars are on my back" (personal communication, May 12, 1990).

WHAT YOU CAN'T CHANGE

The most important attitude for an official to carry into a disaster, however, may be philosophical. Primeval forces are at play. The odds don't support foolproof emergency preparedness: there is neither money nor time enough to prepare adequately for all the twists of wind and weather, no way to know whether the dice will bring the opportunity of flood or the snare of snow. Nor can managers and media coaches properly prep the politician for his or her moment in the crisis spotlight. Fundamental integrity, candor, and energy are the character traits most likely to show and be rewarded. There's a big piece here of trusting, like Milton, to "that power which erring men call Chance." Songwriters called it serendipity; Madison Avenue warns us not to try to fool Mother Nature. To Machiavelli, it was *fortuna*. Regardless of what you call it, political careers are sometimes in the hands of fate.

ACKNOWLEDGMENTS

Paul Albright, communications director of the Western Interstate Commission for Higher Education, provided invaluable research on the key Rapid City and Denver cases. University of Colorado journalism major Michele Heller was responsible for much of the Chicago and New York historical research.

Conclusions

LEE WILKINS AND PHILIP PATTERSON

In the introduction to this volume, sociologist Dorothy Nelkin posed two questions. The first — Why is the media so uncritical of science? — we believe has been answered by many of the essays in this book. Three answers to her second question — Why are scientists so anti-media? — have emerged, each a result of the shifting symbolism of science in the twentieth century.

First, the near reverence with which science as been held in the U.S. media, has been questioned in recent years. Historically, science and scientists were viewed as something to be rallied around. Scientists were regarded as pioneers and crusaders; science itself was seen as a vehicle for societal progress.

But, Americans seem to have changed their attitude about science. The dropping of the atomic bomb on Hiroshima was a watershed event that symbolized the use of science for destruction as well as for the public good. In the decades following, environmentalists would point out that the technological spin-offs of science carried that same capacity for harm.

Thus, the 1980s began with a public more wary of science and scientists than a generation before. The decade ended with mediated images of Challenger, Chernobyl, and the greenhouse effect as reminders that wariness is warranted. The shift had been years in the making. When the enemies were disease and hunger, science was an ally. When the enemy became overpopulation and pollution, science was part of the problem as well as the solution.

Second, as science became more complex, it lost part of its universal appeal. In the previous generation, scientists such as Jonas Salk, Albert Einstein, Charles Darwin, and others made significant, though sometimes controversial, intellectual contributions. While their scientific breakthroughs changed ways of thinking, today their science seems relatively understandable. Contemporary scientists inhabit an arcane universe, populated by government grants and contracts, technologically sophisticated laboratories, and large research teams. They study such delicate issues as recombinant DNA, the use of fetal tissue in medical treatment, nuclear energy, and Acquired Immune Deficiency Syndrome (AIDS), each publicly contentious. The science they produce is viewed not just as a search for knowledge but as a product, capable of making money and influencing public policy.

The mass media, as a creature of its culture, have changed their view as well. Journalists began this century attempting to popularize science. Today, they are more skeptical. Progress is no longer assumed when the news story is one of scientific discovery, nor is progress any longer always assumed to be desirable. While media accounts of various scientific issues are not uniform in this regard, particularly when coverage of the military is at issue, science and technology are no longer covered uncritically by the press.

Third, as the media have changed so has the audience, from passive passengers on the scientific train of progress to citizens active in assessing scientific news and how science may influence their lives. The NIMBY (not in my back yard) movement, the mainstreaming of environmentalism, and movements to ration the kind and quality of medical care are all evidence of an active and sometimes critical public.

Scientists view this change with some alarm. Historically, they connect an active lay participation in the efforts of science with fetters to inquiry and the creation of knowledge. The Catholic Church's excommunication of Galileo and the Scopes trial are but two historic events that have rightly made scientists fearful of nonscientific direction of the scientific agenda. Add to this historical baggage the condition of the modern university, where research and obtaining grants have come to dominate teaching, and scientists see both their careers and their intellectual values challenged in a way that was not the case a generation ago.

Together these three changes represent a shift in symbolism that has become an intellectual battle. On the one hand, science and scientists represent enormous political and intellectual power. They and their work are linked to progress, and they cherish the ability, within the political limits outlined in this book, to set their own research agenda. They connect lay attempts to direct and evaluate scientific findings with superstition.

The public, on the other hand, views science as an activity which has, in some important ways, become disconnected from certain fundamental values. When scientists exclusively control their own research agendas, larger political and social needs are shunted aside. When the scientific elite tells the public what is good for it, that analysis too often omits issues of fairness and control, which the average person also cherishes.

The mass media, more than many other contemporary institutions, reflect this symbolic shift. Journalists are guilty of many small errors in their science coverage, but, more importantly, their increasingly critical coverage of science and technology reflects the larger society's questions about this issue. Just as risk managers have eschewed concepts of lay rationality because they do not match more scientifically derived estimates, scientists eschew journalists because the news they report and write reflects a fundamental challenge to the way science has been conducted during the last half century. So why are scientists so antimedia? Perhaps it is a way of killing the messenger. Scientists can do little about the message, so they've had to settle for second best.

Bibliography

Abney, F. G., & Hill, L. B. (1966). Natural disasters as a political variable: The effect of a hurricane on an urban election. *American Political Science Review, 60*, 974–981.

Abrahamson, D. E. (1989). Global warming: The issue, impacts, responses. In D. E. Abrahamson (Ed.), *The challenge of global warming* (pp. 3–34). Washington, DC: Island Press.

Agnos now a statewide figure. (1989, December 1). United Press International.

Ainby, S. C., Becker, G., & Coleman, L. (Eds.). (1986). *The dilemma of difference.* New York: Plenum Press.

Alexander, T. (1980, July). The unexpected payoff of Project Apollo. *Fortune,* 114–117, 150–156.

Altheide, D. (1985). *Media Power.* Newbury Park, CA: Sage.

Altheide, D. L. (1976). *Creating reality: How TV news distorts events.* Newbury Park, CA: Sage.

Altimore, M. (1982). The social construction of a scientific controversy: Comments on press coverage of the recombinant DNA debate. *Science Technology and Human Values, 7*, 24–31.

American Association for the Advancement of Science. (1989a). *Science for all Americans: Project 2061.* Washington, DC: American Association for the Advancement of Science.

American Association for the Advancement of Science. (1989b). *Biological and health sciences: Project 2061.* Panel Report. Washington, DC: American Association for the Advancement of Science.

Arkin, W. M. (1988, May/June). Prologue to START: New INF numbers cast doubt on standard press tallies. *Deadline,* pp. 1–2, 9–11.

Arnold, M. (1981). CIA tried to get press to hold up salvage media information campaign effectiveness. In R. E. Rice & W. J. Paisely (Eds.), *Public communication campaigns*. Newbury Park, CA: Sage.

Atkin, C. K. (1981). Mass media information campaigns effectiveness. In R. E. Rice & W. J. Paisely (Eds.), *Public communication campaigns*. Newbury Park, CA: Sage.

Ayres, B. D., Jr. (1990, January 19). U. S. agents arrest Washington mayor on drug charges. Washington *Post*, p. A1.

Barabak, M. Z. (1989, November 3). Job performance ratings: Bush gains and Quayle slips. *San Francisco Chronicle*, p. A21.

Barnard, C. (1968). *Functions of the executive*. Cambridge, MA: Harvard University Press. (Originally published 1938).

Barnet, R. J. (1990, January 1). Reflections: After the cold war. *New Yorker*, pp. 65–76.

Barone, M., & Ujifusa, G. (1987). *The almanac of American politics 1988*. Washington, DC: National Journal.

Barone, M., & Ujifusa, G. (1983). *The almanac of American politics 1984*. Washington, DC: National Journal.

Barone, M., & Ujifusa, G. (1981). *The almanac of American politics 1982*. Washington, DC: Barone & Company.

Barone, M., Ujifusa, G., & Matthews, D. (1974). *The almanac of American politics: The senators, the representatives, their records, states and districts, 1974*. Boston: Gambit.

Becker, L. B., & Dunwoody, S. (1982). Media use, public affairs knowledge and voting in a local election. *Journalism Quarterly, 59*(2), 212–218, 255.

Benjamin, G. (1985). The gubernatorial transition in New York. In T. L. Beyle (Ed.), *Gubernatorial transitions: The 1982 election* (pp. 362–375). Durham, NC: Duke University Press.

Billings, C., & Cheaney, E. (1981). *Information transfer problems in the aviation system*. Technical Paper, 1875. Moffett Field, CA: NASA.

Blakeslee, S. (Ed.). (1986). *Human heart replacement: A new challenge for physicians and reporters*. Los Angeles: Foundation for American Communications.

Blong, R. J. (1985). *Public views on disaster response and the news media — some Australian examples*. Mt. Macedon, Australia: Australian Counter Disaster College.

Blumenthal, S. (1982). *The permanent campaign*. New York: Simon and Schuster, Touchstone edition.

Bogart, L. (1981). *Press and public: Who reads what, when, where and why in American newspapers*. Hillsdale, NJ: Lawrence Erlbaum.

Bok, S. (1982). *Secrets: On the ethics of concealment and revelation*. NY: Pantheon Books.

Bolduc, J. P. (1987). Natural disasters in developing countries: myths and the role of the media. *Emergency Preparedness Digest, 14*, 12–14.

Boot, W. (1985). Ethiopia: Feasting on famine. *Columbia Journalism Review, 23*, 47–48.

Booth, W. (1988). Social engineers confront AIDS. *Science, 242*, 1237–1238.

Box, E. P. & Jenkins, G. M. (1976). *Time-series analysis: Forecasting and control* (2d ed.). San Francisco: Holden-Day.

Boyer, P. (1985a). *By the bomb's early light. American thought and culture at the dawn of the atomic age.* New York: Pantheon.

Boyer, P. J. (1985b). Famine in Ethiopia: The TV accident that exploded. *Washington Journalism Review,* pp. 19–21.

Bradbury, J. A. (1989). The policy implications of differing concepts of risk. *Science, Technology, and Human Values, 14*(4), 380–399.

Bradley, B. (1989, November 27). Aftershocks. *The New Republic,* pp. 15–16.

Bram, S. M. (1987, November/December). What reporters think about arms control. *Deadline,* pp. 1–2.

Brenner, D. J., & Logan, R. (1980). Some considerations in the diffusion of medical technologies: Medical information systems. In D. Nimmo (Ed.), *Communication yearbook 4.* New Brunswick, NJ: Transaction Books.

Bucher, R. (1957). Blame and hostility in disaster. *American Journal of Sociology, 62,* 467–475.

Burke, K. (1984). *Attitudes toward history.* Berkeley: University of California Press. (Originally published 1938).

Burkhart, F. N. (1987). Experts and the press under stress: Disaster journalism gets mixed reviews. *International Journal of Mass Emergencies and Disasters, 5,* 357–367.

Burnham, J. (1987). *How superstition won and science lost: Popularizing science and health in the United States.* New Brunswick, NJ: Rutgers University Press.

Burns, J. M. (1978). *Leadership.* New York: Harper & Row.

Callahan, D. (1989). *The limits of medical progress.* New York: Simon & Schuster.

Carey, J.C. (1979). Mass communication research and cultural studies: An American view. In J. Curran, M. Gurevitch & J. Wollacott (Eds.), *Mass communication and society* pp. (409–425). Newbury Park, CA: Sage.

Cassidy, H. (1981). *Using econometrics: A beginner's guide.* Englewood Cliffs, NJ: Prentice-Hall.

Chaffee, S. H. (1972). The interpersonal context of mass communication. In F. G. Kline & P. J. Tichenor (Eds.), *Current perspectives in mass communication research* (pp. 95–120). Newbury Park, CA: Sage.

Chaffee, S. H. (1982). Mass media and interpersonal channels: Competitive, convergent, or complementary? In G. Gumpert & R. Cathcart (Eds.) *Inter-Media* (2nd ed.), pp. 55–57. New York: Oxford University Press.

Chaffee, S. H., & Choe, S. Y. (1979). *Measurement in the March, 1979, NES plot study.* Paper presented at the American Political Science Association, Washington, DC.

Chaffee, S. H., & Roser, C. (1986). Involvement and the consistency of knowledge, attitudes and behaviors. *Communication Research, 13,* 373–399.

Chaffee, S. H., Roser, C., & Flora, J. (1989). Estimating the magnitude of threats to validity of information campaign effects. In C. T. Salmon (Ed.), *Information campaigns* (pp. 285–301). Newbury Park, CA: Sage.

Chaffee, S. H., & Schleuder, J. (1986). Measurement and effects of attention to news media. *Human Communication Research, 13,* 76–107.

Chang, Tsan-Kuo (1989). The impact of presidential statements on press editorials regarding U.S. China policy, 1950–1984. *Communication Research, 16*(4), 486–509.

Check, W. A. (1987). Beyond the political model of reporting: Nonspecific symptoms in media communication about AIDS. *Review of Infectious Disease, 9*(5), 987–1000.

Cheney, G., & Tompkins, P. (1988). On the facts of the text as the basis of human communication research. In J. Anderson (Ed.), *Communication yearbook 11.* Newbury Park, CA: Sage.

Ciborowski, P. (1989). Sources, sinks, trends and opportunities. In D. E. Abrahamson (Ed.), *The challenge of global warming* (pp. 213–230). Washington, DC: Island Press.

Cigler, B. A. (1988). Emergency management and public administration. In M. T. Charles & J. C. K. Kim (Eds.), *Crisis management: A casebook* (pp. 5–19). Springfield, IL: Charles C. Thomas.

Cigler, B. A., & Burby, R. J. (1990). Local flood hazard management: Lessons from national research. In R. T. Sylves & W. L. Waugh Jr., (Eds.), *Cities and disaster: North American studies in emergency management* (pp. 33–56). Springfield, IL: Charles C. Thomas.

Clarke, L. (1988). Explaining choices among technological risks. *Social Problems, 35*(1), 22–35.

Cobb, R. W., & Elder, C. D. (1983). *Participation in American politics: The dynamics of agenda-building* (2nd ed.). Baltimore: Johns Hopkins University Press.

Coblenz, W. (Producer), Ritchie, M. (Director), Larner, J. (Screenwriter). (1972). *The Candidate.* [Film]. Warner Communications Co., Wildwood-Ritchie Productions.

Cocozza, J. J., Melick, M. B., & Steadman, Henry J. (1978). Trends in violent crime among ex-mental patients. *Criminology 16*(3), 317.

Cohen, B. C. (1963). *The press and foreign policy.* Princeton, New Jersey: Princeton University Press.

Cohn, V. (1963). Are we really telling the public about science? *Science, 148,* 750–753.

Cohn, V. (1989a). Reporters as gatekeepers. In M. Moore (Ed.), *Health risks and the press.* Washington, DC: The Media Institute.

Cohn, V. (1989b). *News and numbers.* Ames, IA: Iowa State University Press.

Coleman, J. S. (1957). *Community conflict.* New York: MacMillan.

Cooper, R. T. (1972, June 12). McGovern tours scene of flood, places his staff at city's disposal. *Los Angeles Times.* p. 16, part 1.

Coyne, J. R., Jr. (1970, April 27). Snow job: The politics of anger. *National Review,* pp. 532–533.

Cronin, T. E. (1980). *The state of the presidency* (2nd ed.). Boston: Little, Brown.

Cunnold, D. R., Prinn, R., Rasmussen, R., Simmonds, P., Alyea, F., Cardelina, C., Crawford, A., Fraser P., & Rosen, R. (1986). Atmospheric lifetime and annual release estimates for CFC_{13} and CF_cCl_c from five years of ALE data. *Journal of Geophysical Research, 91,* 10,797–817.

Danielian, L. H., & Reese, S. D. (1989). A closer look at inter-media influences on agenda-setting: The cocaine issue of 1986. In P. J. Shoemaker (Ed.), *Communication campaigns about drugs: Government, media, and the public* (pp. 47–65). Hillsdale, NJ: Lawrence Erlbaum Associates.

Dearing, J. W. (1989). Setting the polling agenda for the issue of AIDS. *Public Opinion Quarterly, 53,* 309–329.

DeFleur, M. L., & Ball-Rokeach, S. (1989). *Theories of mass communication*. New York: Longman.

Demac, D. A. (1984). *Keeping America uninformed: Government secrecy in the 1980s*. New York: The Pilgrim Press.

Denver Post. (1983) 1, 2, 3, 5, 6 January; 28, 29 February; 4, 5, 17, 18 May.

Denver Post. (1982) 26, 27, 28, 29, 30, 31 December.

Denver Post. (1972) 11, 12, 14, 15, 21, 22 June; 25 July.

Dervin, B. (1981). Mass communicating: Changing conceptions of the audience. In R. E. Rice & W. J. Paisley, (Eds.), *Public communication campaigns* (pp. 71–87). Newbury Park, CA: Sage.

DeVolpi, A., Marsh, D. E., Postol, T. A., & Stanford, G. S. (1981). *Born secret. The H-Bomb, the progressive case and national security*. New York: Pergamon Press.

Dewey, J. (1916). *Democracy and education*. New York: MacMillan.

Dewey, J. (1927). *The public and its problems*. New York: Henry Holt and Company.

Dickson, D. (1984). *The new politics of science* (pp. 217–260). New York: Pantheon.

Divine, R. A. (1978). *Blowing on the wind. The nuclear test ban debate 1954–1960*. New York: Oxford University Press.

Dorman, W. A., & Hirsch, D. (1986). Chernobyl: The U.S. media's slant. *Bulletin of Atomic Scientists, 43*, 54–56.

Douglas, M., & Wildavsky, A. (1982). *Risk and culture*. Berkeley, CA: University of California Press.

Downs, A. (1972). Up and down with ecology: The issue-attention cycle. *Public Interest, 28*, 38–50.

Drabek, T. E. (1986). *Human system responses to disasters: An inventory of sociological findings*. New York: Springer Verlag.

Drabek, T. E., & Quarantelli, E. L. (1967). Scapegoats, villains, and disasters. *Transaction, 4*(4), 12–17.

Dunwoody, S. (1980). The science writing inner club: A communication link between science and the lay public. *Science, Technology and Human Values, 5*, 14–22.

Dunwoody, S. (1982). A question of accuracy. *IEEE transactions on professional communication, PC-25*, pp. 196–199.

Dunwoody, S., & Ryan, M. (1985). Scientific barriers to the popularization of science in the mass media. *Journal of Communication, 35*, 26–42.

Dyer, J., & Sarin, R. (1986). Measuring risk attitudes in risk analysis. In V. Covello, J. Menkes & J. Mumpower (Eds.), *Risk evaluation and management* (pp. 221–231). New York: Plenum.

Dynes, R. R. (1988). Cross-cultural international research: Sociology and disaster. *International Journal of Mass Emergencies and Disasters, 6*, 101–129.

Dynes, R. R., De Marchi, B., & Pelanda, C. (Eds.). (1987). *Sociology of disasters*. Milan, Italy: Franco Angeli.

Edelman, M. (1964). *The symbolic uses of politics*. Urbana, IL: University of Illinois Press.

Edelstein, M. (1988). *Contaminated communities*. Boulder, CO: Westview.

Efron, E. (1985). *The apocalyptics: How environmental politics controls what we know about cancer*. New York: Simon & Schuster.

Ehrenhalt, A. (Ed.). (1981). *Politics in America*. Washington, DC: Congressional Quarterly Press.

Elliott, D. (1988). Tales from the darkside: Ethical implications of disaster coverage. In L. M. Walters, L. Wilkins & T. Walters (Eds.), *Bad tidings: Communication and catastrophe* (pp. 161–170). Hillsdale, NJ: Lawrence Erlbaum Associates.

Elliott, D. (1986). Philosophical foundations for newsmedia responsibility. In D. Elliott (Ed.), *Responsible journalism*. Newbury Park, CA: Sage.

The "end" of the cold war? The coming challenge for journalism. (1989, Summer). *Deadline*, pp. 1–18.

Engelberg, S. (1990, January 9). Pentagon looks for ways to stave off budget cuts. New York *Times*, p. A12.

Epstein, Edward J. (1973). *News from nowhere*. New York: Random House.

Ettema, J. S., Brown, J., & Luepker, R. (1983). Knowledge gap effects in a health information campaign. *Public Opinion Quarterly, 47*, 516–527.

Ettema, J. S., & Whitney, D. C. (Eds.). (1982). Individuals in mass media organizations: Creativity and constraint. *Sage Annual Reviews of Communication Research, 10*, 1–160.

Ex-student guilty in campus rampage. (1988, March 4). *Long Island Newsday*, p. 9.

Fahnestock, J. (1986). Accommodating science: The rhetorical life of scientific facts. *Written Communication, 3*, 275–296.

Farquhar, J. (1983). Changes in American lifestyle and health. In J. Hamner III & B. Jacobs (Eds.), *Marketing and managing health care: Health promotion and disease prevention*. Memphis, TN: University of Tennessee Center for the Health Sciences.

Farquhar, J., Fortmann, S., Wood, P., & Haskell, W. (1983). Community studies of cardiovascular disease prevention. In N. Kaplan & J. Stamler (Eds.), *Prevention of coronary health disease: Practical management of the risk factors*. Philadelphia, PA: W. B. Saunders.

Farquhar, J., Maccoby, N., & Solomon, D. (1984). Community applications of behavioral medicine. In W. D. Gentry (Ed.), *Handbook of behavioral medicine*. New York: Guilford Press.

Federal Emergency Management Agency. (1987). *Proceedings of the flash flood mitigation symposium held in Rapid City, June 9–10, 1987*. Denver, CO: Federal Emergency Management Agency, Region 8.

Finnegan, J., & Loken, B. (1985). *The effects of direct mail on health awareness and knowledge in community heart health campaigns*. Unpublished manuscript. University of Minnesota, Minneapolis. Paper delivered to Health Communications Division, International Communication Association Annual Convention, Honolulu, HI.

Fischer, H. W. (1989). *Hurricane Gilbert: The media's creation of the storm of the century*. Working Paper, 67. Boulder, CO: Institute of Behavioral Science, University of Colorado.

Fischhoff, B. (1985). Protocols for environmental reporting: What to ask the experts. *The Journalist*, pp. 11–15.

Fischhoff, B., Slovic, P., & Lichtenstein, S. (1982). Lay foibles and expert fables in judgments about risk. *American Statistician, 36*(3), 240–255.

Fischhoff, B., Slovic, P., Derby, S. L., & Keeney, R. L. (1981). *Acceptable risk*. Cambridge: Cambridge University Press.

Fishman, M. (1980). *Manufacturing the news*. Austin: University of Texas Press.

Foucault, M (1965). *Madness and civilization*. New York: Random House.

Franklin, J. (1986). *Writing for story.* New York: New American Library.

Freimuth, V., Greenburg, R., DeWitt, J., & Romano, R. (1984a). Covering cancer: Newspapers and the public interest. *Journal of Communication, 34,* 62–73.

Freimuth, V., Greenburg, R., DeWitt, J., & Romano, R. (1984b). Information to dispel misconceptions and alleviate public fears is rarely found in newspaper coverage of cancer. *SIPIscope, 12,* 5–9.

Freudenburg, W. R. (1988). Perceived risk, real risk: Social science and the art of probabilistic risk assessment. *Science, 242,* 44–49.

Friedman, B. (1987). *The art of storytelling. The structuring and processing of news during disasters.* Miscellaneous Report, 39. Newark, DE: Disaster Research Center, University of Delaware.

Friedman, R. (1979, July/August). The United States v. the *Progressive. Columbia Journalism Review,* pp. 27–35.

Friedman, S. M. (1989). TMI: The media story that will not die. In L. M. Walters, L. Wilkins & T. Walters (Eds.) *Bad tidings: Communication and catastrophe* (pp. 161–170). Hillsdale, NJ: Lawrence Erlbaum Associates.

Friedman, S. M., Dunwoody, S., & Rogers, C. (Eds.). (1986). *Scientists and journalists: Reporting science as news.* New York: The Free Press.

Friedman, S. M., & Friedman, K. A. (1988). *Reporting on the environment: A handbook for journalists* (pp. 61–80). Bangkok, Thailand: United Nations Economic and Social Commission for Asia and the Pacific.

Friedman, S. M., Gorney, C. M., Egolf, B. (1987, spring). Reporting about radiation: A content analysis of Chernobyl, *Journal of Communication,* pp. 58–79.

From, E., & Keeling, C. (1986). Reassessment of the late 19th century atmospheric carbon dioxide variation in the air of western Europe and the British Isles based on unpublished analysis of contemporary air masses by C. C. Callendar. *Tellus, 38b,* 87–105.

Fromm, J. (1983, Summer). The media and the making of defense policy: The U.S. example. In *Defense and consensus: the domestic aspects of western security, Part 1.* (Adelphi Papers, No. 182). London: The International Institute for Strategic Studies.

Gallup Organization. (1989, June). *The Gallup Report #285: Concern about the environment,* pp. 2–12.

Gans, H. J. (1979, January/February). The messages behind the news. *Columbia Journalism Review,* pp. 40–45.

Gans, H. J. (1980). *Deciding what's news.* New York: Vintage.

Gelb, L. (1989, December 28). Our foreign policy experts. New York *Times,* p. A20.

Gerbner, G. (1973). Cultural indicators: The third voice. In G. Gerbner, L. Gross & W. Melody (Eds.), *Communication technology and social policy: Understanding the new "cultural revolution."* New York: John Wiley.

Gerbner, G. (1961). Psychology, psychiatry, and mental illness in the mass media: A story of trends, 1900–1959. *Mental Hygiene 45,* 89–99.

Gerbner, G., Gross, L., Morgan, M., & Signorielli, N. (1981). Health and medicine on television. *New England Journal of Medicine, 305,* 901–904.

Gert, B. (1989). *Morality.* New York: Oxford University Press.

Gollin, A., & Salisbury, P. (1986). *Newspapers in American news habits: A comparative assessment.* New York: Newspaper Advertising Bureau.

Goodell, R. (1977). *The visible scientists*. Boston, MA: Little, Brown.

Gordon, M. R. (1989, March 23). U. S. opposes release of Soviet nuclear test data. New York *Times*, p. A7.

Graham, L. (1981). *Between science and values*. New York: Columbia University Press.

Greenberg, D. (1974). Let's hear it for science. *Columbia Journalism Review, 13*, 19–24.

Greenberg, M. R., Sachsman, D. B., Sandman, P. M., & Salomone, K. L. (1989). Risk, drama and geography in coverage of environmental risk by network TV. *Journalism Quarterly, 66*(2), 267–276.

Gregory, R. (1989). Improving risk communications: Questions of content and intent. In W. Leiss (Ed.), *Prospects and problems in risk communication*. Waterloo: University of Waterloo Press.

Gruntfest, E. C. (1987). Common ground. In E. C. Gruntfest (Ed.), *What we have learned since the Big Thompson flood. Proceedings of the Tenth Anniversary Conference* (pp. 3–8). Boulder, CO: Natural Hazards Research and Applications Information Center.

Haff, G. (1976). Science writing in American mass media. *Nieman Reports, 30*, 18–24.

Hallin, D. C., Manoff, R. K., & Weddle, J. K. (1989, November). *Sourcing patterns of key national security reporters: A case study in a structural determinant of discourse*. Paper presented at the meeting of the Speech Communication Association, San Francisco, CA.

Halloran, R. (1989, July 17). Stealth bomber suffers from secrecy, high cost and an unclear purpose. New York *Times*, p. A14.

Hanauer, G. (1981, April). The story behind the Pentagon's broken arrows. *Mother Jones*, pp. 23–28, 52–59.

Hart, R. (1984). Shamans and criers: Responsibilities in science reporting. *The Quill, 72*, 24–28.

Hawkins, R., Pingree, S., & Adler, I. (1987). Searching for cognitive processes in the cultivation effect. *Human Communication Research, 13*, 553–577.

Heise, J. A. (1979). *Minimum disclosure. How the Pentagon manipulates the news*. New York: W. W. Norton and Company.

Hentoff, N. (1979, December). The press and nuclear "secrets". *The Progressive*, pp. 31–34.

Hentoff, N. (1969). *A political life: The education of John V. Lindsay*. New York: Knopf.

Herken, G. (1980). *The winning weapon. The atomic bombs in the cold war, 1945–1950*. New York: Alfred A. Knopf.

Hess, S. (1981). *The Washington reporters*. Washington, DC: The Brookings Institution.

Hess, S. (1984). *The Government/press connection: Press officers and their offices*. Washington, DC: The Brookings Institution.

Hiatt, F. (1984, December 20). Weinburg hits shuttle report as irresponsible. Washington *Post*, A1, A14.

Hiroi, O., Mikami, S., & Miyata, K. (1985). A study of mass media reporting in emergencies. *International Journal of Mass Emergencies and Disasters, 3*, 21–49.

Hirsch, P. M. (1981). On not learning from one's own mistakes: A reanalysis of Gerbner et al.'s own findings on cultivational analysis, part II. *Communication Research 8*, 3–37.

Hirsch, P. M. (1980). The "scary world" of the nonviewer and other anomalies: A reanalysis of Gerbner et al.'s findings on cultivation analysis, part I. *Communication Research, 7*, 3–37.

Hohenemser, C., Kates, R. W., & Slovic, P. (1983). The nature of technological hazard. *Science, 220*, 376–384.

Holsti, O. R. (1969). *Content analysis for the social sciences and humanities.* Reading, MA: Addison-Wesley, 1969.

Hull, C. H. J., Thatcher, M. L., & Tortoriello, R. C. (1986). Salinity in the Delaware Estuary. In M. C. Barth & J. G. Titus (Eds.), *Greenhouse effect and sea level rise: A challenge for this generation.* New York: Van Nostrand Reinhold.

If that's not a good job, I'm a Swiss jeweler. (1982, December 27). United Press International.

Inglehard, R. (1984, February–March). The fear of living dangerously: Public attitudes toward nuclear power. *Public Opinion,* pp. 41–44.

The Iraqi breakout. (1989, December 13). *Wall Street Journal,* p. A14.

Iyengar, S., & Kinder, D. R. (1987). *News that matters: Agenda-setting and priming in a television age.* Chicago: University of Chicago Press.

Jacobson, E., & Deutschmann, P. (1962). Introduction. *International Social Science Journal, 14,* 151–161.

Janis, I. L. (1954). Problems of theory in the analysis of stress behavior. *Journal of Social Issues, 10*(3), 12–25.

Kahneman, D., Slovic, P., & Tversky, A. (1982). *Judgment under uncertainty: Heuristics and biases.* New York: Cambridge University Press.

Kahneman, D., & Tversky, A. (1979). Prospect theory: An analysis of decision under risk. *Econometrica, 47,* 263–291.

Kasperson, R. E., Renn, O., Slovic, P., Brown, H. S., Emel, J., Goble, R., Kasperson, J. X., & Ratick, S. (1988). The social amplification of risk: A conceptual framework. *Risk Analysis, 8,* 177–187.

Kates, R. W., Hohenemser, C., & Kasperson, J. X. (Eds.). (1985). *Perilous progress: Technology as hazard* (pp. 91–123). Boulder, CO: Westview.

Keeling, V. (1984). *Atmospheric CO_2 concentration, Mauna Loa Observatory, Hawaii, 1958–1983.* U. S. Department of Energy Report NDP-001. Carbon Dioxide Information Center, Oak Ridge, TN.

Keeney, R. (1980). Equity and public risk. *Operations Research, 28,* 527–534.

Keller, B. (1989, July 9). American team gets close look at Soviet secret. New York *Times,* pp. A1, A17.

Kellogg, W. W., & Schware, R. (1981). *Climate change and society: Consequences of increasing atmospheric carbon dioxide.* Boulder, CO: Westview Press.

Kenney, C., & Turner, R. L. (1988). *Dukakis: An American odyssey.* Boston: Houghton Mifflin.

Khalil, M., & Rasmussen, R. (1985). Causes of increasing atmospheric methane: Depletion of hydroxyl radical and the rise of emissions. *Atmospheric Environment, 19,* 397–407.

Kidder, R. M. (1981, December 9). Urban alchemy: City leaders turn snow to political "hay." *The Christian Science Monitor,* p. 6.

Kinsella, J. (1990). *Covering the plague: The story behind the story of the AIDS epidemic.* New Brunswick, NJ: Rutgers University Press.

Kinsella, J. (1989). *Covering the plague: AIDS and the American media.* New Brunswick, NJ: Rutgers University Press.

Kinsella, J. (1988). Covering the plague years: Four approaches to the AIDS Beat. *New England Journal of Public Policy, 4,* 465–474.

Kneeland, D. E. (1979, March 2). Defeat of a political machine: Years and layers of discontent in Chicago voters surfaced in the balloting against Mayor Bilandic. New York *Times,* p. 1A.

Kneeland, D. E. (1979, February 28). Former city hall official upsets Daley successor in close contest. New York *Times,* p. 1A.

Kneeland, D. E. (1979, February 25). Thaw raises hopes for embattled Chicago mayor. New York *Times,* p. 1A.

Kneeland, D. E. (1979, Jan. 31). Snow plagues Chicago mayor's campaign for re-election. New York *Times,* p. 8.

Kondracke, M. (1975, May). The CIA and "Our Conspiracy." *MORE,* pp. 10–11.

Kotok, C. D. (1987, March 7). Former mayor suffers heart attack after performance: Senator Zorinsky dead at 58. *Omaha World-Herald,* pp. 1, 14.

Kotulak, R. (1989). Sorting through the chaff. In M. Moore (Ed.), *Health risks and the press.* Washington, DC: The Media Institute.

Kraus, S., Davis, D., Lang, G. E., & Lang, K. (1975). Critical events analysis. In S. H. Chaffee (Ed.), *Political communication* (pp. 195–216). Newbury Park, CA: Sage.

The Kremlin apology: Excerpts from speech. (1989, October 25). New York *Times,* p. A12.

Kreps, G. A. (1980). Research needs and policy issues on mass media disaster reporting. In *Disasters and the mass media* (pp. 35–74). Washington, DC: National Academy of Sciences.

Kress, G. (1985). Discourses, texts, readers and the pro-nuclear arguments. In P. Chilton (Ed.), *Language and the nuclear arms debate: Nukespeak today* (pp. 65–87). Dover, NH: Frances Pinter.

Krieghbaum, H. (1967). *Science and the mass media.* New York: New York University Press.

Krimsky, S., & Plough, A. (1988). *Environmental hazards: Communicating risks as a social process.* Dover, Mass.: Auburn House.

Kueneman, R., & Wright, J. (1976). News policies of broadcast stations for civil disturbances and disasters. *Journalism Quarterly, 53,* 670–677.

The lady and the machine: Rebellious Jane Byrne knocks out the mayor of Chicago. (1979, March 12). *Time,* p. 22.

Laetsch, W. (1987). A basis for better public understanding of science. In *Communicating science to the public.* New York: John Wiley.

Ledingham, J., & Masel-Walters, L. (1984). Written on the wind: The media and Hurricane Alicia. *Newspaper Research Journal, 6,* 50–58.

Leventhal, H., & Scherer, K. (1987). The relationship of emotion to cognition: A functional approach to a semantic controversy. *Cognition and Emotion, 1,* 3–28.

Lichtenstein, S., Gregory, R., Slovic, P., & Wagenaar, W. A. (in press). When lives are in your hands: Dilemmas of the societal decision maker. In R. M. Hogarth (Ed.), *Insights in decision making: Theory and application.* Chicago, IL: University of Chicago Press.

Linsky, M. (1986). *Impact: How the press affects federal policymaking.* New York: W. W. Norton.

Logan, R. (1989). The unworkable compromise: The knowledge tablet, ethics and public policy for the future. *Mass Comm Review, 16,* 14–26.

Logan, R. (1985). Rationales for investigative and explanatory trends in science reporting. *Newspaper Research Journal, 7,* 53–58.

Maccoby, N., & Alexander, J. (1980). Use of media in lifestyle programs. In P. Davidson & S. Davidson (Eds.), *Behavioral medicine: Changing health lifestyles.* New York: Brunner/Mazel, Inc.

McCombs, M. E., & Shaw, D. L. (1972). The agenda-setting function of mass media, *Public Opinion Quarterly, 36,* 176–187.

McConnell, M. (1987). *Challenger: A major malfunction.* Garden City, New York: Doubleday.

McLeod, J. M., & Becker, L. B. (1981). The uses and gratifications approach. In D. D. Nimmo & K. R. Sanders (Eds.), *Handbook of political communication* (pp. 67–99). Newbury Park, CA: Sage.

McLeod, J. M., Becker, L. B., & Byrnes, J. E. (1974). Another look at the agenda-setting function of the press. *Communication Research, 1*(2), 131–165.

McLeod, J. M., & McDonald, D. (1985). Beyond simple exposure: Media orientations and their impact on political processes. *Communication Research, 12,* 3–34.

McPhail, T. (1981). *Electronic colonialism: The future of international broadcasting and communication.* Newbury Park, CA: Sage.

McQuail, D. (1984). *Mass communication theory: An introduction.* London: Sage.

Manoff, R. K. (1988, July/August). Reporting the nuclear news in an era of U.S.-Soviet accord. *Deadline,* pp. 1–2, 11.

May, P. J. (1985). *Recovering from catastrophes: Federal disaster relief policy and politics.* Westport, CT: Greenwood Press.

Mazur, A. (1987). Putting radon on the public risk agenda. *Science, Technology, and Human Values, 12*(3–4), 86–93.

Merriam, J. E. (1989). National media coverage of drug issues, 1983–1987. In P. J. Shoemaker (Ed.), *Communication campaigns about drugs: Government, media, and the public* (pp. 21–28). New Jersey: Lawrence Erlbaum Associates.

Miller, J. (1989). *Scientific literacy.* Unpublished manuscript presented to the American Association for the Advancement of Science, 1989 Annual Convention, San Francisco, CA.

Miller, J. (1987). *Scientific literacy in the United States. Communicating Science to the Public.* New York: John Wiley.

Miller, J. (1986). Reaching the attentive and interested publics for science. In S. Friedman, S. Dunwoody & C. Rogers, (Eds.), *Scientific literacy: A conceptual and empirical review.* New York: The Free Press

Miller, J. D. (1987). *The impact of the Challenger accident on public attitudes toward the space program.* Dekalb, IL: Northern Illinois University, Public Opinion Laboratory, Report to the National Science Foundation.

Molotch, H., & Lester, M. (1974). News as purposive behavior: On the strategic use of routine events, accidents and scandals. *American Sociological Review, 39,* 101–112.

Monahan, J. (1984). Personal interview, July 10, 1984, by phone from Boulder, CO.

Monahan, J. (1981). *Predicting violent behavior.* Newbury Park, CA: Sage.

Mooney, M. M. (1980, March). Right conduct for a free press. *Harper's,* pp. 35–44.

Morentz, J. W. (1979). Communication in the Sahel drought: Comparing the mass media with other channels of international communication. In *Disasters and the mass media* (pp. 158–186). Washington, D.C.: National Academy of Sciences.

Morgan, M. G., Florig, K., Nair, I., & Hester, G. (1987). Power frequency fields: The regulatory dilemma. *Issues in Science and Technology, 3,* 81–91.

Morgan, M. G., Slovic, P., Nair, I., Geisler, D., MacGregor, D., Fischhoff, B., Lincoln, D., & Florig, K. (1985). Powerline frequency electric and magnetic fields: A pilot study of risk perception. *Risk Analysis, 5,* 139–149.

Morland, H. (1981). *The secret that exploded.* New York: Random House.

Name? Age? Address? Race? (1965, Spring). *Columbia Journalism Review,* pp. 40–41.

National Governors' Association, Committee on Criminal Justice and Public Protection. (1985). *The role and responsibility of the governor in emergency management.* Washington, DC: National Governors' Association, Committee on Criminal Justice and Public Protection.

National Research Council. (1989). *Improving risk communication.* Washington, DC: National Academy Press.

Nelkin, D. (1988). *Communicating the risks and benefits of technology.* Unpublished paper presented at 1988 Symposium on Science Communication: Environmental and Health Research, Los Angeles.

Nelkin, D. (1987). *Selling science: How the press covers science and technology.* New York: W. H. Freeman.

Nelkin, D. (1985). *Science in the streets.* New York: Twentieth Century Fund.

Nelkin, D. (1984). *Science in the streets.* New York: Priority Press.

New York: A Trumanesque comeback. (1969, October 13). *Newsweek,* p. 17.

New York Times Co. v. United States, 403 U.S. 713 (1971).

Newcomb, H. (1978). Assessing the violence studies of Gerbner and Gross: A humanistic critique and suggestion. *Communication Research, 5,* 264–282.

Newspaper science sections spreading nationwide. (1986). *SIPIscope, 14,* 1–17.

Nieburg, H. (1966). *In the name of science.* Chicago: Quadrangle.

Nimmo, D. (1984). TV network news coverage of Three Mile Island: Reporting disasters as technological fables. *International Journal of Mass Emergencies and Disasters, 2,* 116–143.

Nimmo, D., & Combs, J. E. (1985). *Nightly horrors: Crisis coverage in television network news.* Knoxville, TN: University of Tennessee Press.

Nisbett, R. E., Fong, G. T., Lehman, D. R., & Cheng, P. W. (1987). Teaching reasoning. *Science, 238,* 625–631.

Nunnally, J. C., (1961). *Popular conceptions of mental health.* New York: Holt, Rinehart and Winston.

Ogles, R. M. (1987). Cultivation analysis: Theory, methodology and current research on television-influenced constructions of social reality. *Mass Communication Review, 14,* 43–53.

O'Keefe, G. J., & Atwood, L. E. (1981). Communication and election campaigns. In D. D. Nimmo & K. R. Sanders (Eds.), *Handbook of Political Communication* (pp. 329–357). Newbury Park, CA: Sage.

O'Keefe, M. (1970). The mass media as sources of medical information for doctors. *Journalism Quarterly, 47,* 95–100.

O'Leary, D. (1986). Physicians and reporters: Conflict, commonalities and collaboration. In S. Friedman, S. Dunwoody & C. Rogers (Eds.), *Scientists and journalists: Reporting science as news.* New York: The Free Press.

Omaha City Planning Department. (1977). *Disaster response: The 1975 Omaha tornado.* Omaha, NE: Author.

Omaha World-Herald. (1975). 13, 15, 16, 27 January; 7, 12, 13, 14, 19 May; 5, 18, 21, 23 June.

Patterson, P. (1989). Reporting Chernobyl: Cutting the government fog to cover the nuclear cloud. In L. Walters, L. Wilkins & T. Walters (Eds.), *Bad tidings: Communication and catastrophe.* New York: Lawrence Erlbaum.

Pavlik, J., Wackman, D., Kline, F. G., Jacobs, D., Pechacek, T., & Pirie, P. (1985). *Cognitive structure and involvement in a health information campaign.* Unpublished manuscript delivered to Health Communications Division, International Communication Association, Honolulu, HI.

Payer, L. (1988). *Medicine and culture.* New York: Henry Holt.

Peirce, N. R., & Hagstrom, J. (1983). *The book of America: Inside 50 states today.* New York: W. W. Norton & Co.

Pell v. Procunier, 417 U.S. 817 (1974).

The pentagon vs. the press. A Harper's forum. (1985, November). *Harper's,* pp. 37–52.

Perlman, D. (1974). Science and the mass media. *Daedalus, 103,* 207–222.

Perrow, C. (1984). *Normal accidents: Living with high-risk technologies.* New York: Basic Books.

Perrow, C. (1979). *Complex organizations: A critical essay.* Glenview, IL: Scott Foresman.

Peters, R. L. (1989). Effects of global warming on biological diversity. In D. E. Abrahamson (Ed.), *The challenge of global warming* (pp. 82–95). Washington, DC: Island Press.

Pettegrew, L., & Logan, R. (1987). Health communications, review of research and theory. In C. R. Berger & S. H. Chaffee (Eds.), *Handbook of communication science.* Newbury Park, CA: Sage.

Pfund, N., & Hofstadter, L. (1981). Biomedical innovation and the press. *Journal of Communication, 31,* 138–154.

Plough, A., & Krimsky, S. (1987). The emergence of risk communication studies: Social and political context. *Science, Technology & Human Values, 12*(3 & 4), 4–10.

Ploughman, P. (1984). *The creation of newsworthy events: An analysis of newspaper coverage of the man-made disaster at Love Canal.* Ph.D. thesis. Buffalo: State University of New York at Buffalo.

President's Commission Report on the Challenger (1986). *Report to the President by the Presidential Commission on the Space Shuttle Challenger Accident.* Washington, D.C.

Prewitt, K. (1983). Scientific illiteracy and democratic theory. *Daedalus, 112,* 49–64.

Prewitt, K. (1982). The public and science policy. *Science Technology and Human Values, 36*, 5–14.

Quarantelli, E. L. (1989). The social science study of disasters and mass communication. In L. Walters, L. Wilkins & T. Walters (Eds.), *Bad tidings: Communication and catastrophe.* Hillsdale, NJ: Lawrence Erlbaum.

Quarantelli, E. L. (1985). *Organizational behavior in disasters and implications for disaster planning.* Report series No. 18. Newark, DE: Disaster Research Center, University of Delaware.

Quarantelli, E. L. (1981). The command post point of view in local mass communications systems. *International Journal of Communication Research, 7*, 57–73.

Quarantelli, E. L. (1980). Some research emphases for studies on mass communication systems and disasters. *Disasters and the mass media* (pp. 293–299). Washington, DC: National Academy of Sciences.

Quarantelli, E. L. (1979) Some needed cross-cultural studies of emergency time disaster behavior: A first step. *Disasters, 3*, 307–314.

Ramanathan, V. (1989). Observed increases in greenhouse gases and predicted climate changes. In D. E. Abrahamson (Ed.), *The challenge of global warming* (pp. 239–247). Washington, DC: Island Press.

Rapid City Journal. (1972). 11, 13, 15, 19, 20, 23 June; 7, 9 November.

Redding, W. (1985). Stumbling toward identity: The emergence of organizational communication as a field of study. In R. McPhee & P. Tompkins (Eds.), *Organizational communication: Traditional themes and new directions.* Newbury Park, CA: Sage.

Redding, W., & Tompkins, P. (1988). Organizational communication: Past and present tenses. In G. Goldhaber & G. Barnet (Eds.), *Handbook of organizational communication.* Norwood, NJ: Ablex.

Reese, S., & Danielian, L. (1989). Intermedia influence and the drug issue: Converging on cocaine. In P. Shoemaker (Ed.), *Communication campaigns about drugs: Government, media and the public.* Hillsdale, NJ: Lawrence Erlbaum.

Reid, T. R. (1986, June 23). Babbitt delights in details; Arizona governor wins issues, respect with his command of the nitty-gritty. Washington *Post*, p. A1.

Reynard, W., Billings, C., Cheaney, E., & Hardy, R. (1986). *The development of the NASA aviation safety reporting system.* Reference Publication 1114. Moffett Field, CA: NASA.

Rice, R. E., & Atkin, C. K. (Eds.). (1989). *Public communication campaigns* (2d ed). Newbury Park: Sage.

Ritz, W. R. (1980). A case study of newspaper disaster coverage: The Big Thompson Canyon flood. In *Proceedings of the Committee on Disasters and the Mass Media Workshop* (pp. 195–201). Washington, DC: National Academy of Sciences.

Riffe, D., & Stovall, J. G. (1989). Diffusion of news of shuttle disaster: What role for emotional response. *Journalism Quarterly, 66*, 551–556.

The right to know. (1975, March 25). *The New York Post*, p. 35.

Ritz, W. R. (1980). A case study of newspaper disaster coverage: The Big Thompson Canyon flood. In *Proceedings of the Committee on Disasters and the Mass Media Workshop* (pp. 195–201). Washington, DC: National Academy of Sciences.

Rogers, E. M., & Kincaid, D. L. (1981). *Communication networks: Toward a new paradigm for research* (pp. 57–60). New York: Free Press.

Rogers, E. M., & Dearing, J. W. (1988). Agenda-setting research: Where has it been, where is it going? In J. A. Anderson (Ed.), *Communication yearbook 10* (pp. 555–594). Newbury Park, CA: Sage.

Rogers, E. M., Dearing, J. W., & Chang, S. (1990). *Media coverage of the issue of AIDS.* Unpublished paper, Annenberg School for Communication, University of Southern California.

Rosen, J. (1988, July/August). The campaign press and nuclear issues. *Deadline,* pp. 6–8.

Rossi, P. H., Wright, J. D., & Weber-Burdin, E. (1982). *Natural hazards and public choice: The state and local politics of hazard mitigation.* New York: Academic Press.

Rourke, F. E. (1977). Government secrecy in ten democracies: The United States. In I. Galnoor (Ed.), *Government secrecy in democracies* (pp. 113–128). New York: New York University Press.

Runes, D. (1962). *Dictionary of philosophy.* Totowa, N. J.: Littlefield, Adams.

Russell, C. (1990, January 30). The riskiest of times? *Washington Post Health,* p. 9.

Russell, C. (1986). The view from the national beat. In S. Friedman, S. Dunwoody & C. Rogers (Eds.), *Scientists and journalists: Reporting science as news.* New York: The Free Press.

Russell, M. (1987). Risk communication: Informing public opinion. *EPA Journal, 13,* 20–21.

Salmon, C. T., (Ed.). (1989). *Information campaigns.* Newbury Park, CA: Sage.

Sanders, J. (1986). *The Soviets' first living room war: Soviet national television's coverage of the Chernobyl disaster.* Unpublished paper, Washington DC: Annenberg School of Communications.

Sandman, P. M., & Paden, M. (1984). At Three Mile Island. In D. A. Graber (Ed.), *Media power in politics.* Washington, DC: CQ Press.

Scanlon, J., & Alldred, S. (1982). Media coverage of disasters. *Emergency Planning Digest 9,* 13–19.

Scanlon, J., Luukko, R., & Morton, G. (1978). Media coverage of crises: Better than reported, worse than necessary. *Journalism Quarterly, 55,* 68–72.

Schmidt, W. S. (1983, November 30). New snow stalls Denver recovery. New York *Times,* p. A29.

Schmidt, W. S. (1983, March 1). Denver mayor, 72, announces reelection bid for fourth term. New York *Times,* p. A14.

Schneider, K. (1988, November 13). How secrecy on atomic weapons helped breed a policy to disregard. New York *Times,* p. D7.

Schneider, S. H. (1989a). *Global warming: Are we entering the greenhouse century?* San Francisco: Sierra Club Books.

Schneider, S. H. (1989b). Personal interview, Boulder, Colorado, October 6, 1989.

Scott, A. (1978, March 4). Weather patterns defy the computer. Washington *Post,* p. A7.

Sears, D. O., & Chaffee, S. H. (1979). Empirical studies. In S. Kraus (Ed.), *The great debates: Carter vs. Ford 1976* (pp. 223–261). Bloomington, IN: Indiana University Press.

Shabad, T. (1986). *The Soviet Press and Chernobyl.* Unpublished paper.

Shaw, D. (1987a). Coverage of AIDS story: a slow start. *Los Angeles Times,* December 20, pp. 36–39.

Shaw, D. (1987b). Hudson brought AIDS coverage out of the closet. *Los Angeles Times,* December 21, pp. 20–31.

Shepard, G. R. (1981). Selectivity of sources: Reporting the marijuana controversy. *Journal of Communication, 31,* 129–137.

Shepard, G. R. (1979). Science news of controversy: The case of marijuana. *Journalism Monographs,* No. 62.

Sheppard, N., Jr. (1979, January 19). Chicago struggles to get out from under. New York *Times,* p. A12.

Sherwood, T. (1987, February 1). Barry's defense melts like snow; criticism stings mayor into aggressive action on street cleanup. Washington *Post,* p. A23.

Shilts, R. (1987). *And the band played on: Politics, people, and the AIDS epidemic.* New York: St. Martin's Press.

Shoemaker, P. J. (Ed.). (1989). *Communication campaigns about drugs.* Hillsdale, NJ: Lawrence Erlbaum Associates.

Shoemaker, P., Wanta, W., & Leggett, D. (1989). Drug coverage and public opinion, 1972–1986. In P. Shoemaker (Ed.), *Communication campaigns about drugs: Government, media and the public.* Hillsdale, NJ: Lawrence Erlbaum.

Short, J. F. (1984). The social fabric of risk: Toward the social transformation of risk analysis. *American Sociological Review, 49,* 711–725.

Signorielli, N. (1989). The stigma of mental illness on television, *Journal of Broadcasting & Electronic Media, 33*(3), 325–331.

Simpkins, J., & Brenner, D. (1984). Mass media communication and health. In M. Voight & B. Dervin (Eds.), *Progress in communications sciences 5.* Norwood, NJ: Ablex.

Singer, E., & Endreny, P. (1987). Reporting hazards: Their benefits and costs. *Journal of Communication, 37*(3), 10–26.

Sioux Falls Argus Leader. (1972). 12, 19 June.

Skelton, G. (1989, October 20). Bay area quake: Politicians often tripped by natural disasters. *Los Angeles Times,* p. A3.

Slovic, P. (1987a). Perception of risk. *Science, 36,* 280–285.

Slovic, P. (1987b). Ripples in a pond: Forecasting industrial crises. *Industrial Crisis Quarterly, 1,* 34–43.

Slovic, P. (1986). Informing and educating the public about risk. *Risk Analysis, 4,* 403–415.

Slovic, P., Fischhoff, B., & Lichtenstein, S. (1980). Facts and fears: Understanding perceived risk. In R. Schwing & W. A. Albers Jr., (Eds.), *Societal risk assessment: How safe is safe enough?* (pp. 181–214). New York: Plenum.

Slovic, P., Fischhoff, B., & Lichtenstein, S. (1985). Characterizing perceived risk. In R. W. Kates, D. Hohenemser & J. Kasperson (Eds.), *Perilous progress: Technology as hazard* (pp. 91–123). Boulder, CO: Westview.

Slovic, P., Fischhoff, B., & Lichtenstein, S. (1982). Psychological aspects of risk perception. In D. Sills, C. P. Wolf & V. Shelanski (Eds.), *Accident at Three Mile Island: The human dimensions* (pp. 11–19). Boulder, Colo.: Westview Press.

Smith, B. (1986, July 27). Decade erases marks, not memories. United Press International.

Smith, K. A. (1987). Newspaper coverage and public concern about community issues: A time series analysis. *Journalism Monographs*, No. 101.

Smothers, D. (1981, November 25). Don Rose: The Rasputin of Chicago politics. United Press International.

Snepp v. United States, 444 U. S. 507. (1980).

Snow and politics. (1979, March 2). Washington *Post*, p. A10.

Sontag, S. (1989). *AIDS and its metaphors*. New York: Farrar, Strauss, and Giroux.

Sood, R. (1982) *News media operations in natural disasters*. Ph.D. dissertation. Department of Communication, Stanford, CA: Stanford University.

Sood, R., Stockdale, G., & Rogers, E. M. (1987). How the news media operate in natural disasters. *Journal of Communication, 37*(3), 27–41.

Sparks, G. G., & Ogles, R. M. (1990). The difference between fear of victimization and the probability of being victimized: Implications for cultivation. *Journal of Broadcasting & Electronic Media, 34*(3): 351–358.

Stallings, R. A. (1983). *Making decisions about disaster: Policies, politics, and the costs of relief*. Unpublished manuscript, School of Public Administration, University of Southern California.

Starr, P. (1982). *The social transformation of American medicine*. New York: Basic Books.

Stephenson, W. (1973). *Lake Ozark symposium on science news*. Columbia, MO: National Science Foundation.

Stephenson, W. (1967). *The play theory of mass communication*. Chicago: University of Chicago Press.

Stone, D. A. (1989). Casual stories and the formation of policy agendas. *Political Science Quarterly, 104*, 281–300.

Stone, G. (1987). *Examining newspapers: What research reveals about America's newspapers*. Newbury Park, CA: Sage.

Supperstone, M. (1985). Press law in the United Kingdom. In P. Lahav (Ed.), *Press law in modern democracies. A comparative study* (pp. 9–78). New York: Longman.

Swindel, S. H., Lindstrom, S. A., & Sathoff, R. C. (1988, July). *Media use and knowledge about science and technology: The effects of general exposure, focused exposure and focused attention*. Paper presented to the Association for Education in Journalism and Mass Communication convention, Portland, OR.

Tankard, J. W., & Adelson, R. (1982). Mental health and marital information in three newspaper advice columns. *Journalism Quarterly, 59*(4), 592.

Teplin, L. (1985). The criminality of the mentally ill: A dangerous misconception. *The American Journal of Psychiatry 142*(5), 593–599.

Teplin, L. (1984). July 18, personal interview from Boulder, CO.

Thinking about the unthinkable: A world without nuclear weapons. (1987, January/February). *Deadline*, p. 6.

Tichenor, P., Olien, C., Harrison, A., & Donohue, G. A. (1970). Mass communication systems and communication accuracy in science news reporting. *Journalism Quarterly, 47*, 673–683.

Titus, J. G. (1989). The causes and effects sea level rise. In D. E. Abrahamson (Ed.), *The challenge of global warming* (pp. 161–195). Washington, DC: Island Press.

Tobey, R. (1971). *The American ideology of natural science*. Pittsburgh: University of Pittsburgh Press.

Toman, J. K. (1972, June 7). *Rapid City observes 10th anniversary of flood that killed 238.* United Press International.

Tompkins, P. (1978). Organizational metamorphosis in space research and development. *Communication Monographs, 45,* 110–118.

Tompkins, P. (1977). Management qua communication in rocket research and development. *Communication Monographs, 44,* 1–26.

Tompkins, P., Fisher, J., Infante, D., & Tompkins, E. (1975). Kenneth Burke and the inherent characteristics of formal organizations: A field study. *Speech Monographs, 42,* 135–142.

Trachtman, L. (1981). The public understanding of science effort: A critique. *Science, Technology and Human Values, 36,* 10–15.

Tuchman, G. (1978). *Making news: A study in the construction of reality.* New York: Free Press.

Turow, J. (1989). *Playing doctor: Television, storytelling and medical power.* New York: Oxford University Press.

Tyler, T. R. and Cook, F. L. (1984). The mass media and judgments of risk: Distinguishing impact on personal and societal level judgements. *Journal of Personality and Social Psychology, 47*(4), 693–708.

U. S. Army Corps of Engineers (1971). *Shore protection manual.* Fort Belvoir, VA: Corps of Engineers, Coastal Research Center.

United States v. Marchetti, 466 F.2d 1309 (4th Cir.), cert. denied, 409 U. S. 1063 (1972).

United States v. Morrison, 844 F. 2d 1057 (4th Cir.), cert. denied, 109 S. Ct. 259 (1988).

United States v. The Progressive, Inc., 467 F. Supp. 990 (W. D. Wis.), dism'd, 610 F. 2d 819 (7th Cir. 1979).

Walters, L. M., Wilkins, L., & Walters, T. (Eds.). (1989). *Bad tidings: Communication and catastrophe.* Hillsdale, N.J.: Lawrence Erlbaum Associates.

Warner. K. (1989). The epidemiology of coffin nails. In M. Moore (Ed.), *Health risks and the press.* Washington, DC: The Media Institute.

Washburn, P. S. (1990 April). The office of censorship's attempt to control press coverage of the atomic bomb during World War II. *Journalism Monographs,* No. 120.

Washington Post. (1987). 1, 3, 6, 9, 22 January.

Watkins, J. J. (1990). *The mass media and the law.* Englewood Cliffs, NJ: Prentice-Hall, Inc.

Waugh, W. L., Jr. (1990). Emergency management and state and local government capacity. In R. T. Sylves & W. L. Waugh, Jr. (Eds.), *Cities and disaster: North American studies in emergency management* (pp. 221–223). Springfield, IL: Charles C. Thomas.

Waxman, J. (1973). Local broadcast gatekeeping during natural disaster. *Journalism Quarterly, 50,* 751–758.

Weber, M. (1978). In G. Roth & K. Wittich (Eds.), *Economy and society.* Berkeley: University of California Press.

Weick, K. (1979). *The social psychology of organizing.* Reading, MA: Addison-Wesley.

Weinstein, N. (1989). Optimistic biases about personal risks. *Science, 246,* 1232–1233.

Weiss, R. (1981). The temporal and spatial distribution of tropospheric NO_2. *Journal of Geophysical Research, 86,* 7, 185–187, 196.

Wenger, D., & Friedman, B. (1986, November). Local and national media coverage of disaster: A content analysis of the print media's treatment of disaster myths. *International Journal of Mass Emergencies and Disasters,* pp. 27–50.

Wenger, D. E., & Quarantelli, E. L. (1989). *Local mass media operations, problems and products in disasters.* Report Series #19. Newark, DE: Disaster Research Center, University of Delaware.

Whelan, E. (1985). Toxic error: Not all the muck is in the air and water: Some is in books, magazines, newspapers and broadcasts. *Quill, 73,* 10–16, 18.

Whelan, E., Sheridan, J., Meister, K., & Mosher, B. (1981). Analysis of coverage of tobacco hazards in women's magazines. *Journal of Public Health Policy, 2,* 28–35.

Whitman, D. (1986). The press and the neutron bomb. In M. Linsky, J. Moore, W. O'Donnell & D. Whitman (Eds.), *How the press affects federal policy making. Six case studies* (pp. 145–217). New York: W. W. Norton & Company.

Who's writing the science sections? (1988). *SIPIscope, 16,* 16, 24.

Wilkins, L. (1989). Accidents will happen. In L. M. Walters, L. Wilkins & T. Walters (Eds.), *Bad tidings: Communication and catastrophe* (pp. 171–177). Hillsdale, NJ: Lawrence Erlbaum Associates.

Wilkins, L. (1989). Bhopal: The politics and mediated risk. In L. M. Walters, L. Wilkins & T. Walters (Eds.), *Bad tidings: Communication and catastrophe.* Hillside, NJ: Lawrence Erlbaum Associates.

Wilkins, L. (1987). *Shared vulnerability: The media and American perception of the Bhopal disaster.* Westport, CT: Greenwood Press.

Wilkins, L. (1985). Television and newspaper coverage of a blizzard: Is the message helplessness? *Newspaper Research Journal, 6*(4), 51–65.

Wilkins, L., & Patterson, P. (1990). Risky business: Covering slow-onset hazards as rapidly developing news. *Journal of Political Communication and Persuasion 7*(2), 11–23.

Wilkins, L., & Patterson, P. (1987). Risk analysis and the construction of news. *Journal of Communication, 37,* 80–92.

Wines, M. (1989, December 31). It's still business as usual for spies, even as the Eastern Bloc rises up. New York *Times,* p. A15.

Winsten, J. (1985). Science and the media: Boundaries of truth. *Health Affairs, 4,* 5–23.

Wolensky, R. P. (1984). *Power, policy, and disaster: The political-organizational impact of a major flood.* (National Science Foundation Grant No. CEE 8113529). University of Wisconsin - Stevens Point: Center for the Small City.

Wolensky, R. P., & Miller, E. J. (1983). The politics of disaster recovery. In C. E. Babbitt (Ed.), *The sociological galaxy: Sociology toward the year 2000* pp. 259–270. Harrisburg, PA: Beacon's Press-Pennsylvania Sociological Society.

Wolensky, R. P., & Miller, E. J. (1981). The everyday versus the disaster role of local officials: Citizen and official definitions. *Urban Affairs Quarterly, 16,* 483–504.

World Health Organization. (1958). *The first ten years of the World Health Organization.* Geneva: World Health Organization.

Wright, C. R. (1986) *Mass communication: A sociological perspective.* New York: Random House.

Wright, K. R. (1987). State response to the Big Thompson Canyon disaster. In E. C. Gruntfest (Ed.), *What we have learned since the Big Thompson Flood. Proceedings of the Tenth Anniversary Conference* (pp. 9–15). Boulder, CO: Natural Hazards Research and Applications Information Center.

Yankelovich, D. (1982). Changing public attitudes to science and the quality of life. *Science, Technology and Human Values, 39,* 23–29.

Ziphorn, T. (1988). *Disease in the popular American press: The case of diphtheria, typhoid and syphilis, 1870–1920.* Westport, CT: Greenwood.

Index

About the Contributors

Soon Bum Chang is the Director of Research at the Hanmi Bank, headquartered in Los Angeles. He earned his master's degree at the Annenberg School for Communication, University of Southern California, in 1989, where he was a teaching and research assistant.

Sharon Dunwoody is the Evjue-Bascom Professor of Journalism and Mass Communication and Head of the Center for Environmental Communications and Education Studies at the University of Wisconsin-Madison. Long interested in all aspects of the communication of scientific and technological information to the public, she has most recently engaged in research on how individuals use information to reach judgments about risks. In addition to publishing articles in such journals as *Journalism Quarterly, Science, Technology, & Human Values,* and *Newspaper Research Journal,* she co-edited (with Sharon Friedman and Carol Rogers) the widely acclaimed book *Scientists and Journalists.* Her record of scholarship and research has been honored by the Association for Education in Journalism and Mass Communication.

Deni Elliott earned an interdisciplinary doctorate at Harvard University where she studied philosophy, education, and moral theory. She now directs the Institute for the Study of Applied and Professional Ethics at

Dartmouth College and teaches for the philosophy department there. She is the author of a monthly column in *FineLine,* the journalism ethics newsletter; is the writer and co-producer of a documentary film, "A Case of Need: Media Coverage and Organ Transplants"; and is the editor of and contributor to *Responsible Journalism* (1986). She has served as an ethics coach at newspapers and television stations throughout the country.

Sharon M. Friedman is the chairperson of the Department of Journalism at Lehigh University in Bethlehem, PA, where she directs its 12-year-old Science and Environmental Writing Program. A consultant to the President's Commission on the Accident at Three Mile Island, Friedman has studied media coverage of nuclear power and radiation issues since 1979. She and her husband-colleague Ken Friedman were consultants on environmental journalism to the United Nation's Economics and Social Commission for Asia and the Pacific in Thailand. Their book, *Reporting on the Environment: A Handbook for Journalists,* has been translated into six languages and widely distributed throughout Asia. Friedman was named a fellow of the American Associate for the Advancement of Science for her "contributions to bettering public understanding of science and technology," has served as a Fulbright lecturer and is chairperson of the Science Writing Educators Group, a national organization of university professors who teach science writing courses.

Robin Gregory received his B.A. in economics from Yale University and his M.S. and Ph.D. degrees from the University of British Columbia. His fields of specialization are behavioral decision making, environmental risk management, and natural resource policy. Dr. Gregory has worked at Decision Research, Inc., in Eugene, Oregon, since 1984. During 1988–89 he served as the program manager of the Decision, Risk and Management Science Program at the National Science Foundation in Washington, D.C. He has published articles on risk management, decision making, and strategies for evaluating environmental resources in *Policy Sciences, Journal of Environmental Economics and Management, Risk Analysis, Public Choice, Journal of Environmental Psychology,* and the *Journal of Economics Behavior and Organization.*

Robert A. Logan is an associate professor and director of the Science Journalism Center at the University of Missouri-Columbia School of

Journalism. Logan's research interests include science journalism, journalism ethics, the social impact of new media technology and reactions to the introduction of computers among physicians. He is editor of *Inquiry* and *Sciphers* and a member of the editorial boards of the *Journal of Mass Media Ethics* and *Mass Comm Review*. Before entering the academy, Logan was a science writer and news editor at three midwestern newspapers. His major publications include: "The Unworkable Compromise: The Knowledge Tablet, Ethics and Public Policy for the Future," (*Mass Comm Review,* Summer 1989); "Health Communications, Review of Research and Theory," (in *Handbook of Communication Science*); and "Rationales for Investigative and Explanatory Trends in Science Reporting," (*Newspaper Research Journal,* Fall 1985).

Kurt Neuwirth is a doctoral candidate at the University of Wisconsin-Madison School of Journalism and Mass Communication. His research interests include public opinion with special focus on the spiral of silence theory and on risk communication. His articles have appeared in the *Journal of Broadcasting* and in *Journalism Quarterly*.

Sue O'Brien's career spans both journalism and public affairs. A former political reporter and editor, she has also served as a gubernatorial press secretary, emergency management liaison and campaign manager. She was a reporter assigned to cover the Big Thompson flood and she coordinated Colorado's emergency management response to the 1982 Denver blizzard. She holds faculty appointments at the University of Colorado-Boulder School of Journalism and Mass Communication and at the University of Colorado-Denver Graduate School of Public Affairs. She earned a master's degree in public administration from the Harvard University John F. Kennedy School of Government, and she is co-editor of a Ford Foundation-sponsored study of governors' responses to the New Federalism. During her journalistic career she founded and edited *The Unsatisfied Man,* the first and only journalism review focused on Colorado media.

Philip Patterson wrote his doctoral dissertation at the University of Oklahoma on television coverage of the Chernobyl disaster. He is head of the Department of Communication at Oklahoma Christian University of Science and Arts where he teaches a variety of journalism courses, including media law and ethics. He is a member of the editorial board of the *Journal of Mass Media Ethics* and his articles have appeared in the

Journal of Communication and *Political Communication and Persuasion.*

Julie Phillips is a communications consultant and freelance science journalist from Boulder, Colorado. As a writer or ghostwriter, she has written articles for *Science, Scientific American, Smithsonian's Air & Space, Alternative Sources of Energy,* the *Boulder Daily Camera,* and other newspapers. Her areas of special interest include mental health, renewable energy, space and the physical sciences. She has a bachelor's degree in zoology-chemistry from Pomona College and a master's degree in journalism from the University of Colorado. She is currently working on a book entitled *Harvest of Silence,* which examines the psychological and social ramifications of child abuse.

Henry (E. L.) Quarantelli's distinguished research career dates from 1949 when he first began to examine disasters from a sociological perspective. Since then he has written about 150 articles, reports, and books on disaster topics. He co-founded the Disaster Research Center in 1963 and was its director until 1989, when he retired to become a research professor at the University of Delaware. He is currently at work on a joint research project with Chinese scholars to examine community level earthquake preparedness and response as well as completing a study of the atypical looting behavior in St. Croix after Hurricane Hugo. Among his many publications, those that focus directly on the role of the mass media in disasters include: *Local Mass Media Operations, Problems and Prospects in Disasters* (1989); "The Social Science Study of Disasters and Mass Communication" (*Bad Tidings: Communication and Catastrophe,* 1989); and "What Should We Study? Questions and Suggestions for Researchers about the Concept of Disaster" (*International Journal of Mass Emergencies and Disasters,* 1987).

Everett M. Rogers is the Walter H. Annenberg Professor at the Annenberg School for Communication at the University of Southern California. A scholar of international stature, Rogers's interests span a variety of fields, including health communication, the development and diffusion of new technology, and media coverage of a variety of technology-related events. He is the author of numerous books and articles, the best known of which are *Diffusion of Innovations* (1983), and with Judith K. Larsen, *Silicon Valley Fever* (1984).

David M. Rubin is the dean of the S. I. Newhouse School of Public Communications at Syracuse University. He was founder of the Center for War, Peace, and the News Media at New York University, which studies news media coverage of national security issues. He teaches communications law and was, until 1990, the Chair of the Communications Media Committee of the American Civil Liberties Union. The committee helps set union policy in such areas as access to information and government control of information in wartime. His publications include: "How the News Media Reported on Three Mile Island and Chernobyl" (*Journal of Communication,* Summer 1987); "Nuclear War and Its Consequences on Television News" (*Journal of Communication,* Winter 1989); and *Report of the Public's Right to Information Task Force* (The President's Commission on the Accident at Three Mile Island, October 1979).

Russell E. Shain is dean of the College of Communications at Arkansas State University. He formerly was professor and dean of journalism at the University of Colorado. His research and teaching interests are in culture, communication, and technology. A former newspaper reporter and editor, Shain earned his doctorate at the University of Illinois. His scholarly work has included: "The Effects of Pentagon Influence on War Movies" (*Journalism Quarterly,* 1972); "Hollywood's Cold War" (*Journal of Popular Film,* 1974); and "It's the Nuclear, Not the Power, and It's in the Culture Not Just the News" (*Bad Tidings: Communication and Catastrophe,* 1989).

Phillip K. Tompkins specializes in the study of organizational communication. He is the past president of the International Communication Association and has served as editor of *Communication Monographs.* Before he became a professor in the Department of Communication at the University of Colorado-Boulder, he was associate dean of liberal arts at Purdue University as well as serving as a fellow at the Center for Humanistic Study there. He has written numerous books and articles including *Communication As Action* and *Communication Crisis at Kent State* (with Elaine Anderson). His 1966 article, "In Cold Fact" which was published in *Esquire* has recently been reprinted in *Contemporary Literary Criticism* (1990). His current projects include guest lectures at Helsinki University of Technology, Helsinki, Finland.

Dennis Wenger is director of the Hazard Reduction and Recovery Center at Texas A&M University. From 1985 to 1989 he worked with E. L. Quarantelli at the Disaster Research Center, University of Delaware. Wenger holds joint appointments in urban planning and sociology at

A&M and has written or edited over 50 books, articles, and research reports about all aspects of hazards and disasters. His work has been funded by the National Science Foundation and the National Academy of Sciences. Wenger holds a Ph.D. in sociology from The Ohio State University.

Lee Wilkins is a professor and the associate dean for undergraduate studies at the University of Missouri School of Journalism. A former newspaper reporter and editor, she earned her doctorate in political science at the University of Oregon. Her study of media coverage and public perception of the Bhopal, India, chemical spill — *Shared Vulnerability: The Media and American Perceptions of the Bhopal Disaster* (Greenwood, 1987) — was named an outstanding academic book of 1987 by the library journal *Choice*. Her research has been supported by the Environmental Protection Agency and the National Science Foundation. Her other scholarly interests include political biography and media ethics, and she is currently working on a project to study the professional values and norms that have helped to frame media coverage of the greenhouse effect.